DYNASTIES OF THE SEA

The Untold Stories of the Postwar Shipping Pioneers

LORI ANN LAROCCO

Foreword by Rajesh Unni
Preface by Jeff Parry
Afterword by Dr. Martin Stopford

Marine Money, Inc.

Published by Marine Money, Inc.
100 First Stamford Place, 6th Floor
Stamford, Connecticut 06902
www.marinemoney.com

First Edition: June 2018

ISBN 13: 978-0-9862094-9-9 (Hardcover edition)
ISBN 13: 978-0-9978871-3-6 (Paperback edition)

Cover design by Johnny Miltiades Kulukundis, 2018
Sextant by Joaquim Alves Gaspar - Own work, CC BY 2.5

To my father, Richard LaRocco, you have instilled a love for all things of the sea in my children and myself. May you be catching the "big one" every day with the angels. Love you, Daddy.

CONTENTS

FOREWORD

Global trade has helped to bring the world closer together while creating tremendous economic benefits among both the developing and the developed nations of the world. In a time when globalization and the current structure of free trade are in question, it is easy to forget how global trade is underpinned by the incredible cost efficiencies of seaborne transportation and logistics. This second volume of *Dynasties of the Sea* tells the stories of shipowners, financiers, and entrepreneurs who are impacting the global shipping industry and continuing the quest for further globalization through innovation and optimization in the manufacturing, operation, logistics, and financing of oceangoing vessels. Their stories are highly entertaining in their own right and provide insights into what is required to be successful in one of the world's most competitive industries today and in the future.

We are fortunate that Lori Ann LaRocco once again shares her brilliant storytelling abilities to shine a light on the extraordinary personalities, mindsets, dreams, and achievements of these leading shipping men and women. Lori Ann's enthusiasm for the shipping industry, combined with the trust and respect she earns as a senior editor of guests at CNBC business news, allows her to draw candid and intimate portraits of how these business leaders succeed in the global, volatile, unpredictable, but also exciting and rewarding shipping industry.

In my career, I have had the fortune of meeting with and learning from a number of the outstanding people profiled in this book. They are a true reflection of the diverse and global nature of the shipping industry we all love. Sabrina Chao represents the new generation of Asian shipping as chairman of Wah Kwong Maritime Transport Holdings Ltd., one of Hong Kong's largest privately held shipowners. Claus-Peter Offen heads the Hamburg-based Offen Group, a fully integrated, traditional, family-controlled shipowning firm that has been a pioneer in the development of containerized shipping. Miles Kulukundis is the former head of the International Association of Independent Tanker Owners (INTERTANKO) and of London & Overseas Freighters, a company that was in the middle of the emergence of London- (and later U.S.-) based Greek shipowners during the post-World War II rebuilding years, and which later became part of the Frontline group. Felipe and Ricardo Menéndez Ross are the brothers behind some of the most successful shipping companies throughout the Americas and capital markets. Michael Hudner is a shipping capital markets entrepreneur who developed access to the U.S. bond and equity markets to acquire and finance more than 100 vessels (he has probably forgotten more about the bond and equity markets than most people will ever know). Martin Stopford, the British economist, teacher, writer, and information provider, built Clarkson Research over a twenty-year period to be the industry's leading shipping information and forecasting hub. Herbjørn Hansson, the Norwegian shipowner, created the counterintuitive all-equity, full-dividend payout public shipping company model. And Paul Leand, as head of New York-based AMA, has spent a career explaining Wall Street to shipowners and shipping to Wall Street, while also demonstrating superb dealmaking with the well-timed acquisition and sale of the Chembulk Tankers fleet, as one example.

This is by no means an exhaustive list of those profiled; I hope to meet them all in the future, as their reputations precede them.

While reflecting on these stories, I am reminded of my own upbringing and career in shipping. Growing up in a small town in the southern part of India, seafaring gave me the opportunity to learn from this diverse world, where each culture brings its own uniqueness. Along the way, I learned to appreciate Scandinavian utilitarianism and pragmatism, American ingenuity, Singaporean execution acumen, and Japanese collaboration between regional shipowners, shipyards and banks. These experiences taught me what Lori Ann so eloquently explains: that these individuals are successful because they constantly evolve to meet the challenges and opportunities of the day, and they do so in partnership with the right talent and expertise across the globe. When I ponder how the shipping industry will face future challenges, including digitalization, environmental concerns, and how to care for the next generation of seafarers, I can think of no better inspiration than the insights gained from the driven, entrepreneurial, innovative people so well described in this book.

Rajesh Unni, CEO, Synergy Group

PREFACE

Some friends and I gather at a club every so often to celebrate our continued existence and share stories. I listen with some pride and affection to their accomplishments, though my smile occasionally belies something else: a stifled inner voice saying, "That's nice, but have you ever bought pirate insurance?"

Life in ocean shipping can be somewhat unconventional. It's a 3 a.m. message saying the 25,000 tons of cement your ship's carrying across a wintry Atlantic "have gotten a little wet." A night drive through bandit country to inspect a ship on the Black Sea. Nighttime ascents of storm-slick ladders in Singapore or Lagos. Ordering a raki in Piraeus and a pilsner in Hamburg on the same day. Pulling a boiler suit over a business suit. Or soaking up the impossible vastness of the sea from the bridge of a supertanker.

It wasn't always this way. For millennia, politicians and generals lived secure in the conviction that the sea separated and protected us from the onslaughts of other cultures. The sagas of Odysseus and the early Vikings were cautionary tales of dangerous oceans and unmerciful gods. Normal beings did not tempt the Fates.

Eventually, of course, technological advances in shipping led to ever-greater expansions in exploration and trade. Colonial nations accumulated massive wealth often in correlation to the quality and quantity of their ships. The ceaseless competition led to two world wars and finally a great peace. The sea had connected us, and in profound ways.

The Pax Americana, which continues today, provides the crucible for the stories contained in this book. In the decades after World War II, world trade grew geometrically and demand for ocean shipping soared. Standing at the ready were the descendants of Odysseus and the

Vikings who had been quietly trading ships for centuries. The age of the Golden Greeks, Scandinavians, and Hong Kongers had begun.

But the stories here are not about men and women who were led to a gold mine and handed a shovel. Here's where the pirate insurance comes in. Despite modern technology and process, the oceans still seethe with danger, and the gods—very much alive—remain mercurial. The intrepid souls that devote their time and money to shipping have a particular temperament.

Ocean shipping presents challenges that lie beyond the comprehension of most land dwellers. The price of a ship can rise or fall by 60 percent in months. Freight rates can move farther and faster. Shipowners and courageous seafarers face hurricanes, wars, debt crises, floods, pirates, icebergs, sanctions, collisions, injuries, blockades, tsunamis, mutinies, terrorists, infestations, breakdowns, reefs, drug traffickers, strikes, commodity swings, spread cycles, restraints of princes, promotions of democracy, and the persistent corruptions of men and steel.

The people in this book embody the strange combination of constant motion, patience, iron will, adaptability, charisma, grit, and relentless optimism required to deliver 90 percent of the world's trade on time and in perfect (usually dry) condition. They are among the leading lights of a small global community whose shared experiences and values transcend national boundaries. I am proud to know them and delighted that you will have a chance to meet them too.

Jeff Parry, Mystic Marine Advisors, LLC

CHAPTER ONE

Cesare d'Amico and Paolo d'Amico

A chi vuole, non mancano modi

(Where there is a will there is a way)

After the Great Depression, countries including Italy were economically decimated. Their banks, along with countless other world financial institutions, went bankrupt. Benito Mussolini's Fascist government abandoned Italy's laissez-faire economic policy and created the economic model "corporatism"—a partnership between the government and major businesses, in which the government chose winners and losers. Those companies considered "too big to fail" were saved by government capital, while others were left to flounder in the private sector. On May 26, 1934, Mussolini boasted to his Chamber of Deputies, "Three-fourths of the Italian economy, industrial and agricultural, is in the hands of the state."[1]

By 1939, Italy was ranked second in the world after the former Soviet Union in having the highest percentage of state-owned enterprises. When asked that year by Grover Whalen, New York's police commissioner and president of the World's Fair Corporation, to define Fascism, "Il Duce" responded, "It's like your New Deal!"[2]

---

[1] Gianni Toniolo, ed., *The Oxford Handbook of the Italian Economy Since Unification* (Oxford: Oxford University Press, 2013), 59; Mussolini's speech to the Chamber of Deputies was on May 26, 1934

[2] Grover Whalen, *Mr. New York: The Autobiography of Grover A. Whalen* (Literary Licensing, LLC, 1955), 188.

The maritime industry was also propped up by the Italian government. During the 1930s, the banks were ousted from shipping finance and replaced by the state-controlled Istituto per il Credito Navale, created by Alberto Beneduce on the orders of Mussolini. By 1939, the government controlled over four-fifths of the country's shipping and shipbuilding.

But not all those considered "too small" for government intervention perished. In the early 1930s, in Salerno, Italy, off the Amalfi Coast, Massimino Ciro d'Amico was looking for ways to grow his family's small timber-trading business. The large Italian family had seven sons: Ciro, Oronzo, Vittorio, Carlo, Salvatore, Antonio, and Giuseppe, the oldest, called Peppino by his family. Born in the 1910s and '20s, the brothers saw the struggles in the Italian economy. The d'Amicos did not settle with their financial aspirations. Giuseppe, along with his father, wanted to improve their business by moving its timber supplies from chartered vessels to owned vessels. So, with small schooners and auxiliary-powered twin-masted sailing barges of up to 120 feet in length, Giuseppe transformed the d'Amico timber business.

Massimino Ciro d'Amico

2

The very first d'Amico vessel was the motor sailer *Sette Fratelli* (Seven Brothers). The fleet then increased with the addition of the company's first steel-built steamship, *Peppino Palomba*. An additional 3,000 tons' worth of ships soon followed.

The first d'Amico vessel: Sette Fratelli (Seven Brothers)

On April 8, 1948, the Marshall Plan was enacted, which removed trade barriers and helped rebuild war-torn countries after World War II. The United States hoped this act would prevent the spread of communism and encourage capitalism. The d'Amico brothers had access to the Marshall Plan because they lost four vessels during the war. In that same year, the brothers purchased surplus Liberty dry cargo and T2 tankers from America. The Liberty ships *Harvey Cushing* and *Edward P. Alexander* were renamed *Eretteo* and *Orizia*, and the T2 *Quebec* was renamed *Maria Cristina D*. Over the next four years, the d'Amicos were on a strategic buying binge, picking up the *Alcione* (ex *Fort Gibraltar*), *Atlanta* (ex *Fort Simpson*), *Ariella* (ex *La Orilla*), *Citta di Salerno* (ex *Benvrackie*), *Paestum* (ex *'Liberty' Samspeed*), and *Marialaura* (ex *Empire Eddystone*). In 1950, the Braathan tanker *Braconda* was acquired and renamed *Linda Giovanna*.

With an office now in Rome, the d'Amico brothers were buying additional secondhand tankers. The next two years were characterized as a period of momentous growth for the family-owned company. In 1952, the seven brothers decided to split and go their separate ways to pursue their own shipping interests.

Ciro and his brothers Salvatore and Antonio left and co-founded the shipping company d'Amico Società di Navigazione S.p.A., based in Rome. Giuseppe and his brothers Oronzo, Vittorio, and Carlo remained with Fratelli d'Amico Armatori S.p.A., also based in Rome. Together, they revolutionized the maritime transport industry with the order of the first two "supertankers" to be built by Cantieri Riuniti dell'Adriatico, in Trieste. Both companies continued to prosper. During the 1960s, d'Amico Società di Navigazione transitioned from tramp trade to scheduled services and shipping refined products. The opening of an office in Genoa marked the company's key logistical expansion to start their liner services, which were always supervised by the youngest brother, Antonio d'Amico.

Salvatore, Ciro, and Antonio d'Amico

Ciro and Antonio d'Amico also played an important role at Confitarma, the Italian Shipowner Association. Ciro's role in the in the '70s helped to unify three different shipowner associations, which merged into Confitarma. Antonio presided over the association during two mandates, from 1989 to 1995. Besides being the first president to be a shipowner (before him, presidents were politicians and diplomats), during his mandate he relaunched the image of Confitarma, which also adhered to Confindustria, the main Italian association representing manufacturing and service companies, by opening the shipowner association to a wider, more international public beyond the maritime sector.

Teaching the Second Generation

Ciro's son, Paolo d'Amico, discovered his love of shipping at eight years old when his father took him on a tanker. "It was really something," he said, laughing. "It was a huge piece of steel with a lot of people on board. There were all these pipes and valves, and it moved around the world! It was a tanker, so it was not the most beautiful ship in the world, but, geez, I loved that ship."

MT Cielo di Gaeta

MV Cielo d'Italia

That love burned inside Paolo throughout his young adulthood. When he finished school in 1971, his father asked him what he wanted to do. "I said, 'Can I come to the office?' " Paolo said. "He said, 'Of course! Come!' That was it." In 1981 he was appointed as a director of d'Amico Società di Navigazione, with particular focus on the product tankers segment of the business. Since 2002, he has been chairman of the company. From 2011 to 2013, he presided over a three-year term of the council of Confitarma, pursuing the commitment of the d'Amico family to the worldwide recognition of the Italian shipping sector.

While book knowledge was necessary for Paolo's success, his father's guidance and wisdom during the crisis of 1973 was indispensable. "I learned things you could never get from a textbook," Paolo said. "I moved into the business when the business was sinking. But I learned a lot, and I learned the necessary strategies to surviving the down cycles. My father taught me the dynamics of the industry. As a shipowner, you need to do multiple things at the same time. You need to know how you can defend yourself," he explained, "how you must look at your investment in the future. And you need to ask yourself if you should be bullish or bearish. I learned that when things go right, we all make money—it's very easy. When things go wrong, you need to start looking at a different area of business for survival. That cycle taught me all aspects of what it takes to be a shipowner."

Unfortunately, in April 1974, the company and the family suffered a devastating loss when Salvatore, the company's co-founder, passed away. His son, Paolo's younger cousin Cesare, was just seventeen at the time, and had until then lived a very strict life away from the family business, attending a Jesuit school. "It was a sad time," he recalled with a sigh. "I was still in school, but I decided then that I wanted to pursue a career in shipping. After I graduated, I went to London for four months to start to learn English, which at the time was not done."

Cesare joined the company in 1976 in the technical department. It was a bittersweet moment for him. One of his first acts of business and the guidance he was given are forever ingrained into his business philosophy. "Unfortunately, I had to be eighteen years old to legally put my signature as a personal guarantee on bank loans," he said. "Paolo's dad, my uncle Ciro, told me, 'Remember, any dollar that we are taking from the bank is a dollar we have to give back, because as long as you are able to give back the money, you can remain in this business. The moment that you do not give back the money, you are out of this business. It's your choice.' I have never forgotten that."

Ciro and Antonio took Cesare and Paolo under their wing. It was very important to Ciro that the next generation learn the technical aspects of the ships. "My uncle told me, 'You go there and learn,' so in the beginning of my career I was staying in the shipyards," Cesare said. "Looking back, it has made me a better shipowner."

Over the next seven years, Paolo and Cesare learned all the aspects of the business. "My cousin and I were very lucky because we learned the business during a difficult time of the shipping market," Cesare said. "The downturn was long, but the knowledge and experience we got was invaluable."

Vision

In 1977, Cesare was told by Ciro to go to a "small city" called Singapore. "At the time it was more half-village, half-town," Cesare said. "My uncle Ciro wanted me to go with our technical inspector and stay there because he believed Singapore could grow a lot in the next ten, fifteen, twenty years and would become very important for oil trading. He said the atmosphere of Singapore was the driver." He paused. "Also, my uncle Antonio had a vision about Genoa and the success of the liner service in the '70s. I am proud and impressed to tell these stories, because my uncles had a vision of this city's growth, and shipping is always about vision. The successful shipowners are the ones who have a vision in their life," he continued. "No illusions but real, concrete visions. And when shipowners have a concrete vision, and they act on that vision, they are always successful."

In 1978, Paolo graduated from Rome University (La Sapienza) and added to his role in the company. Cesare also found himself expanding his position. His passion for the liner segment of the business led him to move into the liner services department, where he became general manager. "I was impressed by the fact that while we were a relatively small company, we were able to have contacts all around the world, with important companies," Cesare explained. "I remember we were making deals with Chevron, with Mobil Oil (now Exxon-Mobil), and then also Eni, which was then Agip. On the container side, among other important clients, we had Fiat (today FCA). By working in the liner services department, I was able to travel around the world. I gained a lot of experience."

Cesare's travels were concentrated between Central America and the West Coast of North America, especially San Francisco, Seattle, Portland, and Vancouver.

Like Paolo, during his early years at d'Amico Cesare attended Rome University (La Sapienza), where he also studied business and economics, graduating in 1982.

Hard Work Trumps Birthright

In January of 1981, the cousins suffered another loss, when Ciro died. Cesare, then 25, and Paolo, 27, were faced with the responsibility of showing their board they were up to the task of leading the company. Wisely, their uncle Antonio pushed them into the operative management of the company, while he concentrated on his institutional role and his appointment in Confitarma.

"Our top management at the time was represented by five people," Cesare explained. "They were very strict and hard. They were not going to give us any discount because we inherited the business. Their mission was that we become top shipowners, not their top management right away. We needed to learn how to be successful shipowners and *then* learn how to be successful managers."

"My father told us never to believe in our own hype," Paolo said. "You may be smart, but there will always be others who are smarter. We needed to work hard and show our board we had earned the right to lead the company."

This is advice Cesare has passed on to his sons. "Remember one thing: Forget your last name, because your last name in this situation is a disadvantage. The condition is, if you want to become a shipowner, if you want one day to become the leader in this company, the management and the company in its whole must *choose* you. You have to work hard, or you will never be able to run a shipping company as a family business."

"My father taught us one of our greatest lessons, and that was to be humble," Paolo added. "Don't pretend to know everything, because you don't, and even if you think you know it, question yourself five times. He also said to try to take things the way they are. Never hide things. If there are problems, don't run away, because even if you run away the problem will run after you, so it's not a solution. And of course, be extremely transparent with your people and in the job you are doing."

Their hard work paid off, and the board members, together with their uncle Antonio, who kept always a vigilant eye on his nephews, continue to reward the cousins. When Antonio passed away, in 2002, Paolo was appointed chairman of the board of directors of d'Amico Società di Navigazione, which is today the ultimate holding company of d'Amico Group.

In 1992, Cesare was appointed chief executive officer of d'Amico Società di Navigazione, and in 1993 he launched the d'Amico Group's bulk division.

The second-generation leaders also made their mark on the Italian stock exchange. In May 2007, Paolo and Cesare successfully managed the listing of d'Amico International Shipping S.A., the holding company of the tanker business unit, on the STAR segment of the Milan stock exchange.

Cesare also played a prominent role in the privatization of Italia di Navigazione S.p.A., in 1997. He was named chief executive officer (CEO) and held that position until the company was sold to CP Ships Canada in 2002. Since then, he has played a leading role in the development of the fleet of d'Amico Dry d.a.c. (formerly d'Amico Dry Ltd.), the dry bulk segment of the d'Amico holding.

Since Paolo and Cesare took the proverbial reins of the company, the cousins have led through a multitude of cycles, with the advice from Ciro and Antonio echoing in their minds.

"When you are at the bottom, things can only go in one direction," Paolo said. "You know that the opportunities are out there, but you have to be extremely careful about at what point of the cycle you move in. Even if the assets are devalued, it doesn't matter. This is not an easy game. It's very much up to how much debt you take on your assets, when you buy your assets, and if you can liquidate them easily. You don't want to get stuck with assets you cannot sell, because at the end of the day, capital is most important."

Seal of d'Amico Approval

The leadership model of d'Amico is unique in today's shipping era. The pair lead together at the top but manage their own operations and always commit strongly to sharing a common view of the business, as making decisions together can sometimes be very important. For example, the acquisition of the public company Italia di Navigazione showed how the two cousins get along: Paolo managed to convince Cesare and their uncle Antonio to launch the d'Amico Group in this new adventure. "We do exchange a lot information," Paolo emphasized. "We just don't interfere. This is normal for us because we grew up this way. Now this is a model that, I have to say, has been admired by a lot of people, especially some bankers, and it is not easy to resell it to the new generation because it was a totally different world when Cesare and I started. It was just the two of us."

When the cousins began on their maritime journey, corporate governance, security issues, and environmental regulations were not part of the equation. Cesare said that while the regulations are good for making ships safer, they add a layer of formality that was never there. "In the old days, you would see the captain on deck supervising the loading or the unloading of the vessel. Nowadays, the captain, he's confined in his office, always filling out papers. He's becoming a bureaucratic guy. His experience is to fill out papers to do with audit and costs, and to make sure that everything is in order instead of overseeing what is going on inside the port."

Today, Paolo and Cesare are navigating the company through a new wave of management standards, and they are building the future of the company, together with their children, to carry on the d'Amico legacy. Their bar of management excellence? A d'Amico must be responsible for every facet of business.

"We do this because we want the company growing and working in a specific way," Cesare said. "Today you must follow certain rules, so we both decided there always needs to be a family member responsible. Our name is in the company name. We are ultimately responsible."

"Our managers are very good," Paolo added, "but I think the fact that there is always the family behind it is important. I think the clear example of this is Maersk, the A.P. Møller family. The A.P. Møller family stands behind the company, which is now a huge company."

"The family gives a long-term interest in the company, what they do, in what they pursue, and so on," Cesare stressed. "That long-term interest can be seen in a company's culture."

One of the ways the cousins foster such culture is through an internal academy Cesare leads. The academy is for crew development. Approximately 40 to 45 mariners go through the program, where they start out as a cadet and then become third officers. "They board our vessels and become third officers for our vessels, but also for other companies," Cesare said with pride. "This is a big commitment. The investment in this academy is very important. Investors in a public company would not value that kind of spending. But this is an investment in the long-term success of your crews. More generally, d'Amico Group is very committed to the development and growth of its people, because this makes the success of the company."

Melting Pot

Through the decades, the cousins have expanded their family's company into an international shipping leader. Long gone are the days when the company had one office and every employee was Italian.

"I would say that Italians are the minority at the company, in the sense that there are Italians, Indians, Americans, British, Filipinos, and Chinese," Cesare said. "Thanks to globalization, we have all sorts of nationalities working with us today. The population of d'Amico is also relatively young and very attached to the company."

Because of this melting pot, Cesare said, their family culture has helped transcend the cultural divide many global companies face when expanding into different countries. "It is always very difficult to choose a top manager," he said. "Not because of their capability or knowledge of the business. It is more about if they are able to fit into a family company and embrace our long-term growth philosophy."

One of the key indicators to Cesare that he's made a good hire? "I like to think that our people leave the office each night when I leave. Yes, it's a bit of romanticism, but that's what I wish for the company. But I am aware that this cannot always occur. I had to learn that people are coming from different cultures, and it is not necessarily easy to share the culture of a family business. Therefore, my cousin and I, we work hard on this aspect with our people."

The Future

As Ciro and Antonio taught Cesare during his formative years at the company, through the example of Singapore, understanding human behavior is the key principal in having vision and creating strategies to capitalize on that vision. Echoing his father, Paolo explained that as a shipowner, yes, you need to have the right ship to do the right job, but you also need to understand people's behavior and what they are consuming. What is the next big thing for humanity?

"You need to be aware of what's going on around you," he said. "One of the biggest examples in the change of human behavior was the smartphone. The mobile phone industry started with Motorola and Nokia. They monopolized the market by the end of the '80s and made fantastic phones. But when the smartphone came in, that product changed the mobile landscape in a matter of a decade—not centuries. Nokia and Motorola were thrown out. The iPhone revolutionized the mobile market. It was not only a phone, it was everything—email, entertainment, games, as well as a communication tool."

Because of innovation and globalization, Paolo said, his advice to the next generation is to keep their eyes open, be humble, and try to understand where the world is going. "This world is very different than when my father founded the company," he said. "My father fought in World War II, and he saw firsthand the reconstruction of Europe and the growth in Japan. The change was slow and long-term. In my lifetime I have seen the collapse of Russia and the growth of China. Today's world is smaller and more connected. The Far East is growing. We are watching Africa. I'm afraid we do not have the luxury anymore of looking at history as a guide, because what we are living in is something already different. Technology has sped things up and has made things more complicated. Even financial instruments like the subprime market created a crisis no one could have predicted. I don't envy my children. It's incredible, the speed, how technology's evolving, and that is the big challenge for entrepreneurs today."

Connectivity has also transformed the way fleets are managed. "It is less hands-on and more computer communicating," Cesare said. "When I joined the company, you only communicated with telegrams, which were slower, so a ship was basically a floating entity in and of itself. Today ICT is a very important asset for the business, as it changed the management of the vessels and the life on board."

One of the most significant changes Paolo has seen is the move toward electric cars. "It's going to happen," he said, "so the question for us is how much oil will be imported tomorrow? The guy who was running a chariot with the horses at the end of the nineteenth century at a certain point ended up being overtaken by the steam car. That happened in a matter of years, not centuries. We are leading an industrial revolution, and we must understand where we are in this industrial revolution," he continued. "We don't even realize how many jobs are disappearing just because of the applications we have on our smartphones, and how many new ones are being made, along with new skills and know-how very different compared to the past. Multiply that by a global number and you see that is a whole lot of people out of work only for that, so it's a world in a very strong revolution. The world is changing under our feet in a totally speedy way."

The positive cycles of 2005, 2006, and 2007, and the hard ones, left Cesare staring up at the ceiling at night, pondering how the next generation will lead the company. Their children have entered the company at different moments but always during the so-called supercycles of the shipping sector. Both Paolo and Cesare underline how important it is to have a strong and united family by their side.

"We have instilled the prudence, passion, and commitment our children will need to have to lead d'Amico Group in the years to come," Cesare explained.

The cloudy geopolitical environment is one of the biggest difficulties Paolo and Cesare say their children will have to tackle. "It's more than China," Cesare said. "You have U.S. energy independence and its exportation of natural gas and oil. There is India and Europe. You have natural disasters like Katrina. Many things can affect the business. You have to learn to remain calm and committed to business."

Coraggioso (Courage)

Loss may have been the golden thread that bound the cousins together as they took on the herculean task of growing their family business, but it was the tough love and wisdom from Ciro, Salvatore, and Antonio that fortified Paolo and Cesare on their path to prosperity.

"I sometimes ask myself, If I did not lose my father at seventeen, would I have been able to reach what I've reached on my own without him there? I don't know," Cesare said with a sigh. "I don't know. I've always had this question in my mind. I'm very happy for what we have done. My cousin and I are very strong together. We were able to run through difficult waves—the market cycles, internally, dealing with management, even my uncles, who were not easy guys. The real strength for me and Paolo has been the fact that we were able to have Ciro as our teacher and Antonio as our wise guide. They were both tough, but it made us strong."

"We accepted all types of sacrifice," Paolo added. "My father was a tough man, but I would not change any of it. It made me who I am. This business needs a level of courage that sometimes can lead you to be overconfident and make mistakes."

"In Italian we call it *coraggioso*," Cesare said. "You need a lot of courage to be in the shipping industry, but there is a fine line between that and being over-courageous and reckless. You cannot be stupid.

While I learned a lot in school, our journey in business has taught us humility. That is one thing I remember my father teaching me. Because if you are humble, you always think that you have something new to learn every day. Without humility, you are blind to the mistakes you can make."

Paolo d'Amico

Cesare d'Amico

CHAPTER TWO

Sabrina Chao

The Learner

The shipping industry has been responsible for both the creation and the destruction of massive wealth for many maritime families. As in any industry, the members in charge of shipping's privately-owned family businesses have a direct influence on their company's strategy and direction. The next generation chosen to take over is groomed for years. The lessons learned from the company's successes and failures are taught in the hopes of not making the same mistakes again. Best practices are entrenched and nurtured.

But sometimes things don't go according plan, and instead of a smooth transition, the next generation is thrust into the role. It's up to those individuals to either rise to the occasion or step aside.

Sabrina Chao, chairman of the family-owned Wah Kwong Maritime Transport Holdings Ltd., chose to take on the challenge when she was propelled to leading the company started by her shipping-legend grandfather, T.Y. Chao. Headlines have called her a "Shipping Heiress," and one of the "Next Hong Kong Tycoons," but this self-described "learner" did not take her place at the helm of the company as the result of bloodline entitlement. She learned on the job, surrounded herself with mentors, and through hard work, dedication, and an awareness of the mistakes that had almost torn apart her company in the past, helped grow Wah Kwong through one of the most volatile times in the shipping sector.

Wah Kwong didn't start with a grand epiphany of an entrepreneur with a yearning to be out on the sea. Instead, one of the largest privately owned shipping companies in Hong Kong started with a winning hand of poker. Sabrina fondly remembered stories told by her father, George Chao, T.Y.'s youngest son, about how her grandfather liked to play poker with his boss and friends. One evening, T.Y. won a sizeable pot, and his boss suggested maybe he should invest in the coal freighter *Kwok Sing* with him. This piqued T.Y.'s entrepreneurial, risk-taking spirit, and he took his boss's offer. As the success of the venture grew, so did T.Y.'s shares in the partnership, with his stake eventually growing to 50 percent.

But fortunes quickly changed when the civil war in China broke out. In 1948, the *Kwok Sing* sailed from Shanghai with precious cargo—the Chao family. They were forced to flee their homeland and find refuge in the then British colony Hong Kong.

"When my grandfather settled in Hong Kong, it wasn't easy," Sabrina said. "He did not have enough capital to start off by himself in the beginning, so he had partners." That shipping company ultimately prospered, and in 1952, Wah Kwong was founded.

"My grandfather saw business opportunities postwar with a lot of infrastructure projects that needed to be rebuilt," Sabrina said. "Wah Kwong was one of the first to start building ships in Japan when most of the ships were still built in Europe. My grandfather saw the industrialization in Japan at the time. He took a lot of calculated risk on this industrialization." Those risks included ventures outside of shipping, such as flour mills.

At the top of the shipping cycle in the 1970s and early '80s, Wah Kwong was listed on the Hong Kong Stock Exchange and had a fleet of more than 60 ships. But the heavy blanket of a global economic recession in the 1980s suffocated the shipping industry. Five years of tumbling freight rates and high oil prices hit the industry hard. The growing prosperity once gained by many of the shipping magnates like the Chaos fell at a precipitous pace. From the Port of Los Angeles stretching to the shipyards of South Korea and Japan to the historic docks of Liverpool, 40 million tons of ships sat idle.[3] Five of Wah Kwong's long-term charters faced significant financial hurdles. In 1986, Wah Kwong was in a painful restructuring plan to settle $850 million in debts. T.Y. Chao sold his collection of jade for $10 million, along with much of his antique collection, to help settle some of those debts.

For the next decade, T.Y. and his eldest son, Frank, who oversaw the technical side of the business, and his youngest son, George, who grew and nurtured the global commercial relationships and the financial aspects of the business, transformed Wah Kwong. The company became streamlined. They strategically consolidated and revitalized their fleet by selling off old vessels and replacing them with newbuildings. George, an early supporter of China's shipbuilding industry, ordered the new vessels from emerging Chinese shipyards. By 1998 the fleet had an average age of two years, compared to its more mature fleet age of thirteen years in 1994.

The late 1990s marked a defining moment for Wah Kwong. To survive, the decision was made to sell increasingly large stakes to outsiders like Singapore's Sembawang Marine and Hong Kong's Pioneer Industries. Meanwhile, T.Y.'s health was in decline, and family in-fighting for control was an additional challenge. To add to the difficulties, the Asian financial crisis in 1997 hit the company hard. The future of the company was severely in doubt within the Hong Kong shipping circle, and T.Y. retired as chairman.

In 1999, Frank retired, too, leaving George in charge. Wah Kwong's financial difficulties attracted the investment interest of Bocimar Far East Holdings Ltd. Bocimar became a large shareholder in the company and was dubbed by the industry as Wah Kwong's "white knight." Bocimar took over Sembawang's 18.2 percent stake, and later, the Bocimar brothers moved into Wah Kwong's office, instating Ludwig Criel as managing director, with George becoming deputy chairman. Under Bocimar's majority control, Wah Kwong was

---

[3] Michael Farlie, director of the Hong Kong Shipowners Association. *The New York Times*, "Shipping Awaits a Rebound," December 29, 1986.

transformed from a traditional Chinese, family-run business into a modern shipping company.

In June 2000, Bocimar made a joint voluntary offer with George Chao to acquire the remaining 57.7 percent of Wah Kwong shares. After the transaction, Bocimar had a majority ownership of 54 percent, and Chao owned the remaining 46 percent. In July of that year, Bocimar delisted the company from the Hong Kong Stock Exchange and took the company private. Between 2000 and 2001, Bocimar quietly sold its shares back to George for $70 million. The announcement of the transaction and that Wah Kwong was back in Chao control surprised the international shipping industry. In 2002, George's eldest daughter, Sabrina, joined the company.

Under George's renewed leadership, a deliberate, conservative growth strategy was laid out. He preferred ordering tonnage against long-term charters. While these long-term contracts may have stopped the company from reaping peak spot pricing, the decision strategically insulated the company from losses during the troughs. Sabrina learned from her father's moderate business approach.

Unfortunately, just two years into Sabrina's career in shipping, George suffered a stroke. While the third generation was to be groomed to eventually take over the company, the then 30-year-old Sabrina found herself thrust at the helm. She was still in shock over her father's illness, but she knew the enormity of her responsibility and understood she could not do it alone.

Ever the student of life, Sabrina looked to two trusted executives to help her lead the company: then Wah Kwong CEO Tim Huxley and longtime director Criel. "To be honest, it was quite scary at the time, especially with my limited experience," she recalled. "Tim was very much my rock. I could always bounce ideas off him, and sometimes I needed to be reminded what was important. We came from very different backgrounds. He came from a purely shipping and shipbroking background, and I came from a more finance background. So, while our expertise and our strengths were completely different, there was a very good synergy that formed between the two of us."

Criel also played a significant role. "Ludwig Criel was very much my mentor when I first joined Wah Kwong," Sabrina said. "We spoke the same language because he also came from a more finance background. I knew I could always rely on both of them to give me guidance and to bounce ideas off. I trusted them enormously."

Eventually George Chao recovered and returned to Wah Kwong, working closely with Sabrina as she slowly took over the day-to-day activities of the company. For eight years, she listened to his advice on the challenges and rewards of leading a shipping company. "One of the biggest pieces of advice he gave me was to never be personal about your assets—when it's time to sell, sell. Don't get emotionally attached to what you own. It is a very cyclical business."

He also advised Sabrina not to take pride in the number of ships and the fleet size. " 'Just go with the flow. Go with the market,' " she recalled him saying. "My father always had a trading mentality when it came to shipping." By 2005, Wah Kwong was back on top, with a fleet of 27 ships.

Through the mid-2000s, Sabrina sharpened her skills alongside her father. One of the most important business lessons she learned from him was not during the highs of the business but rather during the lows. In 2008, the global financial crisis turned the shipping world upside down.

The dry bulk sector sank on the toxic combination of vessel oversupply and economic growth grinding to a halt. In May 2008, at the height of the markets, Capesize dry bulk vessels commanded on average \$200,730 in daily earnings. By November 2008, that price dropped to an average of \$4,800 per day.[4] The slash in prices made it difficult to simply cover operating costs.

Sabrina saw firsthand the devastation the lack of credit, falling asset values, and loan defaults had on competitors. Britannia Bulk Holdings Inc., which had an initial public offering (IPO) price of \$15 per share

---

[4] Maritime Analytics AS, 2017, Oslo, Norway, www.maritimeanalytics.com.

in June 2008, posted a huge third-quarter loss in October 2008 and announced that it was considering liquidation or bankruptcy protection. "It was a challenging environment," Sabrina said, "but we saw this as an opportunity to build a reputation as a best-in-class shipowner as we saw the 'daisy-chain' disappear from the markets and top commodity houses preferring to charter ships directly from head owners."

In 2010, the financial crisis continued to shake out the bulk shipping market, but Sabrina would face her own personal challenges. During that year, her father suffered a debilitating stroke.

"Having had the experience in 2004, when my father fell ill again in 2010, I knew exactly what I needed to do," Sabrina said. "The six years of working closely with my father, between 2004 and 2010, definitely prepared me to step up into a leadership role. I also had the support of everyone at Wah Kwong, including the board."

In January of 2013, Sabrina was promoted by the company board to chairman. She was 39 years old—a stark contrast to the male, 70-something Hong Kong shipping leaders.

Now, more than a decade after the historic bulk shipping meltdown, Sabrina said the industry has yet to bounce back, and she is not optimistic that there will be a turnaround any time soon. "To be honest, I think the whole world economy is still in many ways dealing with it, because I don't think ever in history have we had such low interest rates for such an extended period," she said. "For almost 10 years now we have had record-low interest rates, and I think that, in many ways, that is how a lot of companies got through and withstood the crisis. But at the same time," she continued, "the low rates have postponed the problem. Companies should have gone bankrupt. The industry is also being flooded with money chasing these unreasonable yields. The U.S. cannot raise interest rates by itself. Unfortunately, the European banks are not in a healthy enough state to do it. Unless we normalize interest rates, I don't think we can get out of this."

New Challenges

While her father and grandfather had navigated around the boom-and-bust cycles and the plague of overbuilding, Sabrina had an additional host of challenges they did not face: fierce competition from nearby ports, the liberalization of China's trade and cabotage rules, and the shortage of qualified personnel.

The impact of these headwinds has slowly eaten away at the Port of Hong Kong's global business. Once the world's busiest container port, from 1992 to 2004, Hong Kong is now ranked fifth. The regional ports have overtaken the top spots: Singapore is ranked number one in the world, and Shanghai is ranked fourth. "We need to review the current policy and the competition around us, especially with Shanghai and Singapore," Sabrina said. "We are working together with the Hong Kong government on where we can make a difference. Singapore is way ahead of us in that they started their plans for their waterfront properties. We came from such a high point, and then to have our competitive advantage pretty much eroded off, it's quite frustrating at times, but I am a firm believer that the government is willing to meet with us to raise Hong Kong's profile as a maritime center."

As chairman of the Hong Kong Shipowners Association, Sabrina has been a champion for Hong Kong to continue to be an international maritime center based on its positioning between Shanghai and Singapore. "There is no reason Hong Kong cannot be a shipping finance hub like London," she said.

Sabrina became the first female chairman in the history of the Shipowners Association in November 2015, twenty years after her father held the same position. Very early in her shipping career, Sabrina was urged by her father to join the association's executive committee. When she was promoted to chairman, it was around the time of her father's passing. "It was an emotional time for me," she said. "But I kept focused. When I took over I knew exactly what I needed to do. We were in the middle of our ten-year strategic plan. We shifted, realigned the strategic development of the association to get us where we wanted to go, and put our resources for the next ten years.

We have just completed our ten-year strategic planning, so it looks like we're in good shape."

Sabrina has said publicly that, going forward, there needs to be a distinct and separate recognition of Hong Kong's maritime business and the port business. "The port business is only one aspect of our business," she explained. "Our ships trade globally; most of our ships never come to Hong Kong. Our shipping registry is ranked fourth in the world, and we have 100 million gross tons registered under the Hong Kong flag."

Compared to the early and mid-1900s, when her grandfather started Wah Kwong, a career in the maritime industry is not as enticing today and the talent pool of prospective applicants has dramatically shrunk. "There are many other career choices for our young people," Sabrina said. "The situation of inadequate manpower is particularly serious in Hong Kong. We need to work closely with the government to raise industry awareness to the general public and to provide more quality training programs." In 2014, the government set up a HK$100 million maritime and aviation training fund to attract potential talent.

For more than a decade, the rapid transformation of China from an impoverished nation to one of the fastest growing emerging markets has businesses around the world looking for ways to capitalize on the rise of the Middle Kingdom's large middle class. Every economic data point that could provide insight into the heating up or cooling off of the Chinese economy is broken down and scrutinized, from the consumption of copper and oil to the nation's frothy real estate market and rapid credit growth. "China has its own set of problems right now, but fundamentally it is still very much a new economy," Sabrina said. "The government plays an essential part in the success of China today, and policy-wise it is definitely a very strong-willed government. This might not work for other countries, but it has worked for China. It is an economic miracle to see an enormous impoverished country become one of the most dominant economies in the world in such a short period of time."

Sabrina said that one of the early key drivers in China's economic development was investment from overseas Chinese, including Hong Kong residents. "We are investing back into the motherland. If you think about it, you still have the older generation that came out of China back in the '40s and '50s and even the '60s, and they want to give back with the successes they've made overseas. They want to reinvest back in China to give back to the motherland. This is really much bigger than us all put together."

Understanding Trump Trade

With 90 percent of the world's trade transported by sea, the leaders in the maritime industry keep a close eye on trade deals. One of the biggest challenges facing them today is not to get distracted by the tweets or campaign rhetoric of political candidates. Sabrina said that, while the then U.S. presidential candidate Donald Trump had harsh words for China on the campaign trail, she believes the now president's softening of language on China's economic measures, his pursuit of trade deals, and his infrastructure plan could be good for global trade. "Trade has become a negotiation tool for President Trump," Sabrina said. "The trading relationship between the U.S. and China is a very, very important one that cannot be ignored, but to be honest, this is politics. It is very hard to see how this will play out because there are so many forces at play."

Instead of focusing on what she cannot control, Sabrina is concentrated on projects that will create opportunity for the Hong Kong maritime industry. "China has rolled out infrastructure opportunities like the Belt and Road Initiative," she said. "There are a lot of underdeveloped economies within the 60-something countries in this initiative, so we are focusing on the trading activities happening right now rather than be paralyzed in uncertainty."

Sabrina explained that highly populated Southeast Asian countries like Vietnam, Indonesia, and Myanmar offer opportunities because they are still underdeveloped, and the appetite for commodities is there as they grow their infrastructure. She also stressed that while U.S.-China relations are important, you cannot forget Australia and Pakistan, two countries that are also important trading partners with China.

But Sabrina said that one of the most important things to keep in mind when it comes to trade policy is the timeline of a trade agreement's impact. "Even when a certain agreement is reached, it takes time for the agreement to be implemented and really have an impact. Yes, there is an instant effect on the stock market. But for shipping activities there is a cycle, and there is a time lag when we see trade policy impact. For example, the China Open Door Policy was adopted in 1978, but the whole shipping boom came in the early 2000s."

Leading Through the Overbuilding Shake Out

In the boom-and-bust cycles of the maritime industry, overbuilding is always a problem that has slowed down the recovery process. In this cycle however, Sabrina said it has been especially difficult. Despite the number of ships being scrapped peaking again in 2016, there are still too many ships available for hire given the weaker commodity demand and low freight rates. "This is an imminent problem we are facing at this moment," Sabrina stressed. "The oversupply has dragged down the market for the past few years, and unless there is some fundamental weaning out of these shipbuilding capacities, I just don't see how the market can come back to an equilibrium. And if it doesn't come back into some sort of equilibrium over the next few years, to be honest, I don't know why we're even in this business anymore."

Sabrina explained that both the public and the private sectors are to blame for the overbuilding. "Shipbuilding for countries like Korea and China is a strategic industry because it generates employment, and the building is supported by government money. So even with no orders they are still building ships."

On the private market side, the injection of private equity money into the sector starting around 2013 has exacerbated the problem, according to Sabrina. "It has changed the whole game plan for shipping altogether. Before private equity, it was big news for the markets to hear a shipowner ordering six ships. With of all these PE funds entering the market, you were seeing orders of 20, 30 ships! The sad reality is that the fund may have come and gone, but the ships they have ordered to be built remain. These are the ships we will have to deal with over the next twenty years. Between the government money and private equity money, there are no real commercial principles at play here. Low interest rates have also prolonged the problem."

The Future

While the industry has changed a lot since Wah Kwong was founded, Sabrina continues her father's quest to modernize the company so it stays relevant and a tough competitor in all parts of the shipping cycle. She described her modernization strategy as a "three-legged stool. These three legs provide the support Wah Kwong needs to move forward in a volatile shipping world: Professional management, technology to enhance communications, and corporate governance."

One of the legs of the stool Sabrina is particularly optimistic about is technology, specifically the role Big Data could play for both the industry and Wah Kwong. "There's so much inefficiency within shipping right now," she said, "but Big Data, if used correctly, could change all that. We have layers of charterers and layers of agents that we are dealing with day to day. We need to be able to comb through the data better and use that information to improve communication. Unfortunately, though, I think it will probably take an outsider to come in and make that paradigm shift. If we can do that, efficiency would be enhanced."

Sabrina said Wah Kwong is in the early stages of revolutionizing its best technology analysis practices, and acknowledged that the return on its investment will take time. "With the bottom line being squeezed by present market conditions, we are taking strategic baby steps utilizing software that can help us analyze data better between ship and shore. Hopefully meaningful data is generated that can help us improve our efficiency. It will take time to tell if it pays off."

The company's anti-cyclical strategy, created by her father, is something Sabrina follows to this day. "You have to have guts when the market is low, and you need to stick to your convictions," she said. "It's hard, but you have to."

One particular lesson Sabrina learned from her father during a trough in the shipping cycle has shaped her approach to business and is the reason behind every client decision she makes.

"My father was a man of few words, but he always had wonderful pieces of wisdom for me," she said. "One of the most important was, 'You always need to build a long-term relationship through fair deals.' It was needed for the *long-term* success of the company. We don't want to earn every penny from a partner or from a business venture, because we want people to come back. These long-term relationships help Wah Kwong thrive in good or bad markets because we stick by each other."

CHAPTER THREE

Peter Keller

Container and LNG Pioneer

Not everybody is born into the shipping industry, and not everyone in the business went to a maritime academy. Still, it is not too often you hear a leader in the industry say he or she started working in maritime "by accident." But for Peter Keller, executive vice president of TOTE Inc., that's exactly how his story started.

Keller's fresh perspective on the challenges facing the industry have helped push the envelope of the maritime transportation system. Being an "outsider," Keller never settled on the maritime premise of "this is how things have always been done." Instead, he would question, asking what new and innovative processes and technologies could be introduced to move the balance of trade faster on the high seas.

Keller studied civil engineering and later finance at Lehigh University. "I was also an ROTC guy," he said, "and because I had bad eyes I wound up in the U.S. Army Transportation Corps in 1965. When I graduated from college, I was lucky enough to be assigned to Army transportation in Germany. There, I got involved in some of the early work in the transportation of containers down from Bremerhaven using military vehicles." Little did he know those experiences would help pave the way for his future.

One day, after Keller left the service in 1968, he was driving up the New Jersey Turnpike to take a banking job with the Irving Trust Company when something caught his attention. "I was driving through Elizabeth, New Jersey, when I saw the Sea-Land Building," he recalled. "I admired the big building, the cranes, and the ship, and I said to myself, Boy, that's got to be a lot more exciting than being a banker. And without thinking twice I pulled off the turnpike!" He chuckled. "I called the HR people at Irving and told them something like, my wife was sick, or the dog ate my homework, and that I'd come next week to take the job, and they said, 'Sure!' I then walked in the door of Sea-Land and walked out about eight hours later with the job of administrative assistant to the general operations manager. I was making a lower salary than I had made as a captain in the military, and definitely a lot less than a banker, but I was happy."

Getting in on the ground floor with the company that founded containerization and intermodalism enabled Keller to learn the intricacies of maritime transport. Over the decades, Keller saw firsthand the liberalization of trade and the growth associated with trade negotiations, as well as the elimination of non-tariff trade barriers and commercial diplomacy. "Global trade just flourished, and containerization was a critical catalyst," he said.

Growing Pains

The number of freight containers being transported on vessels grew exponentially as the global economy flourished. Keller, working in terminal operations, understood the need for better tracking of cargo and the movement of freight on and off ships. He was always involved in terminal operations and transportation data processing at Sea-Land, even when he was running large operations in Europe or the U.S., and he was eventually promoted to vice president of data processing.

"I look back on those days and I say to myself, My goodness, we were trying to figure out where the containers were with punch cards!" he said with a laugh. "We thought we were pretty slick, having those punch cards. We would sort them, and then we would generate basic— and what would now be considered laughably simple—reports." He laughed again. "We have progressed so much today. With satellite tracking, you can know within seconds where a container is anywhere in the world. We are able to do things that we never dreamed of doing just a few years ago."

"In the old days," Keller recalled, "when we wanted to find a container in the yard, we got on the radio, called a longshoreman by the name of Willie Hop, and said, 'Willie, go run around the yard and let me know when you find 36504 and let me know where it is.' It could be anywhere between two minutes and two hours before Willie would call back and say, 'It's in row 36,' or wherever. And now, of course, it's all fully automated, except perhaps for some of the smaller ports, which may still run manually."

To find a remedy for that problem, Keller led a project at Sea-Land that examined other transportation technologies around the country that could speed up the process. "The closest was the railroad," he explained. "In the early '70s, the railroad had put color-coded placards on the sides of their railcars. So we spent millions of dollars on a project to affix color-coded placards on the front of every container so they could be scanned with a mobile unit mounted on a pickup truck. We would then know where that container would be in the yard. That was the start of scanning," he said. "The real lesson learned, however, was that we needed to look more closely at other modes and their technologies. This was one early example of how intermodalism can really help the entire supply chain when all modes embrace similar technologies. Another was the eventual integration and sharing of data through electronic data interchange (EDI)."

Estimating Global Economic Growth, One Container at a Time

Container traffic is one of the greatest leading indicators for gauging a country's economic growth. Ocean freight comprises shiploads of liquids and fuels, dry bulk, grains, automobiles, and consumer goods. The quantities of these products and commodities are based on the appetite of consumers around the world.

The appetite of a country, or even a region, for energy and goods can impact traffic patterns and logistics. Greater appetite means greater demand for goods, which then increases the volume of the product that requires transportation. "This trade growth has been the story of the container industry since day one, when Malcolm McLean sailed the

Ideal X from Port Newark in April 1956," Keller said, referring to the father of the modern intermodal shipping container. "Growth of our international economy demands more sophisticated and faster supply chains, and that is what the container and its systems and vessels have managed to provide to the world. This is the legacy of Malcolm McLean."

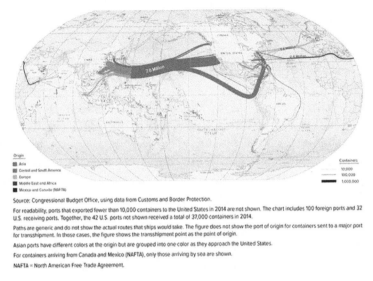

Source: Congressional Budget Office, using data from Customs and Border Protection.

For readability, ports that exported fewer than 10,000 containers to the United States in 2014 are not shown. The chart includes 100 foreign ports and 32 U.S. receiving ports. Together, the 42 U.S. ports not shown received a total of 37,000 containers in 2014.

Paths are generic and do not show the actual routes that ships would take. The figure does not show the port of origin for containers sent to a major port for transshipment. In those cases, the figure shows the transshipment point as the point of origin.

Asian ports have different colors at the origin but are grouped into one color as they approach the United States.

For containers arriving from Canada and Mexico (NAFTA), only those arriving by sea are shown.

NAFTA = North American Free Trade Agreement.

Container Traffic Flow to the United States, 2014

Source: The Congressional Budget Office, "Scanning and Imaging Shipping Containers Overseas: Costs and Alternatives," June 2016

In addition to a country's consumption of goods, the trend of larger ships over the past 50 years has also dramatically changed traffic patterns and logistics planning.

"In the 1960s we had ships that had 360 containers on board," Keller said. "Then the Jumbos came, with 640 containers. The result? The container yard had thousands of these containers and truckers coming in and out all day. These containers on chassis, or trailers, were then going all over the United States and all over the world, but we had to track them. Where were they, and what were they really doing?"

In the early '60s, containerization was still primarily a domestic activity. "The international markets to Europe only opened in 1965 with the sailing of a 226-container-capacity vessel from Port Elizabeth to Rotterdam," Keller said. "Asia opened as a consequence of the Vietnam War and the opportunity to load commercial goods onto ships returning from supplying U.S. forces."

These early vessels were largely converted surplus wartime steamships. They were relatively slow, with maximum speeds of about 15 knots. McLean had dreamed of a faster supply chain, and the vessel to support that was the SL-7, the fastest commercial vessel ever built, with a maximum speed of 33 knots. Launched in the early 1970s, it changed the industry just as the *Ideal X* had some twenty years prior. But with soaring fuel prices, the cost of the added supply-chain speed was not sustainable, and the SL-7s were repurposed for U.S. military service, where they are still active today as part of the rapid deployment fleet. "So much for speed at any expense," Keller joked. "As they say in auto racing, Speed is money—how fast can you afford to go?"

Supply Chain Advancements, Post-9/11

Similar to the airline industry, the container shipping industry often uses a hub-and-spoke system. Smaller vessels, often from smaller regional ports, transport the containers to larger ports, where they are then loaded onto large vessels and shipped across the ocean.

After the terrorist attacks on September 11, 2001, the U.S. government took a closer look at the nation's port infrastructure. Recognizing that the ports could be attractive for terrorists looking to ship nuclear or radiological weapons, Washington ordered an extensive security overhaul.

The 9/11 Commission called for investments in "the most powerful" scanning and imaging technologies. These technologies would inspect containers transported by plane, ship, truck, and rail.

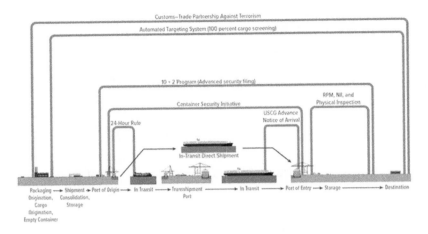

Layered Defense Strategy of U.S. Customs and Border Protection

Source: The Congressional Budget Office, "Scanning and Imaging Shipping Containers Overseas: Costs and Alternatives," June 2016

"After 9/11, there was a rush to install radiation detectors at all ocean terminals around the U.S. to scan cargo," Keller said. "While an interesting concept, it did not really address the problem, as it only identified contraband when it actually hit U.S. shores. It was clear that some extraterritorial process or system was necessary."

The Customs-Trade Partnership Against Terrorism (C-TPAT) was created in November 2001. The voluntary partnership between the U.S. government and private firms offered business incentives to participants that improved the security of their supply chains outside of the U.S., at cargo origin. Everyone joined C-TPAT—lines, shippers, supply-chain partners—as the need for additional security across these ever-growing and massive supply chains became more obvious. "When I was at NYK North America," Keller recalled, "we were a close ally of U.S. Customs and the new Homeland Security organization in this important initiative."

While the industry recognized the need for increased security, Keller said there were concerns that the process would dramatically impede the flow of goods. "While that was somewhat true as new rules and

34

regulations were promulgated, the industry did what it always does: found a way to facilitate this great economic engine called international trade."

Shipping's Shiny New World Trade Toy: Mega-Ships

With the world economy growing, a new buzz phrase was being circulated around the industry: economies of scale. With about $4 trillion worth of goods transported on the world's oceans every year, shipowners were on a quest for the new holy grail—reducing operating and shipping costs through larger vessels.

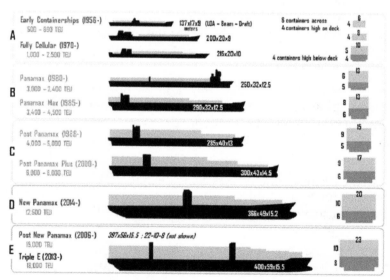

The World Standard Growth

The Panamax vessels the shipowners were using were now considered "too small." The maximum size of those vessels was around 5,000 TEUs, or some 2,500 containers. But there was an important factor about these vessels: They were the *largest* the Panama Canal could handle. Nothing bigger could pass.

"The big question being asked was: Would carriers build vessels that could not transit the Panama Canal, thereby complicating the East-West trade routes?" Keller said. "And the answer was yes! So now current vessel sizes approach 20,000 TEUs!" The race for being the first shipping company to build and use these mammoth vessels was on.

Recognizing the need to accommodate the growth of international trade and these larger vessels, Alberto Alemán Zubieta, then administrator of the Panama Canal, developed ambitious and innovative plans to expand the waterway. If they didn't, the canal would likely see less traffic, and Panama's economy would suffer. The Suez Canal also undertook significant improvements to increase its capabilities so it could embrace this trade expansion. Today, both routes can facilitate significantly larger vessels, and even roll-on/roll-off ships and other classic vessel types have begun growing in size.

In anticipation of those larger ships, ports around the world made significant capital investments to accommodate them and to build out the infrastructure to move the containers off and out of the port without any slowdowns. "The key here is that if the pipeline gets congested and starts backing up, our stores don't get filled," explained Curtis Foltz, former CEO of the Georgia Port Authority. "You can't buy sneakers for your children, you won't be able to get that imported beer, that blouse you wanted—we are basically the conduit and the roadway for all those things to end up on the shelves. Our biggest customers are the big-box stores—Walmart, Target, Home Depot, Lowe's, all these things that people take for granted every day. If we don't continue to invest in infrastructure, there will be problems."

Keller said that one of the challenges for him as a "travel agent" for the cargo was to make sure processes were in place to help alleviate congestion resulting from the increased amount of cargo entering a port. With bigger ships, container yards now accommodate thousands of units, many densely stacked four or five high and five or six wide, making finding an individual container an even greater challenge. Systems today have dramatically improved the process, but problems are still looked at in a piecemeal fashion.

Expediting the whole process is easier to explain than execute, said Keller. "For example, today we have significant delays in some ports because the ships are too big and we cannot move the cargoes through the terminals to truckers or railheads fast enough. Labor is a key component, as is productivity, which is necessary to unload and reload these large vessels in a reasonable amount of time," he explained. "Today we are looking for technologies that can overcome these logjams. Time is money. A port is a very expensive warehouse, so if a container or a shipload of containers sits at a port, everyone loses."

The trickle-down of slow transportation hits all levels of the trade process: the container company that owns the ship and the containers, the customer whose products are not reaching their destination and are incurring inventory costs, and the port itself, which cannot accommodate another vessel. Cargo that is delayed in the logistics chain cannot be stocked on shelves and sold, the ultimate bane of the retailer. Reportedly, the number-one sin at Walmart and Target stores is being out of stock.

This is something Keller has understood since the early years of his career, working in terminal development to untie the knot of congestion at the ports.

"It's all about the time, distance, and money," he said. "When you look at what it costs a particular company, whether it's Procter & Gamble, or Walmart, or Home Depot, or anybody else, for them to first develop a product, manufacture the product, move the product, store and distribute the product, and then finally try to sell the product, that's a huge, huge amount of time and investment. And on top of that, they have to consider the cost of transportation as well as all the other supply-chain costs. That is something customers and service providers are always looking at, trying to find the best time value for their product. One way to try to enhance the process and make it more efficient has been the recent introduction of ever larger vessels. The other is expediting the individual supply-chain links, but that must be undertaken with a view to the entire supply process, not just pieces. The answer is cooperation and transparency across the intermodal range so everyone benefits," Keller stressed.

"We have created these huge ships—18,000, 20,000 TEU behemoths—so the question is: How do we move that much cargo through existing ports efficiently without major changes in assets, automation, and labor relations? These large ships are not just one or two or three trainloads and a few hundred trucks; they are now 50 trainloads and thousands of trucks," he emphasized. "They also require larger more robust cranes, deeper water, larger terminals, wider roads, better productivity, and newer automation and data technologies. Think of the capital and infrastructure required to properly feed this mammoth system! This is not tens of millions of dollars, it's hundreds of millions."

The Future of the Mega-Ship

"I still believe very strongly that the large container ships are possibly going to go the way of the Airbus 380," Keller said. "If you look at the latest production of the 380, I think Airbus is now down to about one a month, and the order book is not terribly healthy. None were ordered in 2016. They're likely going to lose a lot of money on that program. I think there's a strong possibility that this could also be happening with these extra-large containerships," he continued. "The environmental and logistical issues associated with these vessels are huge. Just as the 380 can only operate in certain airports, only the largest deep-sea ports can accommodate the mega-ships. The amount of money that a port needs to spend on infrastructure to accommodate these ships is hellacious."

There is another factor that Keller said could lead to the demise of the mega-ships, and it's not the costs associated with the high price tag of supply-chain expansion. It's the social backlash from communities that live near the ports. Many ports must run 24/7 every day of the year in order to move the extra product coming off those vessels.

"Looking at the supply chain as a holistic system, trucks, like airlines, run ten or twelve hours a day because of work rules—human factors as well as noise abatement rules," Keller said. "Today more and more communities are restricting truck traffic in certain local corridors due to noise and other environmental considerations. You also have labor and other rules that affect warehouses and terminals, thereby restricting their hours of operation. Without changes to each element of the supply chain to allow for seamless constant operations, we will not be able to cope."

Keller explained that these challenges affect the overall transportation system and supply chain all over the world to varying degrees. "With the extra containers that these mega-ships can drop on a port, and with the supply chain essentially being an eight-to-five operation, you will continue to see extremely challenging issues popping up. It's going to be like playing whack-a-mole," he said. "We knock one problem down, but another pops up. The problem is we never have enough hammers to knock them all down at the same time so they stay down."

According to Keller, this is what happens when the supply chain is not viewed holistically, as a long, international factory in which all elements of the process are integrated and interdependent. He stressed that participants in the transport of goods and commodities need to understand that world trade really is about supply chain and ultimately will only be as strong as its weakest link. "It's something that everybody talks about, but no one group has really identified the critical weak links in the supply chain and worked together, on a multimodal basis (marine, truck, rail, warehouses, etcetera), at solving these interrelationships to make the movement of trade more efficient."

Because shipping is a global business, Keller also emphasized the finesse that is needed to keep the logistics flowing from the different cultural bases. "The understanding that time is money is consistent around the world," he said. "But we all have our own speeds and our own investment strategies. We need to remember that there are some parts of the world where you don't want to necessarily use technology to supplant people. Other parts of the world demand more automation and data sophistication. What is productive behavior in one region or country is unacceptable in another. As internationalists in the supply-chain business we need to understand the differences and find a balance that works for the entire factory that is the supply chain."

Strengthening the Supply Chain's Weakest Link

Technology in any industry is a disruptor. It tears open the fabric of innovation and stitches it back up, fortifying an industry's tapestry to make it stronger. While the transport of containers has stayed pretty much the same since containerization started in 1956, with cranes lifting boxes loaded at a shipper's facilities onto ships, the methods of accounting for the process, tracking the boxes, and enhancing productivity to meet the challenges presented by growth have changed. These changes have helped strengthen the supply chain and move boxes faster.

"When I started, the transportation manager was usually somebody on the dock who was actually moving the freight," Keller recalled. "Today it's somebody with an M.B.A. and advanced degrees in data processing, process optimization, and transportation management. That represents a huge, huge change that we often do not think about. That level of sophistication is the reason we have all this emphasis on productivity and optimization of process in the appropriate time-money equation. Then how do I optimize again, and again. A key to logistics is really this continual optimization."

Because of the amount of data and the amount of innovation, the industry now has more tools and sophistication to make logistics more efficient. "We are constantly looking to see how many more gains we can achieve at all levels," Keller said. "We still have far too many weak links in the chain that need to be identified and worked. However, they need to be worked as a system, not individually. It's like a factory. A factory will always move as fast as its slowest process, so in the early days, when we started to automate factories, it started with one robot, but because the other parts of the system weren't automated, the one robot didn't make a difference. The factory didn't see an uptick in productivity until the *whole system* was automated. You need to take a holistic approach when it comes to achieving real logistic gains. I think that's where we are now in shipping. We recognize we need to take that broader view. But can we?"

Keller recognized that getting all parties to the proverbial table to negotiate is a challenge. In order to achieve such synthesis, every member of the logistics supply chain has to be on board.

"It has been hard because everybody is competitive," he said. "Everyone wants to be the best, the fastest, the most innovative, to get the biggest piece of the pie. They are worried if they work together they will lose that advantage. That type of thinking is not helpful."

Keller said it will take some time and a lot of energy to convince the industry and the logistics partners to take a broader view, but he is convinced it can and will be done because the needs are so compelling. One area where he is trying to raise awareness and showing success working together across the different shipping platforms is in the maritime liquefied natural gas (LNG) space.

Energizing Collaboration

"Unity is strength… when there is teamwork and collaboration, wonderful things can be achieved."
—Mattie Stepanek

A powerful example of supply-chain-related collaboration is the shipping industry's initiative to accelerate the adaptation of LNG as a marine fuel through the private sector formation of SEA\LNG. The vision of this international cross-industry coalition is to facilitate the creation of a competitive global LNG value chain that will support the development of an environmentally cleaner maritime shipping industry. "The adoption of LNG as a marine fuel is likely the next major innovation in global shipping, and SEA\LNG will help that become reality," Keller said. TOTE, along with Carnival Corporation & plc, DNV GL, ENGIE, General Electric, Gaztransport & Technigaz S.A., Lloyd's Register, Mitsubishi Corporation, NYK Line, Keppel Gas Technology, Port of Rotterdam, Qatargas, Royal Dutch Shell, and Wärtsilä is a founder of SEA\LNG. The innovative coalition continues to expand its membership to include others in the industry looking to advance the use of LNG technology in maritime.

"We've been able to bring in many organizations from across the value chain of LNG—from the molecules all the way to the Port Authorities that facilitate bunker operations, as well as original equipment manufacturers (OEMs), shipyards, and shipping and cruise lines," Keller said. "We want to address and break down the market barriers to the adoption of LNG, a more environmentally friendly marine fuel. Together we can turn this into a global reality."

As with all technological advances, the transformation needs to be treated as a marathon, not a sprint. Keller emphasized the return on investment (ROI) of converting a fleet to LNG will pay off in the long-term.

"Right now, the ROI is marginalized because the price of bunker fuel oil is so low. However, the volatility of world fuel prices over decades would indicate that is a passing phenomenon, if history is in fact a good teacher," Keller said. "With the International Maritime Organization regulations set to be implemented in 2020, and the existing Environmental Containment Areas (ECAs) currently in place, predominantly in Europe, North America, and now China, we must anticipate that conscientious fleet owners are looking for compliant fuels that will reduce emissions as required by the current and future regulations. From an environmental perspective, the benefits of a ship using LNG versus a similar ship on heavy fuel oil or diesel are dramatic. Compared to existing heavy marine fuel oils, LNG can, depending on the technology used, emit 90 percent less nitrous oxide (NOx), almost completely eliminate sulphur oxides and particulate matter, and emit 20 to 25 percent less carbon dioxide (CO_2)."

Economy of Residual Fuel Oil versus Natural Gas

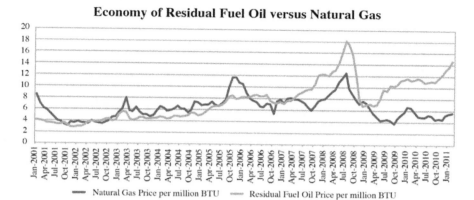

Source: U.S. Energy Information Administration

Keller explained that using LNG as a marine fuel, especially when it is sourced from areas of the world that have readily available supplies of natural gas, such as the U.S., has the potential for significant balance sheet benefits compared to using heavy fuel oil.

"One of the beautiful things about LNG is that the price is about 70 to 75 percent fixed because the main cost element is related to liquefying the natural gas," he said. "For non-LNG-producing locations, the price of transportation also needs to be added. These costs are essentially constant, so the only fluctuation you really have in the cost of LNG over time is the cost of the gas itself. Think about what this means to the maritime executive working on a long-term business plan," he continued. "One of his biggest cost elements is no longer fluctuating wildly, as traditional fuel oil prices have in the past, but rather is now relatively stable—a huge plus."

Comparing international LNG prices with those available for bunkering in the United States is also something Keller said is extremely appealing.

US vs. International LNG Prices
1996-2016

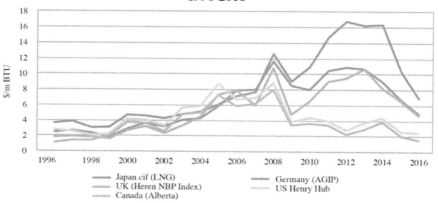

Japan cif (LNG)
UK (Heren NBP Index)
Canada (Alberta)
Germany (AGIP)
US Henry Hub

Source: BP Statistical Review of World Energy

"In the United States, the gas is just across the pipeline, so the price moves in fairly restricted bands. Internationally, the price includes transportation costs, so it is higher. But again, with long-term contracts, the price will be more stable over time. So, as a businessman, I can look twenty years out and say my cost of fuel is only going to fluctuate *this* much, where if I'm in the regular fossil-fuel world, the fuel oil or diesel world, my fluctuation is going to be 100 percent, 150 percent."

To encourage innovation, TOTE's two Marlin-class container ships, operating between Jacksonville, Florida, and San Juan, Puerto Rico, are the world's beta test for the use of LNG as a maritime fuel. "As with so many industries, you've got to prove the case," Keller said, "and I think over the next couple of years, as people look at how the Marlins are performing and how this all works, we will prove our point. LNG is a safe and environmentally friendly maritime fuel."

Keller said he has seen TOTE's competitor Crowley Maritime following in his LNG path, in addition to other LNG-related activity all around the world. "We're seeing a lot of interest on the part of a lot of the shipowners," he said. "But as with any other industry, there's a certain level of caution with new ideas and technologies. Too many business leaders are gauged on quarterly results and not strategies that ensure viable organizations over the long term. The current over-tonnage of worldwide capacity is also an inhibitor in the short term."

This emphasis on generating short-term results, Keller said, is one barrier to the use of LNG as a maritime fuel. "This quarterly—almost monthly—view to please the shareholders, I think, at some point, can be damaging to a company's growth over the long term because it forces leaders to be very, very tactical for just the here and now. It stifles strategic thinking, and the result is missed strategic objectives and potentially becoming less competitive over the long term." Another major concern is the supply of LNG at world ports, but that is being addressed.

Building Out the Supply Chain

When the United States Congress voted in favor of lifting the 40-year-old ban on exporting crude oil and LNG, the shipping industry took a hard look at the nation's ailing export infrastructure and found it unready to take on the opportunity full throttle.

Despite calls from industry experts to invest in LNG infrastructure, little had been done. The industry is now in a game of catch-up. Exporting LNG requires the liquefaction of the gas and the infra-structure capable of loading LNG onto carriers. The Gulf Coast has certainly been building and growing export capabilities, but other areas need to develop their potential. With the largest region of natural gas production, the Marcellus Formation, in the Northeast, the need to have a safe, secure, and strong pipeline to deliver the energy to either the East or Gulf Coast for export is key to United States export growth.

"We need to look at LNG for export as a commodity," Keller explained. "We also need to look at what we call 'Small LNG,' which is that segment that powers trucks, trains, and ships. In terms of our own projects, we learned very early that there was no LNG readily available to us in Jacksonville and Tacoma, the key cities where we operate. So we actually inspired our own projects to fuel our ships."

TOTE developed relationships with existing energy suppliers to construct two small LNG plants, one in Jacksonville and the other in Tacoma. Keller explained that the Jacksonville plant was a joint venture between Pivotal LNG (now a part of Southern Utilities Company Inc.) and Northstar Midstream. In Tacoma, TOTE's partner was Puget Sound Energy. "They are building these plants, initially to supply us but also to become merchant plants to supply trucking, rail, and other parts of the community. Our partners, like us, are looking to the future of LNG implementation, and they want to be a part of this critical infrastructure."

Then there is SEA\LNG, the coalition of energy producers, shippers, component manufacturers, shipyards, and port authorities around the world working to develop an LNG value chain on a global scale.

"You're seeing LNG adoption in a number of ports around the world, including Rotterdam, Hamburg, Singapore, and Scandinavia, as well as the U.S.," he said with enthusiasm. "Ports are realizing that their clients, the shipping lines and their long-term customers, require them to at least facilitate, if not invest in, LNG. It will be good not only for their business but also for the environment of the areas and communities in which they operate. And it will help address the commercial barriers enabling LNG to become a viable bunker fuel that can be readily delivered to a vessel, exactly as other fuels are bunkered."

As another example, Carnival Cruises is investing in a number of LNG-powered cruise ships, at least one of which will be homeported at the Port of Miami. "We have been working with the Port of Miami and others as well as Carnival to help them better understand some of the technical aspects of building out their LNG infrastructure," Keller said.

With no set standardization on infrastructure guidelines, the industry has the opportunity to step up and develop those standards with their regulators. Internationally, SEA\LNG collaborates with the Society of Gas as a Maritime Fuel, which has been working on technical and regulatory issues for a number of years. "In the U.S., we have worked closely with our regulator, the United States Coast Guard," Keller said. "As an industry, we're going to have to standardize fittings, components, processes, and controls. How will a bunker barge connect to the ship?" he asked. "The Coast Guard has their Center of Excellence for LNG, and they have been great because they understand that we are all plowing new ground, and we've been extremely, extremely careful about having our regulators and class society, ABS, in on everything we've done so that there is this important knowledge transfer."

Keller said this information and technology transfer is being put out in the public domain to help others in the industry as well.

Encouraging Proactive Shipping Practices

"The environmental rules facing the shipping industry are coming like a freight train going downhill," Keller warned. "Shipowners need to be able to move more quickly to get ready for these rules. They are not ready. It all goes back to a preoccupation with the here and now as opposed to the longer term. They won't be able to react quickly to the new emissions rules if they don't start strategizing about it now."

Keller said companies that have taken the LNG plunge, including Carnival, MSC Cruises, and the United European Car Carriers (a joint venture between NYK and Wallenius Wilhelmsen Logistics), should be applauded for their strategic view. "This longer-term vision will help get them through these environmental rule changes and set them up for success going forward," he said.

"It's a little bit like what Herb Kelleher, the founder of Southwest Airlines, did many years ago, when he locked in on that long-term fuel contract," Keller explained. "Everybody thought he was nuts. That was, until jet fuel prices went out of sight and there he was making a fortune." He paused. "Sometimes you've got to have a longer-term vision, and you've just got to take it. That's what our leadership at Saltchuk did—they bet on LNG as a viable and cost effective maritime fuel taking a long-term view of environmental and cost benefits when others had not embraced the concept. I don't know if people properly applauded them for that environmental leap, but I am sure they will in the future."

Keller said the shipping world has changed a lot in one key aspect since he joined the industry, and that is in its environmental standards and how it has been responding to create cleaner and more efficient ships. "I always tell people, if I had gone to a major customer twenty years ago to sell my wares and was pitching environmental, I would have been thrown out. Today, if I *don't* mention environmental strategy I would be thrown out!"

Emphasizing that he is not an environmentalist in the classic sense, he said he understands the need for such strategic thinking. "This shows you how the world is starting to change," he said. "I am starting to see more companies look at things more strategically. You've got to walk the walk. You can't just talk the talk."

Looking ever forward, Keller is a walking catalyst for change. Seeing the brilliant horizon ahead and the vast opportunity LNG could provide the shipping industry, he knows the eyes of the industry are on him. Unflinching under the pressure with his beta fleet out on the seas, Keller hopes TOTE's actions will inspire, challenge, and provoke new thinking on the old ways of shipping.

CHAPTER FOUR

Herbjørn Hansson

Shipping Simplicity

Herbjørn Hansson, the charismatic chairman and CEO of the crude shipping company Nordic American Tanker Inc., has been hailed by many as the "evangelist" of the tanker industry, a good salesman, and an industry power player. To those who don't understand his confidence in plotting his own course, he is obstinate, stubborn, bloody-minded, and inflexible. His larger-than-life presence and his passion precede him in the boardroom. Love him or challenge him, Hansson leads his company confidently and unflinchingly.

"I describe him as a sort of a cross between Winston Churchill and the Mad Hatter," Robert Bugbee, president of Scorpio Tankers Inc. and co-founder of Scorpio Bulkers Inc., said, laughing. "He's totally passionate to the core. He has a very simple, consistent message of dividends and profitability. He rows his own boat and is not influenced by what analysts think because they get caught up in monthly numbers. Herbjørn is only steered by his own light, and he uses that light to illuminate his company and shareholders and what he thinks. The simplicity of his message is very calming. He gets everybody back on course."

But before Hansson began connecting with investors and the boardroom, the gregarious Norwegian started out as a deckhand. "During my summers while I was attending my senior high school and business school, I was an able seaman with the DSD," he said.

Hansson worked on coastal cargo ships between Bergen and Oslo. "I had always been interested in international business," he said. "I wanted to try and understand the world. I believe my experiences during those summers at sea helped stimulate my interest."

Hansson, an economist by trade, earned his M.B.A. from the Norwegian School of Economics and Business Administration, and Harvard Business School. From 1974 to 1975, he was employed by the Norwegian Shipowners' Association. In 1975 he began his role as the chief economist and research manager at INTERTANKO, the association of independent tanker owners and operators of oil, chemical, and gas tankers. "During this period I met with all the big names in international tanker shipping," he said. "I found these years so fascinating! It was during that time that I developed my world perspective on oil and energy." It was a perspective that he would later rely on in the creation of two businesses.

In the 1980s, Hansson was chief financial officer of Kosmos/Anders Jahre, which at the time was one of the largest Norwegian-based shipping and industry groups, but it was not enough to fulfill the drive inside him. In 1989 he left in pursuit of expanding his mark on the industry and founded Nordic American, to be renamed Ugland Nordic Shipping AS, or UNS, which became one of the world's largest owners of specialized shuttle tankers.

"When I started my own business, in 1989, after I stepped out of that big Norwegian company where I was CFO, I saw that if you should come anywhere in the world in terms of shipping you had to work internationally," Hansson said. "Norway is a nice country, but the stock exchange in America is 85 times larger than Norway's. In order to grow my business from a global competitive standpoint, I had to go to America."

In the early 1990s, Nordic had about $30 million in total assets. "It was small," Hansson continued, "so I went to my close banking friends at Lazard in New York. I told them I had to be on the stock market in America. I needed to be with the big guys and the big girls."

Hansson credits his confidence for obtaining financial support on Wall Street. "In business, you must have passion and drive, and you must not have internal politics," he said. "That's how you succeed."

The shuttle tanker company thrived under his leadership, and in 2001 it was sold to Teekay Shipping for $780 million.

In 1995, Hansson founded another company, Nordic American Tanker (NAT). The company went public, and with the monies from the first offering and the exercise of warrants, the company acquired three new Suezmax double-hull crude oil tankers. It was a move that many Wall Street observers criticized.

"Many didn't understand what we were doing," Hansson said. "A rule for me has always been to do the opposite of what others are doing. Yes, it's a way of contrarian thinking. Few would have touched the BP deal in the first place, but that was one of the reasons why we went for it."

In September 2004, Hansson decided to work on Nordic American Tankers full-time. "In March of that year we had a general meeting to see whether we should dissolve Nordic and give money back to shareholders," he said.

But that was not what Hansson wanted. He wanted to transform NAT into an operating company. He made his case to the shareholders, and they agreed. "Those who would not like to come along could sell. At that time, the stock was better priced than the steel value of the ships themselves," he said. "Those who believed in my vision stuck with us." And the decision paid off. Those who stayed with NAT saw the stock go from less than $19 to nearly $55 within the year.

NAT Closing Price March 2004 - March 2005

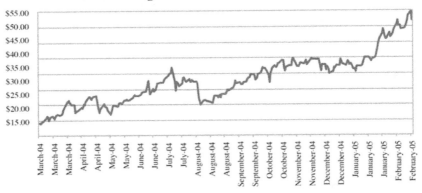

In the Business of Wealth Creation

"I'm not in the guessing business," Hansson said. "Our expertise is not guessing the market. I'm in the business of wealth creation. I work so my 100,000 shareholders and I become wealthy."

In order to achieve that goal, Hansson said, you need to have a business strategy in both strong and weak markets. He broke down his strategy into two parts: Logic and rationality.

"We must have a reason for doing things and a reason for not doing things," he said. The questions he asks himself when approaching an opportunity are something all business leaders, no matter the industry, should be asking themselves: Is it good for the company? Is it bad for the company? Or is it neutral?

"Bottom line, we are three things," Hansson stated. "We are ships, we are capital, and we are people. Together they make a round circle. We are complete."

Acknowledging that including the three pieces in the NAT puzzle is difficult, Hansson said the most important piece is the people. "When you are going to do business with somebody, the first question you must ask is, Who is behind it? And are they good people? Are they bad people?" Hansson said. "Or do you not know about them? And I don't wish to do business with people I don't believe in and people I don't regard as good people."

Hansson sits on the board of the Peterson Institute for International Economics, along with some of the world's top economic minds, including Lawrence Summers, former Secretary of the Treasury and former chair of the National Economic Council; and Jean Claude Trichet, former president of the European Central Bank. "About twenty years ago, I met with Fred Bergstein, the founder of the institute. We got along nicely, and a couple of years ago I was elected to the board," Hansson said. "I'm among these top economists and academicians. The day you do not learn anything is a bad day."

Hansson uses his experience as a research manager and economist when evaluating a region.

Bugbee said Hansson's economic background is one of his greatest assets as a CEO, explaining that his knowledge has strengthened his ability to deliver his message to investors in a very practical and pragmatic way. "Everything he lays out points to wealth creation," Bugbee said. "He's genuinely there to explain how he and his investors will win and create wealth, and I think that's the difference compared to other shipping CEOs. He is prepared even in the worst of times to engage with his shareholders through either the media or his letters. Whereas there are other executives in our industry whom I would consider to be 'fair weather'—they love to talk when they've got great results, but run away when the markets are bad."

Consistency Is the Glue That Binds

Hansson says one of NAT's keys in weathering the tanker cycle for the past twenty years is its unwavering discipline in following a strict regimen of flexibility, transparency, predictability, and accretion.

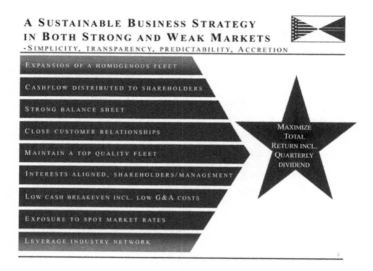

Source: Nordic American Tankers Limited

"We have followed that slide minute by minute for almost twenty years, and we have never deviated from it. Because of these rules, we have a top-quality, homogenous fleet, we have distributed cash flow to shareholders and maintained a strong balance sheet, and we maintain and grow our close customer relationships."

What makes NAT stand out among its peers is the mix of retail and institutional investors. "We have 40 to 50 percent institutions, and the balance is more retail-orientated shareholders," Hansson said. Because of this ownership mix, Nordic American Tankers is the most widely-held shipping company in the stock market. The company is also a favorite amongst yield-loving investors. Since 1997, NAT has also paid a dividend.

Hansson's relationship with his yield-oriented/high-income investors is so important to him that he went against what many shipping executives have called "corporate finance logic" during the worst tanker market trough in history. "Some analysts do not understand the business," he said matter-of-factly. "They use Harvard-type spread-sheets and divide, multiply, subtract, etcetera. They do not see the value of people and the client relationship."

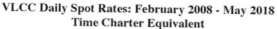

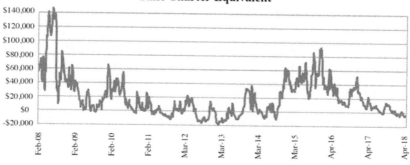

Source: True North Chartering

From the second quarter of 2010 into 2013 the company paid a dividend that was higher than its cash flows. Six of those fifteen quarters had negative cash flow. "Dividend is extremely important," Hansson said. "The value of an asset is the risk-adjusted discounted cash flow."

It's that commitment that has helped NAT sustain a premium valuation. Hansson credits not only his dividend but also his simple message of what the company does as the keys to his wide retail investor base. "We under promised and over-delivered," he said.

With all 30 of the company's tankers on the water spot-trading and on other contracts, NAT is a different type of tanker company. "We explain this in our report to shareholders, and we have a strong following," Hansson said. "We do have institutions. Some have been shareholders for a long time."

NAT can lease its tankers to clients who are looking to either ship or store crude. In times of low crude prices, the tanker business is a good place to be because companies like Nordic not only continue to ship crude, but they also service speculators that use their tankers as floating storage units, waiting for the price of "black gold to go back up so they can sell it," Hansson explained.

The New Buzzword: "Energy Independent"

Since President Richard Nixon, every U.S. president has vowed to make the country energy independent. Thanks to the technological advances in horizontal drilling and hydraulic fracturing to unlock shale oil and gas reserves, the United States has at least 150 years of oil and natural gas, according to energy experts.

Saudi Arabia, the world's top crude-oil exporter, is embarking on its own take on energy independence. They're looking to wean their economy off the go-go juice of their GDP, oil. In April 2016, with projected oil revenues declining, Deputy Crown Prince Mohammed bin Salman unveiled a $2 trillion megafund to make foreign investments and launched the IPO of the kingdom-owned oil company Saudi Aramco. Hansson said the plan will take years. "Saudi will continue to be dependent upon oil for many decades to come."

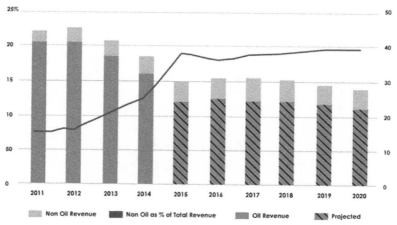

SAUDI'S $2 TRILLION MEGAFUND: HOW TO MOVE ON FROM OIL

The kingdom is looking towards investment as the future of its economy

Revenue as % of GDP

Source: Al Arabiya English, " 'Low oil prices not our battle,' Saudi deputy crown prince tells Bloomberg," 16 April 2016

"Saudi Arabia would like to kill off the shale oil in America because the Saudis cannot afford to have shale oil dominate the whole stage," Hansson said. "The U.S. is underwriting the security of Saudi Arabia. Saudi Arabia is *dependent* on the U.S."

Looking ahead and at OPEC's influence on the oil markets, Hansson scoffed at the organization's perceived "power," saying, "Given their power is low now, with the oil markets becoming freer it's a fact it will be even weaker."

The Hamster Wheel of the Oil Cycle

"I don't think anyone can speculate what will happen with respect to oil prices and gas prices because they are set on the global economy."
—**Ken Salazar**

Since oil prices were first recorded in 1859, analysts and oil CEOs have taken on the herculean task of trying to "predict" the market. The proverbial question "What inning are we in?" is asked by business journalists to such experts. Hansson said he would never answer such a question. "I have met people who *believe* they can see into the future," he said. "I have not met anybody who can actually *see* into the future. All cycles are the same."

But while the cycles may be the same, Hansson added, oil can still be considered a leading indicator when it comes to the health of a country's economy based on its energy consumption. "I started seeing the downturn in Saudi exports to China and the U.S. six to twelve months before the Gross Domestic Product started showing signs of deceleration," he said.

A self-described optimist, Hansson said that while China's economic growth may have passed its peak, he still sees the country growing. "The Chinese work hard. They like money. China is a commercial wonder. Hundreds of millions have become wealthy since Chairman

Deng took over in 1978. We can count on China becoming a richer nation."

Rising Above the Darkest Hour

A contrarian since the beginning, Hansson has never once doubted his ability to lead. When shareholders or fellow board members questioned the future, he stood by his simple message and strategy.

In times of adversity, Hansson always saw the hope, the dawn that would emerge from the darkness of challenge. One career-defining moment was August 2, 1990, when Saddam Hussein invaded Kuwait.

"We had chartered in five (leased) tankers from other owners. At the time, our company was small," Hansson recalled. "We had contracts with the U.S. company Coastal Petroleum, but the contracts had to be canceled because the White House prohibited operators like us from carrying Iraqi oil, which we did for Coastal at the time," he said. "We had several ships chartered in and no work for them that fall. All of the money we lost that fall we got back in the spring, when the market improved and we could charter out the five tankers at a profit."

Hansson recalled a conversation he had years later, in 2008, with a former board member, Harvard Professor George Cabot Lodge. It was another dark shipping time; the company had twenty Suezmaxes with a low market and little work for the vessels. "George asked me, 'Are we in the wrong business?' So I said to him, 'George, I think it's too late to point this out.'"

That time was a learning experience for Hansson. The markets took off again a few years later, and while they made back the money they had lost, Hansson said, the experience was invaluable.

"We learned we needed to be accurate. We could not blame anybody else." Ironically, it was not the first time he was asked about changing his chosen profession. "I have been told ever since I started out in shipping as a young man that I was in the wrong industry," he said, laughing. "But based upon the business principles we follow, Nordic American Tankers has been able to prosper and build a decent company that is about the largest tanker company in the world. And I have no intention of changing a thing."

CHAPTER FIVE

Dr. Martin Stopford

Adventures of a Shipping Cyclist

Shipping's Exuberant Investors

For centuries, leading economists such as Adam Smith and Alfred Marshall have recognized the maritime industry as a vital part of the world economy. With nearly 90 percent of the volume of commodities and products transported by sea, data on gross domestic product and employment numbers are not a sufficient gauge of a country's economic health. To grow, a vibrant modern economy needs commodities and products from overseas. But the shipping industry's uniquely cyclical character presents a challenging collage of opportunities and threats for investors in this trillion-dollar business.

After the Second World War, the world economy embarked on an era of free trade, with sea transport at its heart. Massive investment was needed to build fleets of supertankers, dry bulk carriers, containerships, and specialized vessels of all types to service the needs of multinational companies trading globally. Today, the world is even more reliant on these services, and companies working in the maritime industry must continuously review their strategies for expanding or downsize their fleets.

But reading the economic signals is tricky. Despite its strategic importance, shipping remains a uniquely unpredictable business, facing volatility that even professional gamblers would find daunting. For example, a Panamax bulk carrier ordered for $18.5 million in 1999 and delivered in 2001 could, within six years, have earned its lucky investor $124 million cash![5] But the downside can be just as extreme. Some Very Large Crude Carriers (VLCCs) ordered in the early 1970s for over $60 million each were delivered into layup and eventually sold for demolition at $3 million. An industry founded on, and fueled by, this sort of exuberance needs investors with unshakable confidence and an endless supply of optimism. But to get the balance right, it also needs individuals who can apply a timely perspective on the cycle. For the maritime industry, that economic data go-to person, and the man with an endless supply of cyclical data, is Martin Stopford, non-executive president of Clarkson Research Services Limited (CRSL) and director of MarEcon Ltd.

Stopford is well known to shipbuilders and investors, but also to generations of bankers, shipping professionals, and students who have learned the ins and outs of shipping markets, cycles, and the global economy from his textbook, *Maritime Economics*, now in its third edition. Forty-five years in shipbuilding, banking, and as an executive director of shipbroking giant Clarkson PLC have given him a deep understanding of the "nuts and bolts" of the business. His ability to transform data into a readily understandable message, on which practical and profitable investment decisions can be based, has earned him a reputation as one of the shipping world's leading luminaries. A relentless travel schedule and his love of maritime history have helped him develop this unique perspective on the global maritime village, a community he has come to admire and respect.

Growing Up in Rural England

Born in Bolton, Lancashire, Stopford did not hail from a shipping family. He was the son of a clergyman. In 1947, the family moved to the tiny country village of Whitmore, where Stopford grew up. He went to the village school, which had only about twenty pupils and was very much part of local farming life. Every year in November, the

---

[5] A six-year-old panama bulk carrier could be sold for $80 million in 2008 and would have earned about $44 million trading on the spot market between April 2002 and April 2008, a total return after operating costs of $124 million. If the ship was purchased with a 60 percent loan, the equity investment of $7.5 million increased by a multiple of 16.

school had a week's holiday for potato picking. "We would all go off into the fields and pick potatoes for the local farmers," Stopford recollected with a smile in his voice.

The Peake family were the farmers he worked for. "I vividly remember Old Uncle Tom Peake coming up the back lane with his two shire horses, which the old farmers were still using back then. He gave me four half-crowns for the week, which was less than one dollar in today's money. I was so delighted!"

Young Martin Stopford enjoys a break harvesting grain,
with his father and Fred Latham, probably 1958

He never forgot the glint and weight of the coins. "Half-crowns were big silver coins. Uncle Tom beckoned me up to the back lane behind the house, and I ran up there, and that's where he gave me those four half-crowns. That was the first money I ever earned, at the age of eight."

Stopford knew education was more than just learning from books. In the 1950s his father, Eric, started to farm the "glebe" (the land belonging to the rectory), so that he could get to know his parishioners better during the week. Young Stopford spent much of his free time as a youth working with Eric on the small farm (and, of course, going to church!). They grew barley and built up a herd of pedigree large white pigs. The schoolroom of life shaped the individual. Growing up in a small village, described by Stopford as a "free and easy place that still observed the old country customs," helped form his perspective on life. "It was a very good experience. You got used to a certain way of working with friends and farmers. I learned a lot of things by using my hands and working with others, including the value of persistence. This is what I have tried to do my whole life—get a project to work on, and try and finish it, wherever it took me." Quite a few of those projects involved fixing up old motorcycles, the origin of a lifelong enthusiasm.

Stopford, like the other children in his village, left the village school at the age of eleven. He went on to prep school, then public school. In 1966 he won an Abbott scholarship to Keble College, Oxford, where he studied politics, philosophy, and economics (PPE). When he graduated, in 1969, it was the summer of the Woodstock Festival. "If you didn't go to San Francisco to join the Flower People, you probably went somewhere like India," Stopford said. "I planned a trip with some friends, but being a practical sort of chap, I thought it would be a good idea to arrange a job for when I came back."

One of companies Stopford met with was Maritime Transport Research, the market research arm of the U.K. shipbuilding industry. "I liked them, but they did not offer me a job," he said thoughtfully. "They wanted someone immediately. Little did I know this interview would change the course of my life."

Road Trip to India in the Yellow Van

After graduation and his meeting with Maritime Transport Research, Stopford and his friends John Charlton and Richard Walking purchased an old Comma van for their adventure.

"Those were the days of the hippie trail. So we painted the van bright yellow." He laughed. "But it only drove 40 miles per hour, and we didn't get very far in a day."

Martin Stopford (center), John Charlton, and Richard Walking, with the yellow van, back from India in April 1970

Stopford, Charlton, Walking, and their friend Nick Wright drove on to Turkey, Iran, and Afghanistan. Charlton was a member of the university's bridge team. "He was a very good bridge player," Stopford said. "So if you can picture it, there were the four of us in this van, one was driving, and the other three spent a fair bit of time playing bridge in the back. John, being so good, taught us how to count cards and all sorts of tricks of the trade in bridge. We got very proficient. It was an interesting and a fun way to pass the time as we ambled slowly along the roads and tracks of Turkey, Iran, and Afghanistan."

During their six months on the road, they caught fleeting glimpses of a culture that has long since disappeared. "In the still morning air, we would hear the bells of camel trains tinkling across the desert; and when we drove into Kandahar at dusk one evening in December, it was like being in the Arabian Nights. The fragrant bazaar with merchants lounging on carpeted platforms, smoking hookahs or sipping glasses of black tea, was from an ancient world. Things are very different today." Stopford and his friends arrived back home just after Easter. "Our biggest achievement was getting the yellow van back," he said. "John and Richard dropped me off and drove on to Sunderland. The van never started again. The engine had got mangled up in 50 degrees of frost in the Tahir Pass in Turkey. But amazingly it got us home."

Still with no real idea of what he wanted to do, Stopford got a job with Lyons Bakery driving cake vans. "After all, driving a van was now my main skill!" he said with a laugh. Then, in early 1971, he got a project to convert a disused printing works in Burslem, Stoke-on-Trent, into a cash and carry. "The company delivered wholesale stationery and toys to small shops. The idea was to get the shopkeepers to pick up the goods, pay cash, and maybe spend more when they saw the toys on offer." he explained.[6] Not afraid of physical labor, Stopford rolled up his sleeves and got to work. He moved out all the heavy printing equipment, gutted the warehouse-like structure, built shelving, decorated, and got it ready for the grand opening. "It was not the slickest cash and carry," he reflected with a wry smile, "but it was a great success and very cost effective! We got the customers to do all the work. That's me all over!" With the proceeds, he bought a Triumph TR3A open-top sports car, in British racing green—"a real classic and still my all-time favorite car," he said with a boyish grin.

Launched into the World of Shipbuilding

After six months, the cash and carry project was winding down when Stopford got a call from John Stapleton, the director of Maritime Transport Research in London. "John told me the analyst they hired in 1969 was leaving and asked if I would like the job," Stopford said. "I moved to London and started work on September 21, 1971. That was

---

[6] The printing works had an interesting history. It had been owned by Barnetts of Burslem and was the setting for a novel called *Clayhanger* by Victorian novelist Arnold Bennett. "Although he is now largely forgotten, in his day Arnold Bennett was almost as famous as Dickens. You can still order an *Omelette Arnold Bennett* at the Savoy Hotel in London, where Bennett was a regular visitor," Stopford said.

how I got into the maritime industry, and I have never looked back. I loved it from the first day."

To be an effective analyst, Stopford decided he needed to learn more about economics. In October 1972, he enrolled as an evening student at the new Economics Department set up at Birkbeck College, London University, by two hotshot professors from the London School of Economics, Bertie Hines and John Muellbauer. "I was pretty much their first student," Stopford recalled. "I was interviewed among packing cases!" He did the first year of an MSc in mathematical economics, then switched to a Ph.D. In 1979 he obtained his degree in international economics, having completed his thesis trade matrices for 220 dry cargo commodities over eight years, 1966 to 1972, and a large trade model.[7] "I learned one thing about computing," he said. "You can build big models, but they are not necessarily more accurate. It's just harder to spot the silly mistakes." He grinned. "So keep it simple."

Meanwhile, another opportunity had presented itself. In 1977, the U.K. shipbuilding industry was nationalized—warship yards, merchant yards, engine manufacturers, and ship repairers. The new corporation, British Shipbuilders Corporation, had 87,309 employees and more than 40 companies building everything from fishing boats to nuclear submarines.

Stopford was recruited as group economist and started work on July 1, 1977, the day the corporation started trading.

---

[7] Martin Stopford, Jack Griffiths, Sue Bland, and John Stapleton, *Dry Cargo Ship Demand to 1980* (London: Maritime Transport Research, 1977).

*British shipyards struggled to compete
with big, new Asian yards*

"Shipbuilding was a bare-knuckle business," Stopford said. "But it had a proud history, and when you watch the new ship head down the slipway, you understand why shipyard workers have such pride. It's the same everywhere." A century earlier the British shipyards had built three quarters of the world's ships, but by 1977 that share had slipped to 5 percent and the yards were struggling to compete with the big modern Japanese and Korean yards. For the next ten years Stopford was deeply involved in the efforts to navigate the industry through the 1980s shipbuilding depression, one of the deepest on record.

In 1981, Stopford was made director of business development, responsible for preparing the corporate plan. The world shipping and shipbuilding industries were spiraling into a historic depression, and British Shipbuilders was having a bumpy ride. Cash flow management was crucial but tricky for such a large and diverse business. Personal computers (PCs) were just getting started, and Stopford could see their potential. "We got our first PC, a Commodore Pet, in 1980," he said, "with a spreadsheet called VisiCalc. It only had 80 columns and 250 rows, but it was a giant step forward for anyone handling large amounts of financial data." Corporate planning in a company with 40-plus subsidiaries involved a lot of financial work. Updating forecasts, after reviewing company budgets, was labor intensive and error prone. But spreadsheets worked like magic, allowing Stopford and his team to consolidate and update the financial forecasts submitted by each subsidiary company. "Data on employment, production, productivity, and cash flow forecasts could be consolidated quickly and accurately for the whole corporation, helping us make a real contribution to the management of the business," Stopford said.

Sensing the potential of this new technology, in 1982 Stopford obtained a diploma in accounting and finance from the Institute for Certified Accountants. Over the next five years, in addition to the corporate plan, his department produced the corporation's cash flow forecasts and managed the annual budget, and Stopford served as a member of the corporation's management committee. "Quite an experience for a young man," Stopford said. "I came to grips with the numbers game and learned the value of giving busy decision-makers the information they needed, in an easy-to-understand format. I just wish we had been able to do more."

But by the mid-1980s the recession had become too deep for British shipbuilding to survive. "The combination of the strong pound, due to North Sea oil, and the collapse in shipbuilding prices was unsustainable," Stopford explained. "In 1986 a VLCC sold for $36 million.[8] That might have paid for the materials, but there was nothing left for labor and overhead—an impossible situation," Stopford said. "We lost the battle, and I don't see how we could have won it. My last job was trying to sell Sunderland Shipbuilders' Pallion yard to Sumitomo Shipbuilders in Japan. I went over to Japan with our chairman John Lister and Bill Scott, managing director of the engine-building division of British Shipbuilders. We had a great visit, and they visited us. We shared an enthusiasm for shipbuilding, but their problems were nearly as bad as ours. The writing was on the wall."

---

[8] Worldwide ordered two VLCCs for $36 million each in 1986.

*British Shipbuilders visit Sumitomo February 1988 to discuss
Sunderland Shipbuilders, Stopford third from right*

From Shipbuilding to Ship Banking

In April 1988, Stopford got a well-timed call from Van Mellis, head of shipping at Chase Manhattan Bank. Peter S. Douglas, their eminent global shipping economist, was retiring, and Mellis was looking for a replacement. It was an easy decision for Stopford. At Chase, he saw firsthand how the shipping finance business was transforming itself after the catastrophic recession. "There had been very little lending business done in the mid-1980s. A typical financial transaction was no more than $25 million dollars, and you were lucky if you could get that," Stopford explained. "The banking business was very subdued, and much of the business was still speculative."

Chase had supported many of its European customers through the recession, and as the market recovered in 1988, its shipping department was back in business. But the growing volatility of the shipping market, tighter bank regulation, and the lack of time charters were making conventional mortgage-backed lending increasingly difficult.

An exciting development during this recovery period was the Norwegian KS market.[9] The years following the market trough in 1986 saw one of the best asset play markets on record. Second-hand ship prices rose steadily. A five-year-old Panamax bulk carrier was worth $6.1 million in mid-1986; $10.5 million in mid-1987; $16.5 million in mid-1988; and $21 million in mid-1989. In Norway, the finance houses used the KS structure to set up KS partnership companies to buy second-hand tankers and bulk carriers.

Shares were sold to the Norwegian public, who got a tax break and excellent capital appreciation. As ship prices rose, so did share values and the enthusiasm of investors, helping to fuel the asset price spiral.

When Stopford started at Chase, he inherited an annual course run by Cambridge Academy of Transport from Peter Douglas, course leader on *Ship Forecasting*. "The first one I moderated in 1989 was a bit slim on numbers. Only six people showed up!" Stopford said. "But the banking scene was growing again, and I said to John Doviak, the director of Cambridge Academy of Transport, 'Why don't we turn this into a ship finance course and call it *Anatomy of Ship Finance*? We could give delegates a really broad perspective on the ship finance business and how it works.' " Doviak agreed, and in July 1990, *Anatomy of Ship Finance* was launched, this time with 40 delegates. Stopford, as course leader, persuaded Alan Brauner, one of the industry's most experienced ship financiers, to join as banking advisor, and Doviak ran the ship finance game. "It was a great team," Stopford said. "The three of us worked together on that course for twenty years. Many European bankers attended. One year we had so many delegates from one Dutch bank that they could have fielded their own football team! But given recent events, maybe we didn't get our message across well enough." He laughed. "But it was great fun. We had a fantastic time, and the ship finance game was very realistic."

---

[9] Kommandittselskap (KS) is a single-purpose limited partnership under the Norwegian Companies Act (NCA). A KS must consist of one general partner and several limited partners. The general partner (komplementaren) must hold a minimum share of 10 percent in the KS. The general partner has unlimited liability toward the company's creditors. The obligations of the limited partners' are limited to the total of shares of committed capital (including bank guarantee) of the KS. A limited partner does hold a joint liability toward the KS if there is a default on one of the other limited partners' obligations.

The course started on Sunday, and Stopford piled on the pressure during the week. There were many visiting lecturers, and the ship finance game soon got very intense. By Thursday afternoon, when the game finished, everyone was ready to let their hair down at the farewell dinner. "After dinner, we announced the winners and pandemonium broke loose," Stopford said. "I would dress up as Elvis—honestly! Or sometimes a Johnny Depp–style pirate. It was a lot of fun. Foresight's Ravi Mehrotra used to come to the dinner, as well as Alan Ginsberg, Susan Cook, and Jean Richards."

Delegates on Anatomy of Ship Finance enjoyed letting down their hair after a week of pressure. CATS Director John Doviak (far right, orange wig!) and Stopford (as pirate Johnny Depp, behind him). Guest Ravi Mehrotra, President of Foresight, is an even more convincing pirate (second row, far left). Unfortunately, Susan Cook, (front row, far left) and Jean Richards (front row, third from right) had abandoned their costumes before the photo was taken.

In the early 1990s, the U.S. money center banks were facing a tough time. The savings and loan crisis, fueled by the high-yield bond market developed by Michael Milken in the late 1980s, had created credit problems, and the Fed was determined to tighten standards. This was not good news for ship finance. "There was a credit matrix," Stopford said, "which had risk on one axis and return on the other. Unfortunately, ship finance lay in the low-return and high-risk quadrant, which made the bank's balance sheet a no-go area for loan officers. Annuity income was toast."

Stopford's Dual Destiny: Clarksons and Data

As shipping moved into the 1990s, Stopford could see that digital technology was transforming data collection and distribution.[10] Database programs, PC networks, spreadsheet publishing, and database publishing had all arrived in a viable form. "In the 1980s all this technology was still primitive," Stopford said. "Now it really worked. I also noticed that data suppliers like Fearnleys and Drewry were more interested in consultancy than data, and decided that was the place to focus."

When, in 1990, Hugh McCoy approached him to head up Clarkson Research Services Ltd. (CRSL), Stopford jumped at the opportunity to develop the Clarkson data franchise. "Clarkson brokers covered all the main charter markets including S&P, newbuildings, and demolition," he said. "It was an unrivalled data source waiting to be developed. And Clarkson was a PLC, providing a more stable platform for developing a data system than a private broking company."

Of course, Clarkson also wanted a forecaster, and Stopford had to win his spurs. It doesn't matter what kind of job you have—on your first day, you want to make a good impression. Stopford started as managing director of Clarkson Research on August 2, 1990, the day the Iraqi dictator Saddam Hussein invaded Kuwait. "It was a lively day," he recalled. "I joined a colleague at a meeting with a senior Hong Kong shipowner, who asked us, 'What's the tanker market going to do now?' My colleague, who happened to be Mr. Tony Klima, the

---

[10] Martin Stopford, "The Broker's Role in the Future World of Information and Communications Technology," presented at BIMCO General Meeting, September 20, 1991.

chairman of Clarkson, said it was going to go up, and I said it was going to go down." He chuckled. "Of course, on your first day you don't really want to disagree with the chairman, but in a way it sort of set a good precedent. Luckily, on that occasion, we were *both* right. The tanker market spiked briefly the following February, then collapsed into a long and rather unpleasant trough lasting several years. That's the thing about predicting any of these cycles. You can predict the direction and you can predict the timing, but you really need to predict the direction *and* the timing."

Clarkson Research was a great opportunity, but there was a lot of work to be done. The registers were still produced using paper tapes, downloaded once a year from the company mainframe, and there was only one PC.[11] "Luckily, new spreadsheet publishing software made it possible to automate the production of complex data reports," Stopford said. "I spent my first year working with Cliff Tyler to develop *Shipping Intelligence Weekly* (SIW), which we finally published in February 1992. Such a complex weekly document, with hundreds of data series and complex calculations like time charter equivalents, would previously have needed a big team of analysts. Spreadsheet publishing changed all that. SIW turned into a bestseller, providing the revenue to build Clarkson Research as a business. It also broke new ground in data provision, allowing bankers and investors to see, at a glance, what ships were earning and how markets, prices, time charter rates, and many other variables were performing. "The goal was to make a busy banker, during the cab ride to lunch with his client, a current market expert," Stopford said. "Amazingly, it seemed to work. I still use it all the time myself."

In 1993, the CRSL registers were transferred to database publishing, and World Shipyard Monitor, a monthly report, was published. "At the time, shipbuilding data was only updated a few times a year, so a monthly report was a controversial revolution," Stopford said. "We were told there would not be enough change during a month. Now it's the norm and investors avidly follow monthly changes in prices,

---

[11] Stopford got a lot of support in the early days from a small team of brokers on the CRSL advisory board—Nick Collins, Neil Freeland, Merrick Rayner, and Alex Williams "were real troopers," he said. "Thanks to them all."

contracting and the order book. Other publications followed, and, at the peak of the dot-com boom, in March 2000, Shipping Intelligence Network (SIN), was launched, providing clients with access to the ever-expanding Clarkson database. In 2003, Clarkson purchased Oilfield Publications Ltd., moving into the offshore sector; in 2010, it purchased the World Fleet Monitor, a monthly publication covering all aspects of the world merchant fleet, including ownership. It had taken more than ten years to build and code up the databases to do this.

In 2004, Stopford joined the board of Clarkson PLC as one of three executive directors, an invitation he describes as "a big surprise and a bigger honor." After eight years on the board, in 2012, Stopford turned 65 and decided to retire. "I had a talented team managing Clarkson Research, and it was time they took over," he said. "What I did not expect was that the board would make me nonexecutive president of Clarkson Research, with a mandate to represent the company around the world." This role has given Stopford the chance to carry on his activities in the global maritime village, speaking to companies, conferences, and institutions around the world.

Academic and Author

Another sub-plot to Stopford's career was teaching and his textbook *Maritime Economics*. "I got the idea in the early 1980s, when I was teaching shipping economics and trade at Costas Grammenos's new Institute for Shipping, Trade & Finance at the City University Business School, London," he said. "I became convinced a textbook would make life much easier for everyone." In 1986, Stopford submitted the manuscript for *Maritime Economics* to Allen & Unwin, the Bloomsbury-based publishing company, and they agreed to publish it. "Their office was in Museum Street, London, right in front of the British Museum. Walter Allen, the economics editor, took me out for a literary lunch!" Stopford recalled. "It was really the end of an era for that sort of thing, and I was glad to get a glimpse of it before it disappeared."

The reception area at the Allen & Unwin office was packed with the books by many famous Bloomsbury authors of the 1920s, and Stopford was particularly proud to appear in the same catalogue as Joseph A. Schumpeter, whose *History of Economic Analysis* has a permanent place on his desk.

"The first edition of *Maritime Economics* was published in March 1988, just as I was joining Chase Manhattan bank," Stopford said. "There was a second edition in 1997, and an even bigger, third edition in 2009. It's a privilege to publish a book like this, and I am constantly looking for ways to improve it." The third edition has been translated into Greek, Japanese, Turkish, and Brazilian Portuguese.

Rethinking the Sea Transport Strategy for the Next Investment Cycle

Stopford believes that in tomorrow's world, focusing on speculation will be the wrong business model. "While the past 30 years have been great fun, and the mantra 'We trade ships, not cargo' worked well for some individuals," he said, "this philosophy was the product of the 1980s, when shipowners could buy a Panamax bulker for $6 million and sell it a few years later for $22 million. You can't argue with that, but like winning the slot machine jackpot, it's not really a viable business strategy. Trading ships is *not* the answer. Adding value and dealing with problems like efficient through transport and climate change is where the industry should be focusing."

Stopford thinks the best hope is using digital technology to improve the efficiency of the whole transport operation. "Digitalization adds value because it allows companies to use their resources more efficiently. Just adding ships to the fleet does not. Information and communications technology (ICT) is already extensively used in land-based industries, and with recent improvements in communications, the shipping industry can follow their lead," Stopford explained. "This technology can streamline the scheduling of materials, planning control, and sophisticated statistical quality control, enabling shipping company managers to make better decisions."

Shipping has seen a digital transformation over the past few years, especially satellite communication systems. Global Xpress, the newest satellite system operated by Inmarsat, will allow shipping offices to communicate reliably with their ships almost anywhere in the world, and the whole system will improve.

"But it's not just a single technology that is needed to take a step forward. It's a bundle of technologies, which I call the smart shipping toolbox," Stopford said. "The main tools are telematics. Improved satellite communication technology and subsea cables, cheap cloud-based data storage, smartphone-style apps, touch technology, and artificial intelligence systems—all these will play a part. Most of this technology has been around for a while, but today it works better and costs less."

Stopford added that the technological advancements are particularly important for dealing with maritime environmental issues. "There is a better way to save resources, and I think shipping could be a good example in utilizing technology to measure and monitor performance, using this information to develop strategies to minimize its carbon footprint."

Stopford said that, although the pace of digital change in the shipping industry is faster, this revolution is not going to happen overnight. "The change from sail to steam took about 50 years."

Back to the Farm

Even while looking at the possibilities of the future, Stopford appreciates the value of the past. In 2009, Stopford took a step back to his childhood by purchasing a farm in Staffordshire Moorlands. The farm is in the valley of the River Churnet, with an eighteenth-century farmhouse and farmyard, which he reactivated. "When I bought it, the farmyard was going downhill and had not been used for a few years," he said. "I could have just let the land, but I decided that the farm needs a farmyard at its heart, and so we renovated the buildings and got things started. So, in a way, I'm back where I started—it's organic and we are still farming the old way! But there's no potato picking, and the money isn't so good. Farming cattle is a bit like running Capesize bulkers—you feed money in one end and shit comes out of the other," he joked.

"Maritime economics is still my real passion, but I feel good back on the farm."

Stopford back farming in 2013

CHAPTER SIX

Claus-Peter Offen

Seizing Opportunity in the Troughs

The face of opportunity can reveal itself at any time in a business cycle. For distress investors, the trough is a time to strike. With an educated and discerning eye, quality companies can be cherry-picked at a fraction of the cost. Consolidation is a natural part of the fallout process and is often the healthiest way for an industry to rebalance. After suffering one of the biggest downturns in its history, the shipping sector is slowly recovering through consolidation.

Germany is just one of the many regions where the maritime industry is realigning in the consolidation process. The number of container operators has shrunk in response to a glut of tonnage. Years of plunging freight rates and the February 17, 2017, bankruptcy of Hanjin Shipping (a substantial percentage of the company's container fleet was owned by German banks and investors) added further pressure on the already distressed region.

One of the country's largest shipping debtors, Rickmers Holdings AG, filed for bankruptcy on June 2, 2017. A wave of consolidation took place, with the world's twenty largest container operators condensing into around a dozen companies.

Claus-Peter Offen, founder, sole shareholder, and CEO of Offen Group, has strategically taken advantage of the shipping turmoil and acquired companies as a part of his strategy to expand Offen Group's footprint in the container, bulk, and product tanker market. Offen buys distressed assets at steep discounts, turns them around, and reaps the rewards of a larger, stronger company.

Born in Germany, Offen sharpened his skills by working for shipping companies in England and France as a young man. His career eventually took him back to Hamburg, where he lives to this day. He knew at the tender age of eight that he wanted to be like his father, who owned cargo freighters. "I remember I was with my mother for the naming of a ship," he said. "I found it exciting and fascinating. I loved it and was hooked. When I turned 27, after I had worked in the industry for a while, I thought I could easily do it all myself."

Offen saw his opportunity to realize his dream in the newspaper. A freighter called the *Annie Hugo Stinnes* was up for auction as part of a bankruptcy liquidation. On June 1, 1971, Offen went to a Hamburg court and purchased the ship. "The freighter came from a medium-size but fairly famous shipping company that was part of a steel conglomerate," he said. "The bankruptcy got a lot of publicity. So I went to court and came out owning a small ship." He baptized her in Holstein.

"I never forgot that feeling I had," he recalled, his eyes twinkling. "I said to myself, Wow, now I am a shipowner! I spoke with a private banker who was helping me finance the ship in the beginning a little bit, and he congratulated me and gave me one piece of advice I will never forget. He said, 'You are a lucky man today. If I were you, I would go out on the street and the first poor devil you see, give him a hundred dollars, just to say thank you to your God for helping today.' And I thought this was good advice. When I walked home through the streets there was some poor guy sitting there. I pulled a hundred dollars out of my wallet and gave it to him. He looked at me puzzled." He chuckled warmly.

With no personnel hired for the ship, Offen worked closely with a friend whose father had a steamship company to manage and select a crew. "It did not make a lot of sense to do it on your own for just one ship," he explained.

But there was one thing Offen did want to do on his own, and that was go to America to register his first ship. "It was amazing. I'd never been to the U.S. before. The Liberian Registry is in New York, and I wanted to do it personally," he said. "I had a funny feeling inside when I drove from my home to the airport. I was so excited. I flew economy class. It was a big deal back then because people didn't fly as much as they do today. That whole time on the plane only one thought went through my mind, over and over—that soon I would be in New York! I flew into Idlewild Airport, which is now JFK Airport, and took a taxi to the Waldorf-Astoria, where I stayed."

He smiled nostalgically. "I never forgot the feeling when I arrived in the early evening, checked into the hotel, and walked along Park Avenue. I saw the all the shops, the cafés, the people, and I thought everybody must know I just came from Germany." He laughed. "Of course, nobody looked at me. I must have looked like a stranger, and they didn't care about me at all. I purchased a hamburger, and then I walked up and down on Park Avenue. All these huge buildings were lit. I looked up at all those lights, and said to myself, If there was one place that would be considered the center of the world, this must be it. It really was a great feeling. I was very young then."

The next day, Offen walked into the Liberian Registry and filed the necessary papers. He was now an official shipowner. His company, Reederei Claus-Peter Offen, was founded and chartered under the Liberian Flag.

During the company's formative first year, Offen made close contact with a leading manager of Vereins- und Westbank, a local bank in Germany. He told Offen that some of the bank's major private customers were looking to make investments. "My family was well-known because of my father, and I met with the investors. They believed in me. I was able to buy six ships thanks to their investment. The ships were twice the size of my first one."

With the larger vessels, Offen was able to generate more revenues to add to his fleet. "So I bought one after another six-, ten-, twelve-year-old ships, cargo ships of about 7,000 tons each, from well-known names in those days, like Hapag-Lloyd," he said. "The timing was excellent because when I bought the ships they were very cheap in a crisis, much like today. I was trading them and I was chartering them out to the liner companies. There were a lot of liner companies back then. Much more than we have today. Back then, you would find around 200 that were trading ships. Today, you'll find only 20 or 30 companies in the world."

The rates recovered and were so high Offen could pay dividends of 20 percent every two months to his investors. "We paid 120 percent in a year," he said, smiling. "The vessels were bought at the very bottom of the market, and when I bought them the rates were between $3,000 to $4,000 a day, and all of a sudden they were $12,000 a day, but the investment price was still very low."

For three years Offen paid those tremendous dividends, and after three years he got a feeling that the general cargo trade would slowly end and that the container would probably be the technology of sea transport in the future, so he sold those ships. "We got excellent prices and sold them at about three times the price we paid, so all of the sudden we were a fairly wealthy company, and the company was only three years old!"

Offen placed his first order for six containerships at a German shipyard, which for the mid-seventies was a big jump in volume. The cost: $200 million. "The fleet was considered to be the most modern and largest tramp ships of their time. They were small 600 TEU ships," he said, chuckling. "Today they would be very, very small, and you would call them 'coasters.'"

The ships were delivered in 1978 and '79, and he chartered them out to various liner companies, mostly Ivaran Lines, a Norwegian-owned company. It was the trade routes that appealed to Offen. "They were a very important carrier between the two Americas," he explained. "They were trading from the U.S. East Coast down to South America. I found both interesting places to go, so I did a few trips on the ships from New York down the East Coast all the way to Brazil and Argentina."

Over the years, the company grew. The six newbuildings were delivered and chartered out. Offen purchased some more secondhand ships, and they ordered more newbuildings. The company steadily grew to become the largest commercial customer of the German shipbuilding industry in the 1980s and '90s. "Nobody else ordered more ships in German shipyards than I did in those years, so we were really growing fast," Offen said. "And then, around the year 2000, I decided that there were big problems in the German ship industry, and I saw that the Asian companies were doing great progress, especially in South Korea. I then started ordering the first ships in South Korea. By now, I would say, by now I must have ordered at least 120 ships. We are probably one of the biggest customers of the South Korean shipbuilding industry today."

Between 2004 and 2007, Offen looked for more opportunities to grow. He ordered very big ships, up to 14,000 TEU, which at that time were the largest ships being built in the world. "I chartered them out to the major liner companies like Maersk, MSC Geneva, and CMA-CGM in France," he said, "and the fact that we had ordered all those ships against long-term charters helped us a lot to survive the present shipping crisis."

"Happy" Birthday

It was 2008, and Offen was set to celebrate his 65th birthday on September 15th when the unthinkable happened. Lehman Brothers filed for bankruptcy, sending the global markets into turmoil. The Dow Jones closed down just over 500 points (−4.4 percent). It marked the largest drop of points in a single day since the days after the September 11, 2001, attacks. On September 29, 2008, the markets plunged even further: -7.0 percent.

"I have to say, it was the most expensive birthday I have ever had," Offen said, deadpan. "It was not such a good day. On the day itself, you didn't know what was going to happen next."

Offen knew the Lehman bankruptcy would take a long-term toll on the global economy. He looked at his order book and saw he had some 40 ships that would be delivered between 2008 and 2012.

"Fortunately, most of them were chartered out on medium- and long-term contracts. But there was a huge investment volume, something around $4 billion, which we had to pay to the shipyards. We had the credit financing in place, but we did not have the equity financing in place. Many of those ships were planned to be financed by the German KG system."

Since the company was not an issuing house, Offen was working with two major financial institutions for his equity financing: MPC Capital, which was the market leader in Germany at that time, and CoReal, which was a 100 percent subsidiary of Commerzbank. Both had given his company guarantees. "CoReal paid up whatever it had to pay, something like $300 million, $400 million, so those ships were 100 percent financed. But our other partner, MPC Capital, did not have the funds to come up with for such a major disaster, so we had to talk to the shipyards about how to solve this equity problem," Offen said.

"They all urgently needed these orders, because if the orders failed, they, too, would have a huge problem. So we sat down and came up with solutions."

In the end, Offen agreed to the order. "The ships needed to be built, especially because they all had very good long-term charters, up to 2027, and from a business perspective we needed to build them to keep those charters."

Offen agreed to put up part of the financing to fulfill the order. The largest part was financed as sellers' credits by the shipyards over a longer period so Offen could take all of the 42 ships he had ordered when they were completed. Offen admits they overcame the financial crisis quite well. "Unfortunately, many of my colleagues delayed, delayed, delayed the delivery because they could not put the finances together."

Growing in the Troughs of the Cycle

By the first half of 2010, the shipping market had stabilized. Volumes were recovering. The entrance of new "smart" money—private equity firms and hedge funds—added to the exuberant feeling that the worst was over and the market and global economy would recover to pre-Lehman levels. The private equity firms and hedge funds started to order ships along with others like Offen in the industry.

"Prior to the collapse of Lehman, the market had grown up to 12 or 14 percent every year," Offen said. "Those in the industry had worked out that if this type of growth came back, there would not be enough ships to handle the demand. So the order books were growing again."

But the economy did not meet expectations. Globalization and containerization never recovered to the pre-crisis level. "Instead of having 12 percent growth, we had 2, 3, 4 percent growth. So in addition to all the excess of new ship orders, everybody was fighting for market share. Shipbuilding prices fell dramatically, so ordering ships was much more attractive, and there was a lot of money in the world with zero interest. The orders just piled up."

The cheap money and cheap ships created a glut like the shipping industry had never seen. By the end of 2015, the market realized there was huge overcapacity and newbuildings had to be laid up. There were also a large number of ships running on charter rates that were reduced by 80 percent. "In 2016 and 2017 there were hardly any new orders, but there's still an overhang of ships that have yet to be delivered," Offen said.

Despite the challenges facing the industry, Offen's company grew. He realized he needed to have a better structure to run his floating assets. "We had a large number of containerships, tankers, and bulkers," he said, "so we decided to put each individual company under one central roof and separate the subsidiaries I had. Under the restructuring I had a different management team to run each division. The holding company, CPO Holding, is now the mother company, of which I am the president, but I am no longer in the management of any of the subsidiaries. It was a big step forward for us, and it enables us to go to the international finance markets."

Offen's drive for taking on risk to seize opportunity comes from his competitive streak in playing sports. "When I was young, I played soccer. Then I played a lot of tennis. I played in tournaments, at a fairly, reasonably good level, but then I got a knee injury playing tennis. My meniscus was completely gone. So that was the end of tennis."

After hanging up his tennis shoes and racket, Offen looked to a new sport to satisfy his appetite for competition and his passion for the water: sailing. What originally started twenty years ago as a hobby has transformed into a successful side profession. Offen is a keen sailor and the owner of the Y3K, a Wally yacht that has competed in Maxi events in the Mediterranean. "Just like shipping, it's all about building the right team. I put the yacht crew together. It's all about the people coming together for the common goal of coming out on top."

The qualities Offen looks for in his crew are the same ones he looks for in his shipping management team. "You need top people, and they have to be able to make decisions on their own, whether it is for the company or on board the race boat."

These leadership qualities have translated into success for Offen's yachting team. He and his crew have won the Maxi Yacht Rolex Cup in 2005, 2009, 2010, and 2011. Since 2006 he has also been the president of the International Association of Maxi Yachts (IMA).

German Consolidation

Strong leadership is a necessary brick in the foundation of any industry. The history of the rise and fall of the German maritime industry goes back to the turn of the nineteenth century, when Kaiser Wilhelm II set out to make Germany the world's leading maritime power. Since then, the German maritime industry has risen and failed several times.

The glut of tonnage post-Lehman sliced into the container space, with the twenty largest operators shrinking down to around a dozen companies between 2014 and 2016. Plunging world freight rates and the bankruptcy of South Korea's Hanjin Shipping last year created a perfect storm for the sector, and a headache for German banks and investors, who owned roughly 21 percent of the world's container fleet, according to the German Shipowners' Association.[12]

Despite the industry challenges and headlines of maritime elite falling victim to the crisis, the fallout stoked Offen's entrepreneurial spirit. "A crisis always has its victims, but a crisis also provides a good chance to start something new or to expand. I decided that this was the moment to expand the company," he said.

On March 9, 2017, Offen's personal company, Offen Group, announced plans to take over the Munich-based Conti Group. "It is one of the better companies in Germany, and a very healthy one. It's a large company, and a very big jump forward for us to help create a wider basis for our future."

Offen also said they are not done with their shipping shopping spree, indicating they are looking at a couple of other companies to further expand their market share.

The Conti acquisition signaled to the markets that the consolidation in the German maritime space was just beginning. Even with volumes rebounding and positive signs of a recovery, freight rates in the Asia-to-Europe trade route have stayed at break-even levels, further stressing the industry. After the Conti announcement on May 23, 2017, the merger between Hapag-Lloyd and USAC was announced. Hapag-Lloyd told Wall Street analysts post-merger that it was looking to cut up to 12 percent of its land-based workforce. The maritime workforce, already being squeezed down, would get another haircut.

---

[12] German Shipowners' Association. www.reederverband.de.

The wave of maritime woes continued into June, sending shockwaves to those in the industry. On June 2, 2017, Germany's third-largest shipping firm, Rickmers Holding, filed for insolvency. "Rickmers is maritime royalty," said Basil Karatzas, chief executive of New York–based Karatzas Marine Advisors & Co. "Seeing them file for bankruptcy is like seeing a king get deposed."[13]

The headlines dampened the sentiment of the maritime markets, but for Offen they whet his acquisitive appetite. "This consolidation will continue, and this is a moment of opportunities," he stressed. "Not many of my colleagues are in the financial position to do mergers or acquisitions. Most are very much under pressure. So I am trying to make the most use of this situation. We are fairly well-off for the time being, and we are trying to grow the company during this time and hopefully become even stronger after the crisis."

Offen continued, saying that when it comes to growing a company, timing is extremely important. "With the takeover of Conti, we will be back at number two in the world, behind Seaspan with respect to the container charter fleet. I feel really at home in this space," he said. "The timing now for me is good. We sold two ships in August 2015 for $19 million each, and that was when they had already come down in value from something like $40 million or $50 million. Even though they fell to $19 million, they had had a good charter, so we could still sell them at a small profit. Yes, we lost profit if we sold back at $40 million or $50 million, but my feeling is we are not at the end of the rope, and you never know when you reach bottom. You also never know when you reach the peak. We are confident we know the market in the areas we are in. That makes me happy in my decision."

---

[13] William Wilkes and Costas Paris, "German Shipping Firm Rickmers Files for Bankruptcy," *The Wall Street Journal*, June 4, 2017.

Strategizing for the Next Crisis

"There will be lots of opportunities as a consequence of the crisis in our market," Offen said. "So for the time being I am focused on the opportunities I see now, because I feel the next crisis is already visible on the horizon. There may be a short recovery period, but at this moment it's too early to say if this a long-term recovery or if this is just a brief interval."

Part of Offen's strategy for getting ready for the next crisis is buying secondhand ships right now because of the cheap price. "As long as you get fairly new ships, say ten years old, it's probably a good moment for investment because these ships can have a technical lifespan of 20 to 30 years. Ordering new ships at this moment, I will say, is still a big risk unless you can cover them with long-term commitments, which are not easy to get."

Since the financial crisis, Offen said he has seen a drop-off in charterers taking on ten- and fifteen-year charters.

Instead, the big companies are more focused on financing the ships themselves or going through the Chinese leasing houses or Far East finance funds for their cheap, effective finance. American and European banks have drastically shrunk in numbers, for they cannot compete with the Asian banks' cutthroat financing terms. The risk is too great for them to sign on.

"I'm not certain that the shipping market situation will ever recover to where it was before the Lehman crisis. I think we need to come up with new ideas for how to grow. Maybe we have to do what I did 40 years ago: buy old ships cheap, keep them a while, sell them at a profit. But that's never guaranteed—I may sell them at a loss. Buying cheap ships does not always mean you will make money, because cheap may still be too expensive if the market falls any further," Offen said.

"Nobody ever tells you this is a good moment to buy, and nobody will tell you this is a good moment to sell, and that makes the life of a shipowner quite fascinating. You need a lot of knowledge and experience about the world markets, yes, but you need a lot of stomach to say this is the right moment or the right ship to buy or sell."

Paying It Forward

"I have been growing this company ever since I established it in 1971, and I will always focus on growing. Standing still is *always* a step back," Offen said with infectious enthusiasm. "This is why I'm still doing it and why I'm not going to retire for at least the next two or three years."

Acknowledging that one day he will hand over the company to his predecessor, Offen said he understands he or she might be more cautious than he is. "An entrepreneur is the main engine that drives the company. It's always easier to work with your own money than to work with other people's money, because you don't want to lose it for them. But I think opportunities are all about taking risks."

With a broad smile, he leaned forward when he reflected on his career. A small sigh escaped. A gentle smile emerged. "I have had a lot of luck in my life," he said thoughtfully. "Sometimes it's good to help people who have less luck. This is something I'm always thinking about. So, wherever I can, I do. I think if you've had as much luck in your life as I have, you need to give a part of it to others."

CHAPTER SEVEN

Dr. James S.C. Chao and Angela Chao

Turning the Impossible into the Possible

During the chaos of war, people face two life-defining choices: They can allow their spirit to succumb and fall to the destruction, or they can rise above, nourishing their spirit with hope, love, and encouragement to break the shackles of war and soar untethered. The undying spirit of such survivors looks at life with ever-constant, fresh, grateful eyes, always searching for ways to make the world a better place than how they found it, without seeking fame.

Dr. James S.C. Chao (趙錫成 博士), honorary chairman of the Foremost Group, came of age during the foreign invasions of China, World War II, and the Chinese Civil War. Through it all, Dr. Chao learned from his father, a school principal, Yi-Ren Chao (趙以仁 先生), and his mother, Yu-Chin Hsu Chao (趙許月琴 女士), that a good education was necessary for what he called "the toolbox of life."

As a young student, Dr. Chao earned scholarships to attend middle and high school and ultimately one of the best universities in Shanghai. In addition to doing well in school, Dr. Chao was an all-star athlete and the captain of his school's basketball and soccer teams. He particularly loved the game of ping-pong. "I became a three-year champion in Shanghai. Everyone now knows about ping-pong because it was through ping-pong that China and the United States started their new diplomatic relationship. During the wars that ravaged China, we lost everything," he explained. "But we could still play ping-pong because you only needed a ball and a paddle. We played in the streets. It was a simple game. That's why the game was so popular."

The region where Dr. Chao grew up was a prosperous agricultural area before the decades of successive wars and conflicts inflicted their damage. His family lived in a farming village that planted rice, wheat, and cotton. Potatoes were grown on the poorest soil. During the wars that devastated China, often the only crop they could grow was potatoes. "Relatively speaking, my family was better off than others," Dr. Chao said. "My grandfather was a doctor so sometimes his patients would give him some rice in payment. We were so thankful. But even so, we did not have food every day. Sometimes we had lunch but we wouldn't know if there would be dinner. We ate lots of porridge. When water was added, one bowl of rice could make three bowls of porridge. Thankfully, we had salt. It was the main seasoning for our food."

Sanitation systems were also destroyed, and pestilent epidemics broke out. One took the lives of the young neighbors he played with. They were seven and thirteen. "It was very sad," said Dr. Chao softly. "We survived because I had wonderful parents who taught us to have hope that tomorrow will be better," he stressed. "They emphasized education. Regardless how difficult life was—the lack of food, bombings, and disease—we never, ever forgot the importance of education."

Dr. Chao's father, Yi-Ren Chao, was a teacher who brought education to the children in the rural areas. In 1940, Mr. Yi-Ren Chao had initiated an educational movement in China known as "Education Saves the Nation," in which classrooms were run within private homes, and he founded a private school, Li Feng Primary School, where he served as the principal.

In order to attend schools in larger towns, and eventually Shanghai, Dr. Chao had to take entrance exams. His father taught him so he could pass those examinations.

Dr. Chao remembers studying at night, reading from texts illuminated only by the weak, flickering glow of a burning string inserted in a bowl of vegetable oil. In the wintertime, it was so cold that the black ink he dipped his brush in to write with would freeze. In the summer, the mosquitos would swarm around him, biting him while he tried to study. He was particularly grateful for nights when there was a full moon to provide light for him to study his lessons.

After much hard work, Dr. Chao passed his exams and moved to Shanghai to attend Jiao Tong University.

During this time, many wealthy families were relocating to Shanghai to escape the civil war. Among the displaced was teenager Ruth Mulan Chu. "When we first met, she was very shy. She pretended she didn't know who I was, but I knew she did because her friends told her I was a famous ping-pong athlete in school," Dr. Chao said, laughing. "I would speak to her, and her face would turn red because it was unusual for young men and women to socialize without parental oversight in those days." He chuckled. "Ruth was a dignified girl. She was also very pretty. When she spoke to you, she always gave the feeling she was a special person. I didn't want to date or marry any other girl. I only wanted to be with her."

But Dr. Chao worried their different socioeconomic backgrounds would hurt his chances courting Ruth. "I was a country boy, and Ruth was from a rich city family," he said. "I knew I had to finish school first and get a good job so her parents would be proud of me. I knew the future of maritime graduates was promising because China overall was poor. All the seamen were earning salaries based on the international standard," he explained. "It was very, very attractive."

Dr. Chao was no stranger to the maritime industry. Shipping was in his blood. "Two of my uncles were sea captains," he said. "They never had an accident, and my uncle Yi Chun C Chao spent over 50 years on the sea! That made me very proud of him—and very interested in shipping. It was a really exciting industry, too. I think that's what motivated me."

It would also provide the young Dr. Chao with a rare opportunity for someone raised in a small farming village: seeing the world. "In my time, relatively speaking, there were lots of financial pressures, especially in the Far East, and many of the businesses were still unsophisticated. In shipping, you can go on a ship and have the chance to travel to many, many interesting places."

So Dr. Chao pursued an undergraduate degree in navigation at Jiao Tong University in Shanghai. "In order to graduate with a diploma, I had to go on board a ship to gain some seagoing experience," he recalled. "I left Shanghai at the end of May in 1949. My father came from our village to see me off at the docks. I thought I would see him in two weeks. Little did I know that would be the last time I would ever see him."

While Dr. Chao was at sea, the government changed. The ports were closed, and no one was allowed in or out of the country. Dr. Chao's ship was diverted to Taiwan, where a new chapter in his life was about to begin.

"A journey of a thousand miles begins with a single step." —**Chinese Proverb**

"When I landed in Taiwan, it was pandemonium," Dr. Chao said. "Millions of people from the mainland had come to the island. There was insufficient housing, food, and work, and I was looking for my first job. I figured my only chance to get a job and survive was to do something people didn't want to do, and nobody at that time wanted to go into shipping. The ports you were going into could be in a war zone. It was dangerous," he explained. "But I thought if I could get the chance to show my willingness to sacrifice, I could get a job."

The strategy paid off. Dr. Chao was hired as a second officer aboard a merchant vessel and was quickly promoted to cadet. "I was willing to sacrifice, but on the other hand, I was still trying to make something of myself." Dr. Chao continued to move up the ranks, and by his 29th birthday he was a captain—one of the youngest ocean-faring captains of the time.

When Dr. Chao was not at sea, he was looking for the "love of his life," Ruth Mulan Chu. During one particular four-month period, after his ship was damaged by bombs and in drydock, he searched all over the island to find her. After two years of searching, he finally found her. "I was so happy," he recalled with a warm smile. "The gap in my life was filled." On November 12, 1951, he and Ruth were married.

Dr. Chao's career flourished. "Although the shipowner I worked for trusted me, liked me, and made me the captain of the ship, my salary was less than that of a chief officer," Dr. Chao said. "In the 1950s, a master earned a salary of about $400 a month. In China, $400 was big money. But the shipowner only gave me $180." But Dr. Chao didn't mind getting paid less than half the normal salary for that rank; he was just happy for the chance to prove himself.

Yet despite all his successes, Dr. Chao desired more: In 1958, at the age of 30, he took the Master Mariners exam. "At that time, the grades were still published in the newspaper. It was a public announcement. And, thank the Lord, when I looked to see if I had passed, I found my name at the top of the list." Dr. Chao also found that he had scored the highest grade ever recorded on the exam—a record that has yet to be broken.

Because of his Master Mariners exam score, Dr. Chao was given the opportunity to study abroad in America. By then, he and Ruth had two daughters, Elaine and Jeanette, and were expecting a third child. This was a chance to pursue the next level of his career and give his growing family a better life. However, a quota limiting the number of Chinese immigrants allowed into the United States each year meant his family could not go with him. It was a difficult decision for the young Chao family. Ruth, then seven months pregnant, encouraged him to go. "Ruth was my rock and foundation," Dr. Chao recalled fondly. "Her strength fortified me."

"My father left for America with just his dreams," said Angela Chao, the youngest of Dr. Chao's six daughters. "He wanted to build a business and a life so he could bring my mother and my sisters to America."

"When I arrived, I had all this enthusiasm," Dr. Chao recalled. "I had learned that America was very generous, that there was very good work there. I didn't have any money when I arrived, but that didn't stop me," he said. "I had to survive." Through daily letters, Ruth encouraged and comforted him. "She told me I had the decisiveness, determination, creativity, and diligence to make the impossible possible," Dr. Chao said.

"The Chinese have a saying," he added. "有志者事竟成, meaning, if you have the confidence, if you put in the effort, the Lord won't fail you and you will reach the goal. I think this is the story of Foremost."

Life in America

Dr. Chao knew it would be easier to find work if he had an advanced degree. However, with China closed off to the West, he could not obtain his academic transcripts and had to take many undergraduate courses again. But instead of looking at those years as a waste of time, Dr. Chao saw them as an opportunity to learn more about his new homeland.

"Being forced to retake many undergraduate courses made my educational foundation much stronger," Dr. Chao explained. "I studied common law. I studied American government. It made it easier for me to approach the kind of people I needed to reach, and to understand the government agencies I needed to approach in order to grow my new business. In fact," he recalled, "my business began with contracts with the U.S. government."

In 1961, Dr. Chao began the master's degree program in management at St. John's University, in Queens, New York. That same year, he and his family were reunited after almost three years apart; it was the first time he met his daughter May, then two and a half years old.

"I remember so clearly meeting my father in America," May recalled. "I remember thinking he was a really nice man, and that he made my mother so happy and quick to smile."

In 1964, the year he graduated from St. John's, Dr. Chao founded Foremost Group. At that time, there were more than 100 shipping companies in New York City. Foremost was small, but that didn't deter Dr. Chao from being competitive. "Because there were so many shipping companies, the telephone company made a special phone book just for the shipping industry!" he said. "I tried to find Foremost in it, but we were not there. I checked the second printing, but we still weren't in it."

Later one of Dr. Chao's daughters, Christine, who was still quite young at the time, asked him how they could leave Foremost out. "I told her, 'You rise above your adversities with determination and confidence. You have to believe you will succeed,' " Dr. Chao said. "Today in New York there are only one or two shipping companies. Most have either disappeared or moved to Connecticut. Foremost is still in New York."

Through the years, as Foremost grew so did the Chao family, with the additions of Christine, Grace, and Angela. After college or business school, each daughter worked at Foremost to see if she had interest in taking on the family business. "Shipping is a very hard business, and I think you have to have the interest in order to work in this industry and deal with its challenges," said Dr. Chao. "I did not force any of my daughters to pursue this business. I gave them the freedom to choose their own paths, and I think I made a very good decision because they have each made their own achievements. They are enjoying their lives and are doing well," Dr. Chao said, with a hint of fatherly pride in his voice.

"I joked to my youngest daughter, Angela," Dr. Chao recalled, "that with no more sisters to follow her, she would have to consider working at Foremost seriously." He paused, adding thoughtfully, "Even as a child, Angela always had an interest in shipping. She has a very good heart, and she felt she should help her father and mother."

In her formative school years, Angela would accompany Dr. Chao to work during school vacations to watch firsthand the inner-workings of the business. She quickly embraced and understood her parent's vision of Foremost: to be a leading and trusted provider of services to the world and an integral part of global trade.

Business philosophies aside, one of the biggest leadership lessons Angela learned from her father was not in the boardroom but at home. "One of the incredible things about my father," she said, "is that he has always credited my mother's support and love. He says that without her love and support he couldn't have achieved his goals. My mother didn't go into the office with my father," she continued, "but my father always told us my mother was his full and equal partner. She was his sounding board, his adviser. Seeing this as young daughters, we aspired to be part of the business as well, and to carry on this incredible legacy."

Angela went on to study economics at Harvard, graduating magna cum laude in just three years before earning her MBA from Harvard Business School in 2001.Today, she is chairman and chief executive officer of the Foremost Group. In an industry that is still dominated by men, the lessons learned from her father are held close to Angela's heart as she helps write the latest chapter of the family business.

"Insanity: doing the same thing over and over again and expecting different results."
—Albert Einstein

For more than 50 years, Foremost has weathered numerous shipping cycles. One of the biggest mistakes companies make each cycle is misreading demand and ordering an excess of newbuildings. In the first *Dynasties of the Sea*, Dagfinn Lunde of DVB Bank argued that different people make the same mistakes because they think they are smarter than the individuals who made the mistake the first time. This is something Angela is highly attuned to avoid.

"During the 2016 downturn," Angela said, "we saw a lot of the same mistakes being made in different ways, whether it be with high-yield debt, public money, or private-equity hedge-fund money. But there is a lot of what we call 'silly money' coming in, and shipping is not an asset finance business," she stressed. "Shipping is about people. As a leader, you have to have people and know the people, the individuals, behind your company. Yes, you have to perform, but you have to have faces and names that stand by the product and back up the performance consistently over time."

Since the founding of Foremost in 1964, the industry has seen cycles of boom and bust, with new money flowing in and out of the industry. The graph below is borrowed from the Epilogue Martin Stopford wrote for this book to illustrate where Foremost fell into the shipping cycles.

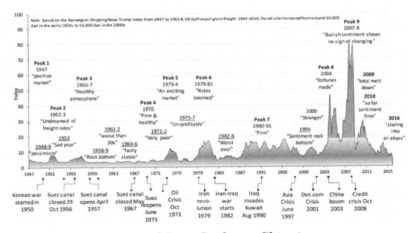

Boom and Bust Cycles in Shipping

"Every shipping cycle has distinguishing features," said Dr. Chao. "I break them down into three, six, and nine years. But now I think these cycles are occurring even faster and deeper."

Shipping Contrarian

Dr. Chao explained that the secret to Foremost's success is to seize an opportunity when the market is depressed. "When the market is down and nobody wants in, that's when we start to develop and expand," he said. "During the good times, we try to be conservative. We always use our money very wisely. We don't speculate. We don't order a ship without the employment in hand."

After Lehman Brothers collapsed in 2008, sparking the world sell-off, an insurgence of new capital from both private equity and hedge funds started to pour into the shipping industry in an effort to chase return on investment.

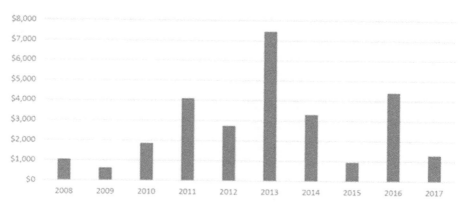

Private Equity Flows into Shipping Post-Lehman Collapse (million USD)

Source: Marine Money

"We have a lot of concerns about it because hedge funds and private equity are not long-term players," Angela said. "These are not people who have the resolve to go through a cyclical downturn. Shipping is not something that you can invest in today and in five years' time get out and make money and just go away," she stressed. "We are providing a service to the world. That requires a long-term viewpoint, and it means you have to be there when there's a downturn."

Controlling One's Destiny

Foremost Group's strategic plans are generally five to ten years out, but that does not mean they are not nimble. "If warranted, they can be revised every six months to address the current environment and provide the direction needed to guide us through the challenges," Angela said, "It's the downturn where you're growing for the future, not at the high point."

Included in each plan are strategies for handling disruptions in trade. From weather to economic events, many disruptions are out of the industry's control, but by employing the proper strategies, companies can help soften the impact of these interruptions.

One strategy Foremost employs to help control its own destiny is building its own ships. "People always go into the shipyard and bargain on price. We build our own ships so we can customize them and not waste money on needless features," Dr. Chao explained.

The Foremost fleet is about 5 million deadweight tons, and it is young, with an average age of less than five years. "Once a ship reaches a certain age, we sell it 'as is.'" Dr. Chao said. "And it is always in very good condition."

These ships are also noted for their environmental stewardship. Dr. Chao has been the recipient of many awards that recognize his and Foremost's contribution to incorporating environmentally friendly designs to their ships. They were willing to take the lead in working with their shipyards to design features that are sensitive to the environment. When other shipowners see that Foremost's designs work, they are willing to add such features to their ships.

"Timing the market is a fool's game, whereas time in the market is your greatest natural advantage."
—**Nick Murray**

Since its introduction in 1985, the Baltic Dry Index has pointed to large downward economic drafts, from Black Monday to the dot-com bubble burst to the 2008 financial crisis and the U.S. Great Recession. A proverbial "canary in the coal mine," the BDI has been a leading economic indicator of global trade expansions and contractions. But banking on economic data and predictions is something the Chao family does not do when plotting their course to navigate around downturns. "Nobody can control the market. We never speculate on the market," Dr. Chao said emphatically.

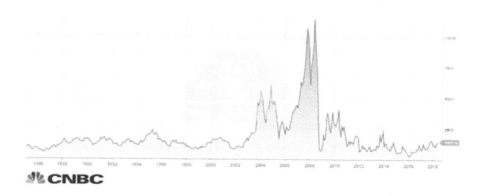

Baltic Dry Index
1985 – 2018
Source: CNBC

"We hedge or we try to mitigate our risks through a three-legged stool approach: performance (which is backed up by good ship design), management, and technology," Angela added.

Foremost's first-class charters range between five and ten years. Because of these timelines, Dr. Chao explained, counterparty risk is one of the biggest risks faced by the company. One of the ways to reduce that risk is to raise the standards of whom Foremost does business with and to stagger the charter parties. "Some are fixed, some are floating," Dr. Chao said. "We manage our market exposure through the contracts on a fleet-wide basis."

As with any cycle, downturns spark a wave of consolidation. Angela views the thinning of the shipbuilders as a way to rebalance and restore high standards and quality in shipbuilding and service. "I think it will be good for the industry," she said. "There were some substandard players that needed to be washed out of the system."

In times of stagnation, publicly traded companies see profits as a result of tightening the balance sheet. But a company cannot grow on cuts alone. A plan needs to always be in place and ready to be executed in order for a company to capitalize during the lows of a cycle. Foremost adheres to such a policy.

"This is not the time to be cutting corners and saving money on crewing or saving money on maintenance," said Angela. "These are the times, actually, when we double down. We invest in crewing because we're now able to retain crew at a higher rate. We can do longer drydocks because the opportunity cost is lower, so we can sandblast all the cargo holds. Yes, it takes more money, but it's during these tough times that we are investing for the future. That's why we also have a healthy newbuilding order book that will be coming out over the next two to three years."

For Dr. Chao, keeping in mind what he can and cannot control has helped him maintain perspective on how to lead during any part of a shipping cycle. "We always ask ourselves, how much do we really have control over? And to be honest, the answer is just about nothing. But one thing we can control is how we maintain a young and healthy fleet," he explained. "We can grow much faster, but we prefer to work with first-class charterers such as large, reputable grain houses, mining companies, etcetera, and to grow at an appropriate rate reflective of our emphasis on a successfully, responsibly managed fleet."

Some of Foremost's charters go back to the 1960s, when the company was first established. Long-term contracts include some of the world's top first-class charterers, such as MOL and Bunge.

"We also invest in our crews," Dr. Chao said. "We have very good, strong crew development programs. We raise them from cadet to officer and finally to captain. They are very, very loyal. We have crew members who will stay with us for more than 25 years. No other company has this history. Nobody can compete against this."

At the company's 50th anniversary, Dr. Chao distributed gold FMC logo pins like the one he wears on his lapel to thank those who have worked for the company for over ten, fifteen and twenty years. Dr. Chao and Angela awarded over 200 crew members and office colleagues for their longtime service.

In a rapid exchange, Dr. Chao and Angela described the importance of "human capital."

"Our crew members and office colleagues are part of the fortifying infrastructure that ensures our clients' cargo is taken care of and delivered properly on a timely basis," Dr. Chao said.

"This takes decades of relationships," added Angela. "Our crewing policy, for example—we literally always consider it as a ten-year plan because you cannot expect a master to be a master without at least ten years of training and experience in your company."

Without skipping a beat, Dr. Chao chimed in: "Most importantly, when a ship comes into port, whether in the Far East or the Western Hemisphere, we always have our staff go on board to visit with the crew, to talk to them, understand their needs, and help them. Angela doesn't just visit a ship to say hello and leave. She will stay on board just like any other office staff at least overnight to make sure everything is addressed."

"My father is a rock star when he goes on a ship," Angela continued enthusiastically. "The crew all lineup and they salute him. We don't ask them to do that, but he's like a living legend, and they just want to meet him and shake his hand," she said proudly. "For instance, there is a very famous tofu dish from Jiading, where my father comes from. If we ever have a chief cook from Jiading, he makes extra tofu for my father to bring home. I mean, that's the kind of extra effort our crew members make for us. They're really wonderful. So you can imagine how well they tend to the ship."

Globalization: The Shipping Industry's Fuel

With 90 percent of world trade transported by the international shipping industry, Foremost is a part of an intricate network of more than 50,000 merchant ships transporting goods and commodities around the world and almost 17,000 bulk carriers delivering the coal, iron ore, and grain countries of all sizes require in order to grow and flourish.

"A good trade deal is one that makes more people better off than it hurts and incorporates measures to limit the negative impact on those it hurts. A bad trade deal is one that makes everyone poorer, and along the way, poisons the well for good trade deals."
—Ian Bremmer, Eurasia Group President

Trade agreements like the Transatlantic Trade and Investment Partnership (TTIP) and the Trans-Pacific Partnership (TPP) have greater impact on containerships than on dry bulk commodities like iron ore, coal, and grain, which Foremost transports. Still, Angela stressed that good trade agreements are incredibly important for world economic health and growth. "We don't live in a world where you can be isolationist anymore. We live in an interconnected, global world, and we need to embrace that as we move forward. Shipping is obviously linked to global trade—it *is* global trade."

"Shipping allows and facilitates global trade," Angela continued. "Building bridges between countries through trade agreements helps facilitate the understanding of different cultures and different languages and different people. Trade helps bring better understanding and less conflict."

Political risk is a reality. The British vote to leave the EU in 2016 shocked the world. Global markets plummeted when the results came in. The lack of clarity on how the country would proceed sent shockwaves of panic through investors and business leaders.

"We are living in pretty amazing times," said Angela. "Because shipping is a fundamentally international business, Brexit does affect everyone Because so much in shipping is English law, and the U.K. was so important in terms of the maritime and admiralty tradition."

"When you have an event like Brexit," she continued, "things like your charter parties or your insurance policy need to be reviewed with a fine-tooth comb. It also depends where your ships are trading and what cargoes they are carrying."

The world is changing, Angela stressed, and shipping needs to be nimble enough for that change. "Look at the impact of the Colombian peace process," she said. "Now our ships have started trading to Colombia again, with coal coming out of that country. It's exciting to see these types of developments."

"You can learn so much about the economic activities and growth of different regions by studying a country's public policy, its trade agreements, and how its government behaves," Dr. Chao added.

Lessons to Live By

As Dr. Chao, his wife, and family advanced in America, they stepped up their role as active and generous volunteers and benefactors. Dr. Chao was Chair of the Chiao Tung University Alumni Association and the Chiao Tung University Alumni Foundation in the U.S.A. "When our mother was alive, she and my father were partners in philanthropy," said Dr. Grace Chao, the couple's fifth daughter. "They gave anonymously, as they were humble people who did not believe in claiming the credit for themselves." With Ruth's passing, on August 2, 2007, Dr. Chao began to make his philanthropic initiatives public in an effort to memorialize his wife's life and legacy.

In recent years, the family has made numerous charitable contributions, including the state-of-the-art Mulan Memorial Marine Simulation Center at Shanghai Maritime University, and the Ruth Mulan Chu Chao Building at Shanghai Jiao Tong University. In 2016, Harvard University dedicated the Ruth Mulan Chu Chao Center, the first building on its campus to be named after a woman or an Asian American in the university's 380-year history.

Dr. Chao's real wealth is in the love of his devoted and accomplished family (in Harvard's own words: "this most accomplished and prominent Asian American family"); the respect of his friends and peers; his excellent reputation and the outstanding reputation of the company he founded in 1964.

"Ruth was the love of my life," Dr. Chao said. "I owe everything to her. She believed in me and encouraged me. With her by my side, I felt I could do anything. I hope her spirit of hope, optimism, and trust will inspire future leaders of the world."

Angela said her parents' advice and the way they lived have helped guide her and her sisters to become the leaders they are today. "When my father arrived to America, he had this thick Chinese accent. He was an immigrant with no money. He knew no one. He basically had to do everything better and cheaper than anybody else in order to get work. That's why, when we were little, he would tell us two things: One, you have to be useful. If you are useful you will generate your own satisfaction and productivity. And two, if someone gives you work, be grateful. They have trusted you with that work, and that means you have an obligation to do a good job."

"I was raised in the philosophy of Confucianism," Dr. Chao said. "Be courteous to others. Live with honor and respect and you will get it back in return. That's how I raised my daughters and built my company."

"It's something we really need more of right now," Angela added. "We are suffering from a fundamental lack of trust in the world. I believe this is great advice for everyone to live by."

CHAPTER EIGHT

Clay Maitland

Free Trade Defender

In every industry, there are those individuals whose knowledge, accomplishments, and charisma transcend others. In the shipping industry, the maestro of maritime is Guy E.C. "Clay" Maitland, managing partner of International Registries Inc. His involvement in two of the world's largest registries, his work to protect the rights and safety of seafarers, and his negotiations to expand and support free trade have garnered him countless accolades. Ask the loquacious Maitland a simple question, and sit back as he takes you on an entertaining journey with his answer.

Maitland was born in England, on December 28, 1942. His mother was from New York, and his British father was a pilot in Bomber Command of the Royal Air Force. His father was lost along with his plane, a B-25 Mitchell bomber, in March of 1943. "One of my earliest memories being in England was when I was three, playing with my uncle. He was mowing the lawn of our house in Waybridge, in Surrey, with an old-fashioned lawn mower. He would joke, threatening to run me over," Maitland said with a laugh. "When you are this young, you can only remember snippets."

But as was the case for all children growing up in England during that time, war interrupted the simple joys of childhood. "I remember cutting my head when I was running into the air raid shelter at our home. Everyone at that time had one," Maitland said. "There was a shovel propped up inside the shelter, and I ran right into it. Because I was three and not very tall, the height of a shovel up against the wall was the right height to cut me on my forehead when I ran into it. I've still got a scar on my forehead from that day."

When it was safe to travel, Maitland and his mother went aboard the RMS *Queen Elizabeth* en route to America in 1946. Maitland remembered the ship was still painted gray—a physical reminder of the "Gray Ghost" duties transporting American troops during the Second World War. "I celebrated my fourth birthday on the ship. It was the first time I ever had ice cream in my life," he recalled. "In wartime England, you didn't get ice cream, you didn't get fresh fruit. I don't remember what flavor the ice cream was, but it tasted great. We also made friends with some interesting people on board the ship."

Once in America, Maitland and his mother settled in her home state of New York. In 1950 she was remarried, to Walter Sachs. They moved to Guilford, Connecticut, just east of New Haven. "My grandmother taught me to read and write," Maitland said. "I didn't learn at school. By the time I started school in Connecticut, I was already about two years ahead of my classmates."

Maitland graduated from Columbia University in 1964 with his bachelor's degree and attended New York Law School, graduating in 1968. He said his entry into maritime law was completely accidental. "My stepfather was a partner at Goldman Sachs, and he said to me, 'Don't go into Wall Street. You don't have the interest or qualifications.'"

Instead, his stepfather steered him to law. "He had some friends in law firms in New York. So he wrote a letter to a man who was about 80 years old at the time. His name was Charles Burlingham, and he was an active partner in Burlingham, Underwood, White, Wright & Lord. It was an admiralty law firm located at 25 Broadway, which is right across from where the big brass bull of Wall Street is located."

The law firm was famous for its representation of the White Star Line in the Titanic case.

"I applied not knowing what I was going to do, and they offered me a job. I later found out that the guy who offered me a job sang in the church choir at the Brick Church with my stepfather, so there was a family connection."

Family connection or not, Maitland did not rest on his laurels and expect things to happen for him. For six years, he went to court to litigate cargo damage cases. "I defended shipowners from all over the world," he said. "Maritime law is a general practice. It's contracts, it's cargo, it's personal injury, it's registration of ships. You name it, maritime law does it." Little did Maitland know that one of the firm's long-term clients would pave the way for his future.

The client was the Liberian Ship Registry. "Back in the 1940s, Edward Reilly Stettinius, Jr., who had been Secretary of State under Roosevelt, had come to the firm and asked them to draft up a maritime law for Liberia. So the firm did, and it was passed into law by the Liberian legislature. Burlingham were the lawyers for the Liberian flag from then on."

The Liberian Registry was created in 1948, under Liberian President William V.S. Tubman, with the direction of Stettinius. On March 11, 1949, the first commercial vessel, *World Peace*, was registered.

By the time Maitland joined the law firm, the Liberian open shipping registry oversaw nearly 75 million gross tons, making the registry the largest in the world by tonnage in number of ships.[14]

"Eventually, I did some work for the Liberian flag, and, lo and behold, they offered me a job in 1974. But I initially turned it down."

Maitland left Burlingham to become admiralty counsel at Union Carbide Corporation (of Chernobyl fame), but his time at the company was short. "Union Carbide moved up to Danbury, Connecticut, and I did not want to go to Danbury. So I quit."

---

[14] GlobalSecurity.org

In 1976, Maitland was commuting on the train with a good friend from Burlingham. "His name was Frank Wiswall," he recalled. "His father-in-law worked directly for Fred Leidinger, who had been Stettinius's chief military aid during World War II and was now in charge of the Liberian Registry. Frank told me he wanted me to speak with Leidinger. He was going to work for them and said I should work for them too. I agreed to the meeting."

He still remembers the meeting well. "It was at the Hay-Adams Hotel, right across from the White House," Maitland said. "Leidinger offered me a job working as his assistant. It later turned out that I was going to be doing a little bit of everything at one time or another."

During the late seventies, Maitland was a Republican delegate for the state of New York and was active in the Ford campaign. Ford lost to Jimmy Carter, and then, in 1980, Maitland was very active in the Reagan campaign. "They did make me an offer to work in the administration, but it was going to be at the Maritime Administration, and I wasn't enthusiastic about working for the U.S.-flag merchant marine and sort of being typecast as a civil servant or political appointee."

Maitland turned down the job offer and focused on his work for the Liberian Registry.

In 1989, the First Civil War broke out in Liberia. During this time, Liberia depended heavily on monies generated by its maritime funds, which accounted for up to 70 percent of government revenue.[15] With the civil war in the headlines, Maitland explained, it was very important to have a good public relations campaign to offset fears and stop a potential run on the Liberian bank they also managed.

"We wanted to be out there to develop a high level of confidence. It's what we call a comfort level," Maitland said. "If you're anonymous and relatively invisible, you can get run over by a crisis of confidence. If your customers don't see you, they don't know you. If you want to

---

[15] GlobalSecurity.org

have that high level of trust and confidence, you need to communicate. We had to keep everybody briefed on everything that was happening in Liberia, and we never closed our commercial bank in Monrovia, Liberia. We kept it open during the First Civil War."

In addition to the war, competition from the Panama and Honduras open registries took a bite out of market share, and Liberia fell to second place.

"Panama's great strength was always Japan, Korea, and China," Maitland explained. "Liberia was losing ground there. Why? Largely because Liberia was inefficient in growing its registry. Panama was quick to serve. If you wanted to register a ship in Panama, you would come to Miami to draw up the paperwork. Laws can be changed quickly to serve client's needs. However, the way Liberia is run, you must go through its government, and that's a big problem because the parliament in Liberia hardly ever meets. So to get a new law or amendment through for a prospective maritime customer, the customer would have to wait a number of years."

Looking beyond the turmoil in Liberia, Maitland and his colleagues saw opportunity. In 1990 they formed International Registries (IR). IR was soon hired to develop a new maritime and corporate program for the newly anointed United Nations member the Marshall Islands.

One of the attractions of the Marshall Islands was the Compact of Free Association. "It's a treaty and their charter for Independence," Maitland said. "What we liked about the Marshall Islands is that it's totally under the control of the United States, and yet it's an independent nation. You can prevent corruption there because it's transparent. It's the only foreign country in the world with a U.S. zip code!"

For ten years, IR ran both registries in tandem. "Finally, for a number of reasons, we realized we couldn't continue with Liberia. The government of Liberia was not sympathetic to our registry business model, which was: We give you the money that you are owed under our contract, and we run the registry. The government wanted to run it," Maitland said. "This was a problem because in the shipping industry they want to deal with people they know." After years of civil wars and an unstable government, "We realized, Holy smoke—if they're going to run this registry themselves, we are going to be strung up by the thumbs by the United States government for violating the Foreign Corrupt Practices Act. So we got out and focused all of our attention on the Marshall Islands."

Leveraging the Marshall Islands' transparency and its proximity to trade routes, IR has grown the Marshall Islands Registry into the largest open registry in the world by gross tonnage. "People in the industry like John Fredriksen are interested in trade routes," Maitland said. "They are always looking for a better mousetrap. They need to be nimble. From my view as a lawyer, I can tell you that with a ship registry you want to have the ability to change the law regularly to reflect the needs of the lending community. We had to have the Marshall Islands Maritime Act amended so we could do that. Efficiency is key. Being nimble to serve the needs of prospective customers is what gives us the competitive advantage."

Defender of Open Registries

The later dramatic growth of the Marshall Islands registry, while good for free trade, might never have happened. Open registries came under fire in the mid-eighties when flags of convenience became the target of the United Nations Conference on Trade and Development (UNCTAD), and the Organisation for Economic Co-operation and Development (OECD). "They wanted to get rid of open registries so they could profit from creating their own shipping agency," Maitland said. "But little did they know we had the support of both Britain and the United States, who understood our value and contribution to the global trade system."

In Geneva, United States President Ronald Reagan and British Prime Minister Margaret Thatcher cut off funding for UNCTAD.

"Our opposition to efforts to get rid of open registries had the support of the U.N. General Assembly, so part of the battle was actually fought in New York," Maitland said. "The U.S. and Britain vetoed the Security Council's attempts to eliminate the open registries. This was a political exercise fought not only in the halls of the U.N. but in the media as well. We took to the media and did lots of interviews. You are not going to convert people to your point of view by sweet reason. You convert them by making it clear that their economic interests are being threatened. Our big enemies were European countries and European academics hoping to get jobs running a sort of U.N. superagency governing shipping. They would say flags of convenience were the tool of Western imperialism. A tool of Western domination," he said. "If they had succeeded, and had flags of convenience eliminated, they would have failed miserably because it would have cost too much to operate. They didn't understand the business benefits of an open registry."

Expansion of Global Trade and the Changing of the Geopolitical Landscape

Fast forward several decades, and Maitland is excited to see the maritime opportunities being created thanks to the advancement of energy production in the United States. In June of 2017, the Trump administration's deputy press secretary, Sarah Huckabee Sanders, announced the first delivery of U.S. liquefied natural gas (LNG) to Northern and Central Europe.

"LNG production and export is a game changer," Maitland said. "It means the United States is energy efficient. OPEC basically goes away. Transporting LNG coastwise is good for the U.S.-flag merchant marine because, according to the Jones Act, a U.S.-flag vessel has to transport the commodities or cargo. We are slowly building out our ability to export, which offers our European trading partners choice in product. They now have another source of LNG to buy from, not just Russia."

The expansion in production of LNG and fracking in the United States has been hailed as the biggest driver in America's energy independence. Oil producers such as the Continental Resources chairman and CEO Harold Hamm have called it a "geopolitical game-changer."

"The fact is, the infrastructure to undertake large-scale overnight LNG exports does not currently exist," Hamm said in his testimony before the House of Representatives Foreign Affairs Committee on March 26, 2014. "If we want to have an overnight impact on today's global events, we can immediately begin exporting crude oil, which does not have the same infrastructure constraints as LNG."

Now, under the Trump administration, with Commerce Secretary Wilbur Ross and Transportation Secretary Elaine Chao, two cabinet members with vast maritime knowledge and experience (Chao's family owns the bulk carrier giant Foremost Group, and Ross's investments include LNG carrier Navigator Holdings LLC., Nautical Bulk Holdings Ltd., and Diamond S Shipping Group, Inc.), the energy markets are optimistic the infrastructure needed to export LNG and U.S. oil will be built out.

The growth outlook for LNG demand is on an upward trajectory. According to Shell's first LNG outlook, LNG demand is anticipated to grow by 4 to 5 percent annually.

New FIDs required to meet demand growth after 2020

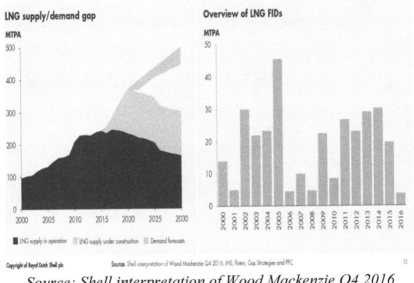

*Source: Shell interpretation of Wood Mackenzie Q4 2016
IHS, Poten, Gas Strategies, and PFC*

Maitland, a big booster of the U.S.-flag merchant marine, said the trickle-down effect of such expansion would be a win for free trade. "I think the U.S. is going to produce a lot of gas. I believe we will have more capacity ashore to liquefy it and therefore to export it. I would like to see us export a lot more LNG, and I would like to see LNG exported on U.S. flag ships. But I'm a realist. It will take time. The U.S. government has neglected our shipping infrastructure for years. It's cheaper, cleaner, and once we have the infrastructure, I think we're going to export the hell out of it."

In May of 2017, the markets were surprised when President Trump announced a trade deal with China's president, Xi Jinping, to negotiate long-term contracts for LNG shipments from American suppliers as well as additional beef and poultry. The previous trade deal prevented LNG developers from approaching Chinese companies directly. Wood

Mackenzie estimated that as China weans off coal, its demand for LNG could triple to 75 million tons by 2030, at the price tag of $26 billion a year.

"We don't know how long the Trump agenda will survive, but it may turn out to be a very long time, with or without Mr. Trump. He represents the polar opposite of what the far-left Organisation for Economic Cooperation and Development likes. I don't disagree with him on free trade. The biggest irony is, here he is talking about putting up trade barriers, but I think what is going to happen is he's going to end up knocking them down!"

War and the Boom-and-Bust Shipping Cycles

Maitland and his partners at International Registries are large monetary supporters of the U.S. maritime academies. While they are excited about the global trade expansion and energy independence of America and how it can help the U.S.-flag merchant marine, they do worry about its ability in times of war. "We would like to see a revival of the U.S.-flag merchant marine, ships painted gray, with enough sealift capacity," Maitland said. "Why would we like to see that? Because we believe there is going to be another war in the Pacific, probably involving North Korea. When I say this to people they look at me as though I'm absolutely nuts, but you know the average American attitude is that, Well, everything is hunky dory today so it will be hunky dory tomorrow. But that's the wrong type of thinking," he said. "I think this crazy little fat guy [North Korea dictator Kim Jong-un] who's firing off missiles regularly is eventually going to try to hit San Diego. I think Jong-un can do it. And I think that there are a lot of people in Washington who agree. When Ronald Reagan started to talk about Star Wars everybody laughed at him. They're not laughing now. So we need military sealift capacity. We need more seafarers—American ones. We need American flag ships that can carry cargoes of various kinds to the Far East and probably elsewhere in the world. But all of this is neglected and allowed to go to seed."

Looking into the future from a five- and twenty-year horizon, Maitland said the industry, which includes the new money of hedge funds and private equity, has to realize that the big booms in the boom-and-bust cycle of the shipping industry have usually been associated with wars. "Whether it was the Arab-Israeli Wars, World War II, or the War of Jenkins' Ear, which was around 1740 and was between the British and the Spanish, trade was affected, which impacts shipping," he said. "Freight rates will first go through the roof, and when that happens you'll see a boom. So will there be a boom and vast fortunes be made? Yes, I do think so. I think the boom-and-bust scenario is very much with us, and it'll be associated with some kind of military emergency. Like North Korea."

Fact vs. Fiction

Maitland characterizes the shipping industry as a business full of optimists. "We always believe we're going to make a profit and that business is going to be better tomorrow than it is today," he said with a smile. "And in relying on that optimism, we go out and build too many ships, we sometimes hire too many people."

Shipping, he continued, is not like any other industry. "Unlike Silicon Valley, which bases its business on research and planning, shipping goes simply by its belief. We don't plan. We just believe that we don't have to do anything to plant fertile seedlings for the future. Very little thought is given to the next month, next year, or even the years after that."

The foundation of shipping, Maitland said, is not the future technologies that will be discovered and utilized but, rather, the people working on the ships. "For us in the Marshall Islands, it's all about the seafarers. We are determined to protect their lives, their safety, and their living conditions, and to raise their wages."

Quality of seafaring life is a top priority for IR. "Yes, our ships are safer," he said, "but we are focused on the mental health of our crews. Right now, we are doing a study on suicide at sea—how many seafarers kill themselves either at sea or ashore over the course of a year and the reasons behind it. Very few countries are doing that. We are. It's important to be proactive and address the causes of this."

One of the problems facing seafarers, Maitland noted, is the advancement in satellite communications. While it has helped industry efficiency, there is a tragic downside. "Most seafarers now are in contact with their homes, and when they get bad news they get it immediately. Compound that with the isolation at sea, it can have a very bad effect on them. You're on a ship with say 20, 25 people, and you're away from home a good part of the year. That is the great drawback of a career at sea. Anyone who does it will tell you that."

Maitland also echoed the concerns of Angela Chao regarding the industry's quest to find talent. "In addition to finding qualified people it is very, very difficult to recruit people to even go to the maritime academies. This is a problem not just in the United States but throughout the world. People want to stay at home," Maitland said. "They want to be with their families. You may have someone who goes to sea but then goes ashore after a few years. Loneliness is part of it, but there are certainly other problems. And the women who come out of Fort Schuyler and Kings Point face additional obstacles, living in such a male-dominated environment. Sexual harassment at sea is a real concern. There's no questions about it."

Funding is another hurdle facing the future of the industry. "Over the years, the U.S. government has given less and less support to its maritime sector," Maitland said. "One example is the maritime academy in Maine. It's almost totally funded by the state of Maine! Very little financial support comes from the federal government. This is something that needs to be reversed."

Lessons Learned

Maitland acknowledged that his path in life and his mark on the world were not carefully planned. He said proudly that everything in his life has been built on coincidence. "If I would offer some advice, as a sort of an imaginary commencement speaker, it would be: Don't try to plan ahead too much, because it's likely that what you're going to end up doing in terms of your career is going to be determined by chance, coincidence, and luck—especially luck," he said. "That doesn't mean you shouldn't work hard, or develop the professional credentials to get ahead in the world. It just means that sometimes you find yourself, like I did, doing things you certainly had no intention of doing or thought of pursuing. That's not a bad thing. It's really just a question of being in the right place at the right time."

Having led through turmoil and numerous shipping cycles, Maitland acknowledges the one thing a good leader must expect is the unexpected. "You never know what the next turn in the road is going to be. Even now, at my age, there are things happening that I never thought would happen, and there are advantages that come my way that I didn't anticipate. Most of the people who do well in life do well because they keep it up. They do not quit or become discouraged," he said.

"When things go bad, you pick yourself up off the ground and continue. You do not allow life to beat you down. That sounds like a very trite and boring commencement speech, but it is true."

CHAPTER NINE

Kishore Rajvanshy

No Substitute for Hard Work

Many maritime leaders can trace their relationship with the sea back to their early childhood. But for Kishore Rajvanshy, growing up in the inhospitable Thar desert region of Rajasthan, India, the only ships he saw until his young adulthood were the ships of the desert—camels.

"Living in a small town I learned very early in my life that there was no substitute for hard work," Rajvanshy said. "My parents were well-off, but we were not rich. We had all the opportunities and health, but we had to work hard. I watched both of my parents and my siblings work hard. To seize on opportunity, you needed to have the combination of work ethic and creativity."

Students at his school were presented with three "career streams": engineering, medicine, and humanities. Based on his academics, Rajvanshy had the option to study medicine or engineering. With a family full of engineers, he decided to follow in their footsteps. For three years at the Birla Institute of Technology and Science, Pilani, he happily studied engineering. Then, in 1968, during his fourth year, while on a study tour visiting various companies around the country that were looking to hire engineers, he saw his first ship.

"We were visiting the cities of Mumbai and Chennai," Rajvanshy recalled. "We took a detour to the ports. It was my first sight of the ocean. I was awestruck by the sheer vastness of it all. Watching the ships enter port, seeing them loading and discharging and setting off for foreign lands fascinated me," he said. "Back in those days, ships were much smaller than they are today, but to me they were huge. I couldn't imagine how these large steel structures could float and navigate the world."

Rajvanshy was interested in the different machines on board such vessels but never thought he would have a career in the maritime industry. Like his relatives before him, after graduation he worked as an engineer. For about a year, he was happy working at an institute in Rajasthan, until a visit from a friend altered his career path and changed his life.

The friend was working for the state-owned company the Shipping Corporation of India (SCI), and he spoke glowingly to Kishore about his career at sea. "He told me that it was very nice living on the ship," Rajvanshy said. "That there were a lot of things to learn, and that it gave you the opportunity to see the world. He said compared to the shore jobs, the salaries were very good."

The visit from this friend made an impression on Rajvanshy. "He was wearing fancy shirts he said he purchased in Singapore," he recalled. "Back then, India was a closed economy. Anything that was not made in India was considered very difficult to buy, and it was expensive—at least three or four times the price. He told me that traveling the world, you could buy whatever you like. He strongly recommended that I give it a thought. That was the first time I seriously considered shipping as a career."

Rajvanshy sent a letter and his CV to the Shipping Corporation of India not really expecting an answer. He had forgotten about his letter when, a couple of months later, he received a reply. He was asked to travel to Mumbai for an interview. But Rajvanshy had started to second-guess his application. "I was not sure whether I wanted to do it," he said. "In those days, there was no internet to gather information on what a career at sea would be like. So I went to one of my college professors, and anyone I thought could help give me more information on a shipping career." After many conversations and fact-finding discussions with relatives and friends living in coastal areas like Mumbai, Chennai, and Kochi, Rajvanshy decided to go for the interview. "I thought there was no harm in attending the interview."

After an hour-and-forty-five-minute interview, Rajvanshy was told he'd been selected to be a trainee engineer on board the ships. He would need to attend a marine workshop in Mumbai for six months, followed by an additional six months in Mumbai. "I would gain hands-on experience and then take written exams for promotions," he said. "They told me that in about ten to fifteen years I could become a chief engineer."

Rajvanshy decided that day to join the company, and after his training he was assigned to a large bulk carrier in Japan to work on board as a trainee engineer. He flew from Mumbai to one of the ports in Fukuoka, where he joined his colleagues. "The experience was really, really different," he said. "The ambience, the weather, the rolling and pitching of the ship, the people on board. Everything was very different and overwhelming. Initially, for a week or two, I thought I had made a mistake. What the hell have I done to choose this career?"

Even though Rajvanshy was busy learning from the senior engineers, when he had downtime, the isolation of a life at sea was hard for him to get used to. "You are in the middle of nowhere," he explained. "All around you, you see water, and you feel that your boat is not connected with anybody. You can't make any phone calls. Back then, there was no communication when you were at sea. Only the captain could communicate, and it was through Morse code."

It took about a month at sea for Rajvanshy to embrace his new life and realize the many opportunities he could take advantage of. "There are so many careers within shipping," he said. "From constructing to surveying a ship, commissioning, fixing, or even running and insuring a ship. The opportunities were endless!" His desire to work hard was ignited.

Fueled by ambition, Rajvanshy took his exams quickly and was promoted yearly. During his last three years at sea, he sailed as chief engineer. "What most people completed in ten years, I achieved in six," Rajvanshy said proudly. "I worked hard and it paid off."

Despite the many months at sea, Rajvanshy found time for romance and met his future wife, Shashi. They were married in 1977, and during the first year of their marriage they made two round-trip voyages on the ship MV *State of Andhra Pradesh*.

*Kishore Rajvanshy, Chief Engineer, on board
SCI's MV State of Andhra Pradesh*

The first voyage had the couple sailing out of Mumbai and traveling to the ports of Singapore, Hong Kong, and Taiwan. On the next journey, the newlyweds voyaged to the west coast of North America, to the ports of Tacoma, Seattle, Vancouver, and Alaska. "While it was good exposure for my wife to experience a life at sea, she did not like it because of the seasickness during the rougher weather. So when the corporation offered me a shore job, it was a welcome change."

In 1978, after seven years at sea, Rajvanshy was brought ashore to work in the company's Mumbai offices as a technical supervisor of ships. There, he supervised four ships, following their performance and maintaining their operational readiness.

At his onshore job, Rajvanshy quickly learned the enormous structure on which the company was built. "We had a union, and it was required that every job had to be a union job, so instead of having one person at a certain position, there would be four people," Rajvanshy explained. "There were many layers of management. Even though I was a supervisor, there were many different people under control, so I was very sheltered. I had many people to guide me when there was a problem."

His onshore position at the Shipping Corporation was short lived, however. After one year, he accepted a ship management position at Univan Ship Management in Hong Kong. "We managed ships for owners who wanted a ship management company to take care of their crews, the ship's technical issues and operational readiness."

Moving to Univan was a defining moment in Rajvanshy's career. "Univan was a lean and mean company," he said. "They had very tight control over their employees, and they were extremely tough bastards. They expected you to do the job of four people. It was very tough, but it also gave me tremendous opportunity to learn the ropes of the trade."

Because of the intense pressure put on the staff, Rajvanshy explained, there was a lot of turnover. Instead of being overwhelmed, he looked at the pressure-cooker environment as a source of opportunity. He took on new challenges and learned all parts of operational ship management. "I would meet with the owners and the insurance companies," he said. "I would be at the shipyards for the repair of the ships, and at crew selection. When there was an incident, I would go and investigate and work with authorities. The exposure was tremendous, but with hard work I was able to grow the business."

Rajvanshy embraced the tough grind culture, and for ten years he thrived and was rewarded. "I got some profit-sharing in the company because the boss was quite happy and the company was doing very well. For fifteen years, I was taking on more and more responsibility, and in the last five years I was almost running the organization by myself." Rajvanshy said that in those five years, the company quadrupled in size, from around 20 ships to 80 ships.

Univan's expansion was marked by historic turmoil in Hong Kong, as the then British-controlled sovereignty was ravaged by Typhoon Ellen in 1983 and the start of the Sino-British negotiations. "Hong Kong and

Shenzhen were of strategic importance to China's economic strategy," Rajvanshy said. "Ship management was also getting more and more focused. By the end of 1994, I had some differences with Univan's owner and decided to quit. I thought I knew everything in ship management, and I wanted to look for new options. There was a new management company in Hong Kong under the umbrella of Noble Group. I reached out to them and then joined Noble Group in November to establish Fleet Management."

Dispersing the Cloud of Uncertainty

During the first formative year of Fleet, a cloud of uncertainty hung over companies operating in Hong Kong, as worries about what the 1997 handover of Hong Kong to China would bring. "Many feared that Hong Kong would become a Communist Chinese city and everything would be controlled by the state, so many corporations decided to move their headquarters and their operations," Rajvanshy said. "Many of them went to Singapore and Australia, some as far away as Vancouver."

Compared to the other companies Rajvanshy had worked for, Fleet was small. With only seven staff members, a move from Hong Kong to another destination would not be difficult, but they decided to stay to see how the transfer would play out. "During this time, China was opening up," Rajvanshy said. "Chairman Deng Xiaoping, the Communist Party leader, was trying very hard for reforms. And he opened China up so much that Hong Kong shipping companies greatly benefited because more ships were needed to transport commodities and goods to China. It was a high growth time in those days, as people who were investing in ships needed ship management companies to oversee their vessels."

Tasked with growing a company from nothing during a time of expansion may sound easy, but Rajvanshy said he did not want to make the same mistakes his prior employer had. Despite the height of Univan's success, Rajvanshy said the company lacked in the human touch. "If you are demanding high performance from your crew, you

126

need to give them a feeling that you really care for them. Good salaries are important, but they need to feel like a part of the organization. They need to feel valued. They also need to know that if they are having a problem, you would always be there to help them."

In preparation for managing three of Noble's ships, Fleet had to put a system in place and write its own procedures and manuals. Because shipping is regulated, everything had to be documented. In three months, Fleet took over the operations of its first ship, the 65,785-deadweight-ton Panamax bulker *Min Noble*.

MV Min Noble, Fleet's first ship under management

"There was the understanding initially that Noble would buy more ships, but they did not buy more ships at that time," Rajvanshy said. "Because of their financial model, they decided to take the ships on charter. This was a kind of disappointment for us, and a step back, because we were set up to run the tonnage, the ships, we had thought Noble was going to buy."

For at least two years, Noble did not buy ships, and a crisis for Fleet ensued. It was not viable to run the company with a handful of ships. The future of the company looked uncertain. In an effort to stay afloat, Rajvanshy and his team decided that the way forward was to try and develop a third-party management business.

Not a stranger to this form of business, Rajvanshy would operate Fleet in a way similar to how Univan operated. Using his connections from his time with Univan, he traveled to Europe and visited prospective clients in Holland and Scandinavia to market Fleet's services. Under his direction, Fleet soon expanded its management to 35 vessels. Vroon Shipping of the Netherlands and Norway's Spar Shipping were some of the company's earliest customers. The future seemed brighter. At its height, under Noble ownership, Fleet would manage 220 vessels and their crews.

MV State of Andhra Pradesh berthed

Leading in Dark Times

On the morning of November 7, 2007, under the cloak of heavy fog, one of the ships Fleet managed, the MV *Cosco Busan*, struck the San Francisco Bay Bridge. National Transportation Safety Board investigators said the licensed bar pilot of the containership, John Cota, had "degraded cognitive performance from his use of impairing prescription medications," and had been speeding. The impact of hitting the tower tore a 150-foot-long, 12-foot-high gash on the portside of the vessel and punctured two of the ship's fuel tanks; 53,569 U.S. gallons of bunker fuel spilled into the bay.

"At the time of the accident, it did not look very concerning, as the amount of oil spilled was not yet quantified," Rajvanshy said. "But once known, it was a big worry, and we mobilized all our resources to face this nightmare."

The accident thrust Fleet into an unwanted spotlight, but a spotlight from which it did not shy away. It is clear that Rajvanshy keeps those days close. "You hear it said a lot, that it is not so much the crisis but your response to it by which you are judged," he said. "This was difficult. It could hardly have been a larger stage. But I was heartened that our team, and those who worked with us, from the beach cleanup through the official processes, were accountable, responsible, and transparent. That is who I wanted us to be, even at the darkest moment."

While Fleet Management plead guilty to a violation of the Oil Pollution Act of 1990 (OPA-90), and a company superintendent plead guilty to making false statements for creating forged documents, the accident, like any major maritime accident, tested management to the extreme. Political debate in Washington over the future role of the U.S. Coast Guard, the passionate environmental sensitivity of the San Francisco Bay area, and ambitions of local officials played out in a most public fashion.

In September 2011, Fleet agreed to pay a $10 million fine and to create a series of training and voyage planning reforms.[16] At that time, it was the largest oil spill settlement of its kind in the United States since the passage of the OPA-90.[17] *Cosco Busan*'s owner, Regal Stone Ltd., and Fleet agreed to pay $44 million to settle the civil case. John Cota, the licensed bar pilot, was sentenced to serve ten months in federal prison.

For Rajvanshy and his team, the accident was a painful experience. Their goal each and every day is to run their ships safely, keeping the care of those on board and the protection of the environment first and foremost. "That is what our customers rely upon us for," Rajvanshy said. "When the accident happened, it was our job to stand up and be

---

[16] United States of America v. Cota et al., case number 08-00160, in U.S. District Court for the Northern District of California. Fleet was represented by Keesal, Young & Logan.
[17] Ignacia Moreno, head of the Justice Department's Environmental and Natural Resources Division.

accountable. Some of the things said hurt our souls, but thankfully no one was physically hurt. We met all our responsibilities, paid our penalty, and eventually the community saw that we were not some offshore entity but real flesh-and-blood people for whom the accident was horrifying. The experience made us stronger. Everyone who was there that day will never forget."

During this time, Noble, Fleet's parent company, was in the midst of a restructuring. Adding to its "Bigger is Better" slogan, the company was moving away from transporting commodities to becoming a producer of them. In 2011, Noble decided to sell Fleet, and Rajvanshy, along with Harry Banga, the former chairman of Noble, bought the company. "Harry has a majority shareholding, and I have a minority shareholding. There was no Caravel at that time," Rajvanshy said, referring to the trading and maritime conglomerate Banga created in 2013, of which Fleet would become one of three verticals.

Fast forward to 2017, Fleet has muscled its way to be the third largest ship management company in the world, managing almost 450 ships.

The Biggest Lesson in Life

Looking back at the founding of Fleet Management, along with the highs and lows he and his colleagues have weathered, Rajvanshy said if it wasn't for the solid foundation of working hard, and the unfailing support of its clients, Fleet would not be where it is today.

Rajvanshy credits the biggest lesson he has learned in life—that there is no substitute for hard work—as the key source of his motivation. It is something he has instilled in his two sons, one now at Microsoft, the other a finance professional in London. "Back when I worked at Univan, I knew that to take on more responsibility would not be easy," Rajvanshy recalled. "You can do that only if you are spending long hours in the office and are working very hard. My kids saw it when they were growing in Hong Kong, and they saw the rewards that come along with it. My children have embraced my ideology, and they both work very hard."

In 2017, Rajvanshy received the Lloyd's List Asia Pacific Lifetime Achievement Award. In the release announcing the thirteen winners, Lloyd's List said it applauded Rajvanshy's ability to grow Fleet organically, without the help of mergers or acquisitions—a rare business strategy in today's economic times. Banga called the award a "true testament" to Rajvanshy's hard work and commitment to the company, but also to his contributions to the maritime industry globally. "I was once told that to accomplish great things we must not only act but also dream; not only plan but also believe. Kishore, this quote resonates true with what you have achieved in your career."

Honored by the recognition, Kishore stressed that a fundamental building block in Fleet's achievements is teamwork.

"Those who joined me at that time knew it was not going to be an easy task to start the company. A lot of hard work was required. The most important piece to Fleet's success was employing top industry talent and rewarding their hard work by inclusion," Rajvanshy said. "If you reward people well and develop a sense of family at work, they like to work harder. They feel a part of the organization. That's the secret to creating a culture that promotes hard work and all-around growth. The results? Success."

CHAPTER TEN

Rod Jones

Niche Master

The evolution of shipping and shipping systems can be traced back to the 4th millennium BCE in Egypt, where images of ships adorned clay vessels and tablets. Ancient civilizations built their societies around the water. As man's desires to expand his world peaked, new technologies to feed that passion were created. Technological advancements, such as the compass and the use of animals to power ships, enabled man to achieve his aspirations of discovering new worlds and civilizations, and trade was born. Eventually, the use of fossil fuels to power ships expedited the flow of trade to the global levels we know today.

As trade expanded, some operators focused on a particular specialty and became experts in their small segment. The shipping world is home to many individuals who have used both information and technology to carve out niches that have shaped the maritime industry. One of the earliest niche masters was Edward "Coffee Man" Lloyd. Lloyd owned and operated a coffeehouse in London in the 1600s that was *the* meeting place for merchants and underwriters. He saw the value of the news being exchanged at his shop and decided there was a need to share that news with others in the maritime industry. In the late 1600s, Lloyd started a weekly newsletter. That newsletter became the forerunner to *Lloyd's List*, the second oldest continuously published newspaper of any kind in the world, after the *London Gazette*, which was first published on November 16, 1665. To this day, Lloyd's publication is a must-read for anyone in the industry.

Simply identifying the need for specialization and creating a niche does not guarantee success. By definition, a niche is not for a mass audience. It requires focus on one particular segment of a market and a determination to perform in that segment better than anyone else. Rod Jones, former president and CEO of CSL Group, the largest owner and operator of self-unloading ships in the world, knows firsthand the amount of work that goes into creating and sustaining a prime position in a shipping niche.

CSL did not invent the gravity-fed self-unloader, but as one of the major carriers on the Great Lakes, it has been operating these highly specialized vessels for almost 100 years. High-efficiency, gravity-fed self-unloading ships have been employed to carry bulk cargo on the Great Lakes for a very long time. (In fact, Jones sailed as a deckhand on a U.S.-flag self-unloader on the Great Lakes almost 50 years ago.) The high volumes and short distances for cargo movements in this unique shipping market demand much higher efficiencies than traditional bulk trades. By the 1960s, self-unloaders were the dominant form of marine transport on the Great Lakes. However, until the 1980s, gravity-fed self-unloaders were not typically in use outside of the Great Lakes, as the benefits of these vessels for longer oceanic trades were less readily apparent. But by the early 1980s, growth on the Great Lakes was petering out and tonnage movements were starting to decline. When Paul Martin bought CSL Group in 1981, he realized the company would have to look outside its core market for growth.

Jones was one of the early pioneers in CSL's entry into the international gravity-fed self-unloading ship niche. These specialized ships are slanted on their sides so commodities such as coal, grains, ores, minerals, salts, fertilizers, and other aggregates can flow, using the power of gravity, through special gates located at the bottom of the ship's cargo hold. The cargo then falls onto a system of conveyor belts, which carries the cargo from the bottom of the ship all the way to the main deck, up to a long (76 meters) boom that can deposit the cargo into the customer's receiving bin or right onto a stockpile on the dock.

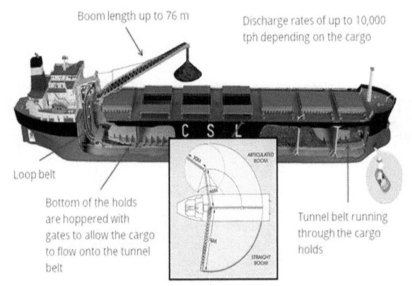

Boom length up to 76 m

Discharge rates of up to 10,000 tph depending on the cargo

Loop belt

Bottom of the holds are hoppered with gates to allow the cargo to flow onto the tunnel belt

Tunnel belt running through the cargo holds

Self-unloading Ship
Source: CSL

Whereas most bulkers discharge at about 500 tons per hour, gravity-fed self-unloaders regularly discharge at 6,000 tons per hour, without the need for expensive shore unloading equipment and shore-based stevedores. They are particularly well-suited for trades in which no shore unloading facilities are available, unloading costs are high, and/or the time saved due to the discharge efficiency is a high percentage of the overall trip time.

"No customer is ever going to carry cargo on a self-unloader if it's not adding value for them," Jones explained. "The way to add value is to reduce the total delivered cost of transporting their goods. Self-unloaders discharge much faster and require much less shore equipment. We just figured out who could benefit most from these capabilities and targeted them. We made it our business to learn the trades of our customers as well as they know them, and then demonstrated how we could save them money. We didn't waste our time on the ones that weren't going to benefit from self-unloaders," he said, adding, "99.9 percent of world shipping doesn't make sense for our vessels. We just tried to figure out the 0.1 percent that could benefit and really focus on them."

But even with just 0.1 percent of the shipping industry as a target, CSL quantified the self-unloading niche as a $1 billion opportunity.

Entry into this market had to be carefully considered. Self-unloaders cost 50 percent more to build than traditional bulk carriers, and are more expensive to operate. The ships also have less cargo volume than regular bulk carriers, so the risks of building the ships and then not having enough added-value cargo are high. "It never makes sense to run a self-unloader in a regular bulker trade," Jones said. "For most shipowners, the risks of entering this new market were just too high. We focused on the trades where it made sense for us to have these niche carriers, and then we quickly got in there to build up a strong market position. We pooled with other shipowners to increase the size of our fleet, which increased our efficiency. It helped us take a leadership position very quickly."

Oldendorff Carriers, Marbulk Shipping Inc., Algoma Central Corporation, and Torvald Klaveness have all been members of the CSL International pool. A series of acquisitions also helped expand CSL's footprint in the niche space: In 1999, CSL bought the Australian self-unloading fleet owned by Australia National Line, and in 2011, CSL purchased the Jebsen Group self-unloader fleet in Europe.

Because of its pooled resources, CSL became efficient in managing the trading patterns of its fleet. "We had cargoes going in all directions," Jones said. "When a ship completed the discharge of a stone cargo, we were likely to have a requirement to load gypsum, salt, coal, or iron ore nearby. We grew very fast from around 1990 to around 2014. We were identifying new markets for these ships every year. I remember having one set of voyages where we had a total of twelve hours ballast time in about two months."

But in the past few years, the market has cooled. In 2014, the dry bulk shipping industry was in the midst of its worst downturn since the mid-1980s. Customers were hit hard, and CSL's growth leveled off. "We faced a quadruple whammy," Jones said. "The overall bulk shipping market was in the cellar. The iron ore boom had leveled off. The global economy was still in a very slow recovery, and Atlantic coal tonnage was in a long-term decline, mostly due to substitution by cheaper and cleaner natural gas. Basically, the bulker earnings were negative, which put great pressure on self-unloaders," he explained. "It reduced our competitiveness in some trades and has certainly slowed our growth. So, for right now, it's all about right-sizing."

Since CSL is not a public company, it does not face the pressure of growing for growth's sake to satisfy investors. "We can make long-term decisions without spending all our time talking to analysts on Wall Street," Jones said. "We are not making quarterly decisions about how to run our very long-term business. Every investment decision we make goes to the board of directors, but the CEO and his team run the business. As long as we have the long-term investment rationale clearly laid out, we can usually count on the board's support, despite the cyclical nature of the shipping business as a whole."

Jones explained that part of CSL's strategy was to take a long, hard look at its fleet. "We've basically curtailed the size of some of our fleets. The good thing about having old, medium, and young ships is that it is not very onerous to recycle or lay-up the older vessels if the market isn't there," he said. "We may have plateaued, and it is hard to tell how much of this is the downturn in the global economy and how much might be a structural change in our market. But when we get an upturn again, I expect there to be more growth. We have a lot of firepower left and a strategy to always patiently look for the next growth leg. We aren't content to sit there and just run the business we have. CSL is always looking for a new opportunity."

The Rebel

Jones's path in shipping was not as straightforward as those of many other shipping leaders. His father, Roger Jones, a shipping consultant, was considered one of the great authorities in the industry. Growing up in Nassau, the Bahamas, Jones remembered the mountains of marine magazines and journals his father read in the predawn hours. His father's writings were widely distributed, and his advice was often sought by many in the industry and commodity companies around the world. Jones's younger brother, Scott, lovingly calls their father the "Google of shipping" because of his vast knowledge.

"We always had a huge procession of shipping luminaries—from Greece, Norway, Canada, America, and Hong Kong—coming to Nassau to speak with my father's shipping consulting firm, Jones, Bardelmeier and Co., Ltd.," Jones recalled. "We used to have a wonderful back patio where he would entertain them in the evenings, and at the time I kind of rebelled against it. I wasn't all that interested."

When Jones was an undergraduate at Colby College, he sailed as a deckhand for three summers on the Great Lakes on self-unloaders for Cleveland-Cliffs Inc. and Oglebay Norton Corporation to earn money and have fun. But when he graduated with a biology degree and his grades were not good enough for medical school, he tended bar for a while in Boston. But he quickly saw that he needed to get moving on his career, so he applied for and was accepted to the U.S. Navy's Officer Candidate School.

During his navy years, Jones realized he loved ships, and he excelled in his position as an engineering officer. "I had 76 people reporting to me in my division at the age of 21," he said. "You learn a lot about yourself when you are leading people, especially in times of crisis."

One particular crisis helped Jones realize what kind of leader he wanted to be. "I remember I was so frustrated by the captain of my ship because he was always so unsure of himself," he said. "He was afraid something bad would happen if someone else was driving the ship. Therefore, he never delegated the conn when the ship was in a maneuvering situation. This was something all junior officers wanted to do. But because of his lack of self-confidence, he would not allow it. We were on our way to the western Pacific from San Diego," Jones recalled, "when he had a stroke on the bridge and was helicoptered off. A chief of staff of the squadron was helicoptered in. He was an old, experienced hand who really knew what he was doing, and the first thing he said was, 'Okay, who's driving the ship into Hawaii?' It opened my eyes. I really saw the difference between someone who was incredibly self-confident, had done it all, and didn't need to prove anything, versus someone who was afraid to empower others because of his or her own lack of confidence. The chief of staff was going to let us develop ourselves. That was the kind of leader I wanted to be," he said emphatically.

"Being a leader is not owning every decision," Jones explained. "When you are a leader you are a part of a team, and you need to allow people to have the opportunity to step forward and shine. You need to have that courage. There are times when things are shaky, or you are not 100 percent sure that something is going to work, but you must soldier through. My navy experience helped me see the value in that and gave me that confidence."

After four years in the Navy, Jones looked for commercial opportunities in the shipping industry. "During my time in the Navy I really began to understand how a ship is a floating town, with sewerage, fresh water, heating and air-conditioning, a restaurant, a hotel, a communications hub, security—not to mention all the cargo-handling and navigational systems. When I got out of the Navy I stopped rebelling against my father's passion and admitted to myself that I shared it. I loved ships and wanted to get a job in the industry."

Between his Navy connections and his father, Jones lined up a series of meetings with various shipping contacts. He landed a job with Navios Corporation and for two years worked as a vessel operator in New York. He quickly realized his degree in biology was not going to be enough for a maritime career. "I didn't really understand accounting, financial statements, or general economics," he said, "so I decided I needed an M.B.A."

Jones enrolled in Dartmouth University's Amos Tuck Business School, in New Hampshire. While during his undergraduate college career he had viewed studying more as a hobby than a job, Jones worked hard at Tuck and earned high distinction as an Edward Tuck Scholar.

In business school, Jones was heavily influenced by Harvard business guru Michael Porter. "He had this concept that you could only achieve long-term success if you built and maintained a long-term competitive advantage," Jones explained. "Good timing alone is unlikely to be a long-term competitive advantage."

Upon graduating, many of Jones's friends were lured into the more lucrative worlds of investment banking, consulting, and fund management. But the financial glamour of Wall Street did not appeal to him. He decided he was more interested in growing a shipping business, but not in just any shipping segment. Jones wanted to work with a long-term oriented and strategically successful company.

"When I looked around the shipping industry, I realized Porter's long-term competitive advantage concept would be incredibly hard to achieve in most of shipping because no matter the segment—bulkers, tankers, containers—they were basically commodity plays," he explained. "A ton of space on one bulker is worth exactly the same as a ton on another. Strategic success in these businesses is basically about cost management and good timing (perhaps by developing better market information). So I decided I wanted to get into a shipping niche and work for a company that I thought could build and defend its niche market position over a long term."

Among others niches, Jones looked at heavy-lift shipping, chemical tankers, and Jones Act container shipping. He targeted six companies that were considered leaders in their specialization at the time. "But there was one niche I had personal experience in, and that was the self-unloaders on the Great Lakes," he said. "My dad was also a big proponent of self-unloaders. I believed the self-unloading technology used extensively on the Great Lakes could be expanded into the Atlantic and beyond. I thought that there could be a way to build and develop that niche. CSL was one of the top self-unloader operators in the world, and I knew the company was interested in global growth. So I targeted CSL."

On June 7, 1981, CSL president and CEO Paul Martin and his friend Laurence Pathy, the owner of Fednav, acquired CSL in a leveraged buyout. Shortly afterward, Martin announced his plans to expand CSL outside of the Great Lakes and St. Lawrence River, focusing on self-unloading vessels.

Martin saw this expansion as necessary for the future of CSL. The Rust Belt was shrinking, and demand for moving bulk commodities on the Great Lakes would shrink with it. Martin's passion for global growth motivated Jones to contact CSL. "I wrote to CSL after I graduated from Tuck and said I wanted to be a part of this expansion," he recalled. "I believed in the opportunity and felt it offered an untapped, high-growth market where the major player could eventually command a very strong market position."

When Jones joined the company, CSL had only three Atlantic-class lake-size self-unloaders that were strong enough to operate in the ocean. They were originally designed so they could operate nine months on the lakes and then three months outside when the lakes were frozen. Martin wanted to expand and strengthen CSL's market share into the ocean waters. During his 30-plus years at CSL, Jones helped lead the charge in growing the company's international self-unloading fleet to over 40 ships, which now account for approximately two thirds of the company's operating profit.

When CSL decided to set up CSL International as a separate operating company in 1992, Jones was offered the role of president, a role he held until 2007, when he became group CEO.

Niche Strategy Benefits

Over the course of his career in shipping, Jones has seen the industry buoy and sink on the economic waves. "You can't be in bulk shipping and not be impacted," Jones said. "But with our niche strategy, we have been able to ride a gentler wave, whereas the rest of the shipping industry has faced much steeper cyclical peaks and valleys."

CSL's industrial customers usually have long-term contracts, and the company typically avoids tramping its ships. Jones acknowledged that the best way to lead through these cycles is to focus on the things he can control, one of which is diversification. "CSL is constantly trying to figure out ways to diversify our business base and smooth things out," he said. "We used to be a Great Lakes shipping company, so we lived and died by the health of the U.S. and Canadian steel industry. Then we expanded out to the ocean, where we were a player in the U.S. construction industry and some coal movement. Our big expansion into Australia was next and is now about a third of CSL's business. Most recently we acquired a small self-unloading company in Europe that positions us well for growth in this region."

In 2008, the shipping industry faced its biggest crisis since the Great Depression. World trade by volume and value collapsed as nations scrambled to keep their financial systems intact, and most Western economies headed for a period of economic recession.

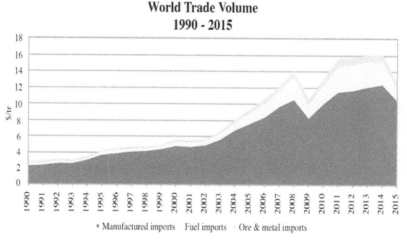

World Trade Volume
1990 - 2015

* Manufactured imports   Fuel imports   Ore & metal imports

Source: The World Bank

"When the 2008 crash happened, I think we had around 28 self-unloaders operating in our international pool," Jones recalled. "Demand dropped immediately to twenty self-unloaders. In the span of one year, we were able to redeploy those ships to Asia, Africa, and

141

Australia. Our Australian expansion helped insulate us from the global financial crisis because they were servicing China and Asia, which were still going strong."

CSL redeployed the self-unloaders that were transporting cargo from the West to be used for the transshipment of iron ore in Africa, Canada, Australia, and South America. "We adapted to avoid the big death punch that was hitting the industry. Our diversification enabled us to be somewhat counter-cyclical in some parts of our business."

After the slow recovery from the financial crisis, the shipping industry saw the entry of new players. Optimism for a market rebound and rock-bottom prices of new fuel-efficient ships wooed private equity and hedge fund investors. Money poured in, and hundreds of eco-ships were ordered. "It was senseless," Jones said flatly. "All these new ships would be coming onto market while most of the old ones were still there. The mini shipbuilding boom of 2012 to 2014 prolonged the crisis for at least three or four years. While shipping has changed a lot over my career, some of the problems it faces are still the same. The biggest problem is the boom-and-bust cycle. I am not naive enough to think this will change any time soon. However, the future leaders of this industry have to try to find ways to make the industry and the companies they operate more sustainable."

The Love-Hate Relationship Between Shipping and Commodities

The maritime industry is the main source of transportation for many commodities. One of the legs supporting the stool of President Donald Trump's energy plan is coal. Trump's support for coal helped him win the Rust Belt in the 2016 election, and in March of 2017 he signed an executive order that started the process of undoing the Obama administration's signature legislation on climate change, which Trump called "Obama's war on coal." But even with the executive orders unwinding energy regulations and President Trump's decision to withdraw from the Paris Agreement, Jones is not optimistic about the future of coal.

Ten years ago, CSL had four ships fully dedicated to shuttling coal across Lake Erie to Ontario-based power stations. Under the Ontario government's green energy plan, all of those coal-fired power stations have closed. This trend is being repeated all over the world, and Jones believes it will continue and, in fact, accelerate despite Trump's political promises to his base.

"I'm one of the people who believe that coal will continue to decline as an important source of energy going forward," he said. "It's already almost gone in Europe, and we used to move a huge amount of coal from South America into the U.S. That's very much dried up. The U.S. power stations have all converted to natural gas or closed. It will be very difficult for anyone to make a new long-term investment decision that relies on coal."

Jones explained that the downward trajectory of coal is a slow but continuous process. "Sure, we might still see some little humps, and ups and downs, but it is never going to rise significantly. We still carry significant volumes of coal, especially coking coal for the steel industry, but in our strategic plans, we see coal volumes continuing a long-term decline."

While coal's share of CSL's cargo volumes is in decline, Jones said the rise in iron ore imports to China has been a bright spot. "Although the rate of growth has declined over the past few years, China still imports more iron ore every year, and this is the engine for most of world shipping. CSL does not participate in the big, long-haul commodity movements from the iron ore exporting nations to China, as this business does not make sense in self-unloaders. However, CSL has found a new niche, using its self-unloaders to transship iron ore from shallow draft load ports into large, Capesize ships."

Total iron ore consumption v seaborne iron ore demand

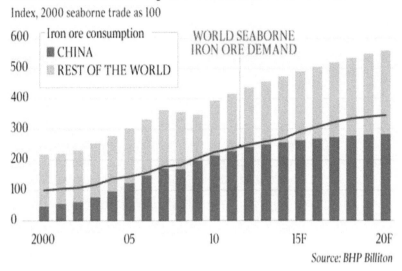

Index, 2000 seaborne trade as 100

Source: BHP Billiton

Jones said these recent developments reminded him of Japan in the 1980s. "When I first got into shipping, what really drove shipping markets was the demand for Japanese steel ore. Back then, if they imported 100 million tons, it was a bad year for shipping. If they imported 110 million tons it was a boom year. Now look at the numbers! Australia exports 650 million tons, mostly to China, in a single year! The demand is just incredible!"

But while China's appetite for iron ore continues to increase, albeit at a slower pace, China's Gross Domestic Product, which grew at double digits for much of the last decade, is slowing down. "The uncertainty about China's ability to manage its economic shift to a consumer rather than export-based economy and its handling of its credit challenges is likely to have a big impact on shipping markets in the years ahead," Jones predicted. "If they are successful, shipping will likely come out of its downturn fairly smoothly in the next few years. If they are not successful, shipping could be in for a prolonged crisis. Despite the strength of the other Asian tigers, there are no other economic engines out there that can replace Chinese demand if it falters."

Jones's Legacy

After almost four decades in shipping, Jones hopes two of his legacies will be his efforts to improve environmental responsibility and to broaden employee diversity. Under his leadership, CSL launched its first Corporate Sustainability Report in 2014, detailing the company's 2013 performance and progress toward its improvement goals. The report was a broader cousin to the company's Environmental Report, first published in 2008. "CSL believes that being a good corporate citizen means going beyond regulatory compliance to better serve customers and contribute to a healthier world," Jones said. "Since 2000, we have kept track of all of our environmental footprints including carbon, NOx, SOx, and waste. We believe that if you want to have a seat at the table and be taken seriously by the regulators, whether they're in the U.S., Canada, Europe, Australia, or anywhere else, you need to be credible. You can't just say no to every effort to clean up the industry. You need to be working hard on reasonable solutions to the problems. CSL has taken its environmental stewardship responsibilities very seriously. Our goal is to become a sustainable company. We have made great progress reducing our footprints, and we are very proud of our leadership position in green shipping."

Jones said CSL's proactive stance has served the company well. "We have a very good reputation in most of the markets we serve for doing the right thing. But we also believe that you need smart regulation." In April 2014, Jones testified before the House Transportation Committee on the then new rule that required the use of high-cost, ultra-low-sulfur fuels in ships operating within 200 nautical miles of the North American coast, designated an Emission Control Area (ECA). In his testimony, Jones told committee members that the new fuel requirement would translate into cost increases for CSL's ships that were ten times the Environmental Protection Agency's estimates. These costs would then raise shipping prices, and customers would be forced to choose less environmentally friendly, land-based shipping modes, like truck and rail. Jones, along with other CEOs who testified that day, hoped that Congress would adjust its policy from 200 nautical miles to 50 nautical miles.

So far the 200-mile limit remains in effect. "This is an example of a one-size-fits-all rule that is actually detrimental to the environment," Jones stressed. "Shipping is by far the most efficient and greenest means of moving bulk commodities. This rule, which was aimed at forcing big, high-horsepower ships to switch to low-sulfur fuel for the last day of their transoceanic voyage, inadvertently caught the coastal shipping fleet. CSL has about twenty ships that trade primarily along the coast of North America, and it moves stone, gypsum, and salt much more efficiently than rail and truck. Just one Panamax can carry the same load as 1,923 trucks or 819 rail cars, saving fuel, reducing greenhouse gas emissions, and preventing congestion on our roads and in our cities. We provided a scientific study to show that, for our smaller engines, there is no difference in the air-quality impact onshore under a 200-mile or even a 50-mile rule. Unfortunately, although our argument resonated with some congressmen, so far our relatively narrow issue has not garnered enough attention to make its way through the complicated congressional process."

While the shaping of environmental policy does not always end in the proverbial home run, Jones is also proud of his role in helping forge a path for women in a historically male-dominated industry. "When I joined CSL, many employees were women, but almost all held secretarial roles. It seemed that most male executives had a female secretary working for them. It was a bit of a *Mad Men* environment."

Since then, Jones said, CSL has made a lot of progress. CSL elected its first female board member in 2011 and promoted the first female senior executives in 2009. "I think 30 percent of our top senior executives are now women, and pretty close to 50 percent of middle management. We've been very open to hiring and promoting women." CSL's internship programs and female recruitment are two platforms Jones helped put in place in an effort to diversify CSL's staff.

The biggest diversity challenge facing the industry, though, is something that he cannot change, and that's the onboard shipping lifestyle. "We still have problems keeping women on board the ships long enough for them to reach senior shipboard ranks. The shipping lifestyle may have something to do with that, which is why we need to better understand the barriers and work to find solutions."

Looking at the rest of the industry, Jones said that while it still has a long way to go, they are no longer in the first inning. "I think we're probably in the fourth or fifth inning in a nine-inning game. The makeup and mindset are changing." Jones is very pleased that his two daughters and his son have promising careers in the shipping industry. With so many baby boomers like him retiring soon, there are likely to be wonderful career development opportunities for the younger generations. "It is time for us old, experienced captains to stand aside and let the younger generations—of both sexes—take the conn. They may bump into a dock or two along the way, but they will be the ones to transition this industry into the coming digital age."

In November 2016, Jones was awarded co-Personality of the Year by the Women's International Shipping & Trading Association (WISTA). "I strongly believe that embracing diversity in all its forms is not only the right thing to do, it's also good for business," Jones said.

Family

With a legendary father, two brothers holding senior positions in the maritime industry, and eight of the next generation working in or close to the industry, the Jones clan has been characterized as a shipping dynasty. But Jones is quick to point out that their dynasty is built on something much more important than a fleet of ships. "I have said many times: We're like a Greek shipping dynasty except we didn't inherit any ships. We only got the love of the business. Inheriting that passion was far more valuable than any ship that we could have inherited!"

Passion was the root of all things in the Jones household, and his father and mother nurtured and encouraged it during their family time. The family had a cabin on an island in Ontario, Canada, that had no electricity. There the kids would talk to their parents about the direction of their lives, their hopes and dreams, and what would make them happy. It was understood that shipping was not a mandatory path. Jones remembers those talks and was encouraged to find something he would love to do.

With three of his own children now in the industry, he finds himself repeating the same advice he heard from his father all those years ago. "My father told me to make sure I do what I love. It's not a job, it's your life, so make sure you love what you do every day. If you don't wake up every day excited, then you are probably not in the right line of work."

CHAPTER ELEVEN

Paul Leand, Peter Shaerf, and Jim Dolphin

Thriving in Chaos

The maritime industry is no stranger to crisis and the chaos that swiftly follows. The disruption may be short-term, but the impact of that turmoil can last for years. For those making deals in shipping, chaos is not considered a spoiler. Rather, if taken advantage of properly, it presents opportunities and can be used as an effective weapon in the arsenal of the shrewdest of negotiators.

Taking advantage of opportunity created by chaos is a natural part of the business for energy and transport merchant bank AMA Capital Partners. Paul Leand Jr., CEO and managing director, has been working with partners Jim Dolphin and Peter Shaerf since the early 2000s. Together they bought out Fearnley Shipping's interest in American Marine Advisors and changed the company's name to AMA Capital Partners LLC. Viewed by many as the "bridge" between the operating and financial worlds, AMA has seen not only an evolution in funding within the various sectors of maritime but also the entrance of new financial players.

In rapid succession, the three finished one another's sentences as they explained the upside of a crisis and their approach to business.

"Shipping has always been an industry of creative destruction," Dolphin explained. "Markets get overbuilt. Established players get into trouble and fail. Assets get re-priced and then new players emerge. The thing that has changed most over the years is that this cycle used to play out almost entirely within the universe of shipowners and shipping financiers, but now professional investors have entered the market in a big way."

"Add to this the fact that chaos tends to be good for shipping," Shaerf continued. "Think of the closing of the Suez Canal, or the Gulf Wars. The short-term disruption of trade lanes and stockpiling of oil drove up short-term rates."

Dolphin jumped in: "While recessions and trade wars are never a good thing, when there are tensions in the world, the uncertainty can drive shipping in a positive way."

"You need to recognize *where* you are in the market," Leand emphasized. "Keeping clear focus on your objectives and executing before the market moves on you, even if you have to give up the last dollar, is just incredibly important."

Dolphin, Leand, and Shaerf have their finger on the pulse of the various segments of the shipping industry through the multitude of publicly traded companies on whose boards they serve: Eagle Bulk Shipping Inc., Genco Shipping & Trading Ltd., Golar LNG Partners LP, Lloyd Fonds AG, North Atlantic Drilling Ltd., Seadrill Ltd., Seaspan Corp., and Ship Finance International Ltd. Previously, the three sat on the boards of OSG America LP, Oceania Cruises, TBS Shipping Services Inc., General Maritime Corp., and MC Shipping Inc. Private boards include Interlink, Ocean Protection Services, and Helm International.

"We are always trying to give our clients honest advice," Shaerf said. "We only like to do *good* deals, so there are plenty of times when we tell people, 'You know, you *shouldn't* do this.'"

So what constitutes a good deal? After much research and analysis, the final box to check off for approval is this: Would they invest their own money in the deal? In many cases, it is not a hypothetical question. "We have a long history of living with risk and investing our own money in deals, so we view everything we do through that lens,"

Dolphin said. "If our advice leads us to not getting paid for something because we thought our client shouldn't do a deal, or if they needed to take an alternative route because we couldn't help them, that's fine with us," he explained. "We're very consistent with that. We review up and down the balance sheet so we understand the alternatives, and we always tell people what we think their best option is."

Shaerf enthusiastically agreed. "There have been times when we've told prospective clients that we wouldn't consider recommending a particular investment and maybe it ended up being successful. It's okay we walked away from it. We've tried to talk people *out* of doing certain things more than *into* them on many an occasion."

The Early Days of Restructurings

Restructuring is one of the organic steps of chaos. Finding the undervalued jewels lumped in among the casualties takes expertise. The shipping high-yield debt crises of 1999 and 2000 was a defining moment for AMA. High-yield bonds, or junk bonds, were relatively new to the industry. In the 1990s, 35 issuances were made. Between 1997 and 1999 alone about $6.5 billion was invested. Unfortunately, most of those 35 issuances failed due to a combination of the weakening freight market, the cyclicality of the bond market, and other economic headwinds. The environment created an undertow that made it impossible for companies to service the debt. Approximately $4 billion was eventually written off or lost, with some bonds never even making a first interest coupon payment. Shaerf captured the mood at an industry conference at the time, saying, "We thought the market had hit bottom, until they started handing out the shovels."

Defaulted/Restructured Shipping Bonds (US $M)

Alpha Shipping	$175
Amer Reefer Co. Ltd. (AMEREE)	$100
American Commercial Lines (VECTUR)	$300
Cenargo Intl PLC (CENINT)	$175
Enterprises Shipholding Inc. (ENTSHI)	$175
Equimar Shipholdings Ltd. (EQUIMA) *(No default – buy-back)	$124
Ermis Maritime (ERMIS)	$150
Global Ocean Carriers (GLO)	$126
Golden Ocean Group (GOLDOG)	$291
Hvide Marine (HMAR)	$300
Millenium Seacarriers (MILSEA)	$100
Navigator Gas Transport (NAVGAS)	$217/87
Pacific & Atlantic (PACATL) *(No default, buy-back at 102.6%)	$128
Pan Oceanic	$100
Pegasus Shipping (PEGSHP)	$150
Premier Cruises (CRUISE)	$160
TBS Shipping (TBSSHIP)	$110
Trico Marine (TMAR) *(No default)	$280

Source: Marine Money

The lessons learned during this part of the cycle were painful for many. But for investors in the distress community, it was a time of great opportunity. AMA realized these distress players were new to shipping and had much to learn about the vulnerable companies and assets they had bought into. These investors needed advisors. For the first time since the company's inception in 1987, AMA expanded into this arena.

"Hedge funds and private equity viewed shipping as a new asset class. Shipping would be a very small percentage of their overall fund allocation, but for the industry, it was a lot of money offered up," Leand said. "That kind of capital was historically unavailable to the industry. This marked a complete departure from the disciplined approach that shipping banks historically took. Gone were the days of financiers with a deep understanding of the industry. These new players looked at shipping as merely a commodity. It resulted in more volatility."

As the instability grew, AMA thrived. Between 1998 and 2004, Leand led the development of AMA's restructuring practice, which worked on 16 of 23 formal restructurings. The creditors were their clients.

Industry-Transforming Deals

This first wave of professional investors into shipping was largely transactional; they were buying distressed debt and then creating some sort of settlement through the restructuring process. One of AMA's most notable transactions at the time was the sale of Fred Cheng's Golden Ocean VLCC fleet to John Fredriksen, which transformed Fredriksen's Frontline Ltd. In this transaction, AMA was working for the bondholders, and Leand drove the sale of Golden Ocean as a means of restructuring.

"What was important in those early restructurings is that we could put the bondholders on equal footing with the shipowners to help drive an actual solution," Leand said. "The conversations were never easy, but defaulting shipowners came to realize they simply couldn't run over the bondholders. The bondholders could and would enforce their rights if need be."

Negotiating the restructuring deals for the new entrants of private equity, hedge funds, and professional debt investors proved to be bountiful for AMA. The company created investment realizations through sales and, on average, improved the value of the underlying securities by over 100 percent.

Picking through the carcasses of distressed assets and finding value can take creativity. After September 11, 2001, AMA found itself with a mandate: Find a home for five brand-new cruise ships that were abandoned by the bankrupt Renaissance Cruises. "The large cruise lines didn't want these ships, and the offers on the table were less than half of the $180 million build cost per ship," Dolphin explained. "Working with the lead bank Crédit Agricole, we came up with the plan of creating a *new* cruise line to prove the value of the ships."

AMA selected a management team led by luxury cruise veteran Frank Del Rio, who raised money for the venture, and Oceania Cruises was born in 2002. Under Del Rio's leadership, Oceania grew, taking a dominant position in the niche upper premium luxury tour market. The hedge fund Apollo Group Management acquired Oceania in 2007 and expanded it with the purchase of Regent Seven Seas Cruises. Apollo was also a majority shareholder of Norwegian Cruise Line Holdings, and the two merged in 2014, with Del Rio eventually being made CEO of the combined entity.

MS Riviera, Oceania Cruises

MS Marina, Oceania Cruises

"Most advisors, particularly those focused solely on process, would have accepted the bankrupt situation of Renaissance and sold the ships at a loss," Dolphin said. "We found a way to capitalize on those vessels and essentially created a profitable return as well as a niche market."

AMA's Natural Evolution

As the market recovered and then began to accelerate in the 2000s, AMA's focus expanded from distressed investing to M&A (mergers and acquisitions) deals and private equity investing. "M&A was a natural extension of our restructuring work, as shipping restructurings often lead to the sale of assets," Shaerf explained.

The firm ran M&A deals that helped build the fleets of General Maritime, OSG, Eitzen Chemical, and Clipper Group. The company also paved the way for private equity investors to purchase TECO Transport in the U.S. and for the sale of Norden out of Denmark. From 2003 to 2008, AMA executed over $4 billion in M&A deals around the world.

Building a business in private equity investments was also a goal of the AMA partners. In 2000, AMA had established an investment fund with GATX and the Dutch bank NIB Capital, which at the time was a small shareholder in AMA. The AMA-managed fund focused on the opportunities in Korea created by the Asian financial crises and proved successful, delivering returns of more than 20 percent.

In 2005, AMA formed the first of another series of investment funds, this time working with the hedge fund Värde Partners. Värde was an active investor in distressed shipping high-yield bonds, and AMA often served as its advisor in the restructurings that followed bond defaults. From 2005 until 2007, AMA was on the hunt for deals that had just the right amount of risk and complexity to scare off other investors, but which it thought it could manage. During that time, AMA managed a series of investments in containerships, dry bulk carriers, tankers, rail cars, and airplanes.

"We were looking for fundamentally good assets where you could buy a dollar for 75 cents due to the circumstance," Leand said. "We liked this sort of risk as opposed to simply going long in a particular asset class."

The early deals all proved profitable, and in early 2007 AMA and Värde, together with industry veteran Bob Burke, purchased Chembulk Tankers LLC. The Chembulk fleet was a mix of owned and long-term chartered ships with Japanese yen-based purchase options. The complexity fit AMA's investment focus, and AMA went to work to try to make the deal successful. "We really liked the company and the fleet," Leand said. "Burke took over as CEO, and industry veteran Jack Noonan was brought in to position Chembulk as a preferred service provider in the market. We then focused on the financial side and purchased the charter in vessels, which increased the EBITDA[18] of the company by removing the charter in expense."

Having increased Chembulk's EBITDA through some creative financial engineering, Dolphin explained, AMA was able to guide Chembulk to more effectively use the capital markets, accessing loans not typically used in shipping. AMA helped Chembulk place a covenant lite loan in the institutional market, which gave Chembulk more flexibility in terms of restrictions on collateral, debt generation, level of income, and payment terms versus a traditional asset-based loan with stricter guidelines. The flexibility proved to be profitable. "We closed a dividend recap refinancing in August of 2007, just as the broader finance markets around the world were starting to come under stress," Dolphin said. "I believe we were the last covenant lite deal done in that market, and the only one ever done for a traditional shipping company."

"The covenant lite deal was important for us because we were expecting a downturn and we wanted a bulletproof balance sheet," Leand added. "It took the pressure off, and it gave us the freedom to ask for the price we wanted when a buyer approached us on Chembulk at the end of 2007." The trio declined to comment on the profitability

---

[18] Earnings before interest, tax, depreciation, and amortization.

of the investment, but sources close to the transaction speak of it as one of the most successful deals of the period.

Cashing in on the Offshore Disarray

The global financial crisis that started in 2007 and erupted in 2008 presented both challenges and opportunities for AMA. While many industrial sectors were hard hit by the crises, the immediate impact on shipping was less severe because certain segments were propped up by Chinese infrastructure stimulus programs.

"We looked at the run-up in the markets from 2004 until 2008, and we simply couldn't believe what we were seeing," Dolphin remarked. "I'm sure we left money on the table, but we were hesitant to invest unless we found the right deal, and by 2008, 2009, we thought nearly every market in shipping was overbuilt."

Shaerf jumped in: "It was hard for us to get excited about shipping. You had high asset prices, falling demand, and a glut of new ships being delivered. It was hard to see how there was going to be a quick recovery."

"As early as 2006," Leand continued, "we thought our business model—combining financial skills with deep industry expertise—could be built out into related areas. At that point we started hiring folks with similar skills to ours but with expertise in rail and oil and gas. As opportunities within shipping closed off, it became obvious we needed to refocus."

Just as the chase for yield had consumed the shipping industry in the late 1990s, investors were flocking for yield again, this time in offshore drilling companies. In 2000, AMA saw numerous Norwegian bonds investing in companies that were either new or had a small collection of assets with little to no track record. Fueling this chase was the belief that the price of crude would continue to climb, and that China would keep on consuming energy. Reality smacked the high-yield investors sideways. The price of crude plummeted, and China's demand pulled back. High-yield investors were left holding worthless paper.

Offshore casualties were littered across the globe, and for AMA, opportunity came knocking once more. AMA's restructuring services were in demand. Leand remembered the company's first offshore assignment. "Honestly, we were hired by bondholders because we *weren't* Norwegian," he said, chuckling. "The bonds had been issued in Norway by a Norwegian sponsor that had a Norwegian law firm and a Norwegian advisor telling the bondholders that the only way forward was a dramatic haircut. The bondholders thought there had to be a better way and called us."

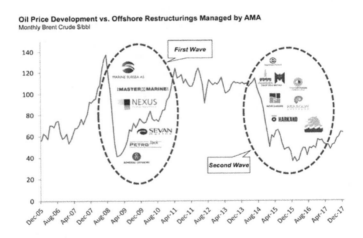

Source: AMA Capital Partners

One thing led to another, and between 2009 and 2013 AMA ended up working on ten of the fifteen deals that needed restructuring. The bondholders were always their clients.

Dolphin said capitalizing on the chaos in offshore was very natural for them. "The banks and investors we knew in shipping were also involved in offshore," he explained.

For nearly three years, offshore restructurings dominated AMA's work. By the end of 2010, AMA was once again involved in shipping restructurings.

The Basics of Restructuring

"All restructurings are essentially about information, about the assets, about the documents, about the jurisdictions, etcetera—and leverage," said Dolphin. "With information and relationships, you can create options. You can then use whatever leverage you have to push the option that works best."

Leand explained that knowing how to leverage jurisdictions to their advantage had been a key for AMA in leveling the playing field between the companies and bondholders so recoveries could be realized, not losses. "Shipping is truly a global business in which companies, assets, and operations can touch multiple countries. Each has its own rules on how creditors are dealt with and what rights they have. One time, we purposely placed a container aboard a ship because we needed to arrest a ship in a certain country because in that country we had the authority to do so," he explained. "So, we tracked our container when the ship got into that specific port so we could arrest it."

Even though the worst of the global financial crisis was over around 2012, the shipping industry and offshore showed little strength. Funding was constrained because banks either left or severely curtailed their involvement in the sectors. Private equity and hedge funds, however, remained interested after seeing supersized returns between 2004 and 2007. Speculation that banks would need to sell off massive amounts of shipping debt quickly never materialized. But that did not squash the alternative investor's hope.

Shaerf remembered a conversation he had had with a secondary investor. "I asked him, 'Why are you looking at this now?' And he said, 'Well, our LPs (limited partnerships) want us to be in shipping.' There was almost this global desire to be in this distressed asset class, sight unseen and not really knowing where any of the bodies were buried or how they'd been buried."

The "new" money that entered the shipping markets shortly after the financial crisis and initial downturn learned a hard lesson in funding. The overbuilding of the previous decade depressed ship values, but not to the levels seen in previous crashes. Leand explained that the glut in investment appetite created an artificial floor in ship values, which did not allow the values and cash flows to come into alignment. "Instead of the natural churning we had seen over the past 30, 40 years in the industry, we saw a flood of cash coming in at the first signal that the market was turning. The investment demand supported the valuation of the asset, but the cash flows did not."

In recent years, a substantial portion of all deals have been made by these alternative investment companies, making them formidable competitors in the capital arena. "Banks have pulled back. Hedge funds and private equity firms are a huge source of money for shipping, and people are still knocking down their doors. We are now looking at a very different finance cycle," Shaerf said candidly.

Private Equity Investments in Shipping, 2007 - 2017 [million USD]

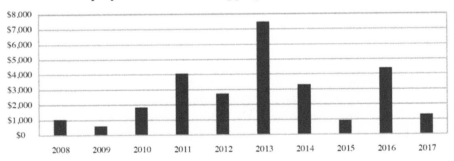

Source: Marine Money

This change caused banks to reset themselves for how they would compete. "We all grew up in a world where there was relative stability and shipowners could get a bank loan priced as investment grade for a noninvestment-grade credit," Dolphin said. "That world seems to be gone, and the providers of credit also seem to be gone. I mean, I hate to say that they'll never come back, but I'm just not seeing it. We're consistently seeing fewer lenders rather than more, even though today is arguably a better time to be lending. The new lenders coming in are not your traditional banks."

Leand agreed. "There is a natural attraction for shipping companies to align themselves with people who provide capital or people they *perceive* to be providing capital," he said. "In many ways, we didn't compete with the hedge funds or private equity firms looking to do shipping deals in the last cycle."

Instead, AMA pivoted its attention to its restructuring business or private equity investing, trying to find assets no one else was paying attention to and going outside of shipping.

The New Life Cycle of Shipping

Since the emergence of hedge funds and private equity, there has been a bifurcation in the expectations of shipping. For the multigenerational families in shipping, it's more long-term, whereas the private equity sponsor is very transaction oriented. These expectations have greatly altered the life cycle of shipping investments. "They [hedge funds, private equity] just care if the deal suits their purposes today," said Leand.

Dolphin jumped in: "The object for financial guys is to make money. If it's not in shipping, it's something else. Families who have been in shipping for generations are beholden to the industry. Some families will take a lower return on equity because they think they can manage the risk better. They are thinking about the long-term."

"It can be more of an emotional issue for family owners," Shaerf said. "They have had employees working with them for years, and they're more likely to buy more ships or continue to operate half-empty ships in order to keep their employees working."

"In the end, it's about helping them come to a decision that's right for them," Dolphin concluded. "You have to understand what their primary motivators are."

Leand explained that when AMA first started, the cycles in shipping were seven years and were relatively predictable. "You could see your way in and out. You could plan accordingly. The cycles you now have are six to eighteen months long. It is more volatile. The worst thing that can happen to you as a sponsor is that you miss the market and the market collapses and you haven't executed anything. You're left behind the eight ball. Understanding the execution risk is incredibly important. You need to be nimble and take in the situation."

The shortened cycle coupled with tremendous volatility and scarce liquidity has forced sponsors like AMA to take a hard look at where they are in these cycles. Leand, Shaerf, and Dolphin all agree that AMA is far more cautious in how it views the market conditions now.

The short-term motivations of hedge funds and private equity have also impacted the investment life cycle. "We are, by and large, cycle analysts of the industry, which sometimes has hurt us on our investing decisions. We tend to look at the industry as a reversion to the mean in terms of rates and values."

"Shipowners make money primarily by buying and selling ships," Dolphin added, "*not* by operating ships. But it's hard to sell ships in any real quantity these days. There just aren't buyers or access to capital. With any investment you do these days you need to be convinced you are buying at a good price but at the same time also figure out how you are going to exit."

But the lack of buyers isn't deterring the shipbuilding industry. In 2017, Japan knocked Korea out of the number two spot, with China still dominating as the number one shipbuilder in the world. While the slump has slowed down the building of ships, Dolphin said the disconnect between shipbuilding and shipping will forever be there. "What's good for the yards is not necessarily good for shipping companies."

Describing what they call a kid's-glove approach to shepherding companies through the rough-and-tumble cycle of the capital markets, Leand said they are far from the dinosaurs of the industry. "The need for us is greater now. The problem is that today these alternative funds raise the capital and convince the shipowners that they have the expertise and people in-house to handle navigating through the cycles. In certain instances, they do okay, but in other instances they don't."

"Whether it's the objectives of your clients or the objectives of the people who sit across the table from you, when you are negotiating you need to understand both of their endgames. Listening is an important part of making deals," Shaerf emphasized.

"I'm really curious about what's next," Dolphin said with a hint of excitement. "Over the last 30 years, we have adjusted our capabilities and the focus of our work multiple times to capitalize on chaos and industry evolution. We've always been very flexible in how to deal with uncertainty and turn it into opportunity. I don't know what lies ahead, but I know whatever it is, I'm confident we will seize on it."

CHAPTER TWELVE

Felipe and Ricardo Menéndez Ross

Family of Innovation

One of the biggest drivers in a thriving business is innovation. It is the foundation of a company's longevity, and it is up to the company's successors to build onto it in order to thrive and remain competitive. For the Menéndez Ross family, their eye for establishing and carving out niches in each generation has expanded not only their company but the movement of global trade as well.

The Menéndez family started in shipping in 1874, when José Menéndez moved with his young family from Buenos Aires to the world's southernmost large city: Punta Arenas, Chile. Through the Strait of Magellan, José Menéndez y Compañía carried sheep from the Falkland Islands, or Islas Malvinas, to Punta Arenas, in the Chilean region of Patagonia.

"When my great-grandfather started, it was a very small ship chandling business," said Felipe Menéndez Ross, co-CEO of Interocean Transportation Inc. "He was fortunate enough to understand the potential that Patagonia had for sheep farming. It was very, very hard at the beginning, but by the time he died, in 1918, he was the largest wool producer in the world."

In 1894, José expanded into cattle ranching and traveled south of the Rio Grande in the Argentine territory. Two years later, he founded Primera Argentina, the first *estancia* of Argentina, with 105,169 acres purchased from the Argentinian Government (that farm today is named after him). After the success of Primera Argentina, José opened a second venture in livestock (Segunda Argentina, since renamed after his wife, Maria Behety). In 1897, he created the Argentinian and Chilean company José Menéndez y Compañía (later renamed Menéndez Behety Sociedad Anónima Ganadera y Comercial).

Menéndez Behety Share Certificate, 1917

Looking to enhance the family's performance on the sea, José's youngest son, Julio Menéndez Behety, started to look for an acquisition to create added value. In 1930, Menéndez Behety acquired Braun & Blanchard, a shipping company that operated a liner service in Patagonia. The merged company was renamed Compañía Chilena de Navegación Interoceánica S.A. (CCNI),[19] and Julio's son, Julio Menéndez, oversaw the newly minted company.

In the mid-1950s, the younger Julio, like his father and grandfather before him, saw an opportunity to branch out and create a new niche in shipping. His contribution to the family expansion would be into energy. Julio saw liquefied petroleum gas (LPG) as a new option to extend the company's business. He started the tanker company Sociedad Anónima de Navegación Petrolera (SONAP), and worked with gas shipping innovator Renè Boudet, founder of Gazocean France, to create Interoceangas, the first LPG shipping company in South America.

---

[19] This was the same entity that was sold to Hamburg Süd in 2015, but the Menéndez family ceased to have any involvement with the company in 1970.

This partnership pushed the envelope in the transportation of energy. At the time of the Menéndez and Boudet venture, LPG was virtually unknown in maritime. "Together, they started the transportation of gas, the installation of tanks, and the distribution of LPG throughout South America," Felipe said. "They brought the logistics that enabled the widespread use of liquefied petroleum gas for residential use in Brazil, Argentina, Chile, and a number of other countries."

From there, the Menéndez energy presence in shipping grew.

Seeds to Seamless Transition

Felipe was born in Chile but lived most of his life in Argentina. As the great-grandson of José and the third youngest son of Julio, he was immersed from a young age in all aspects of shipping. His older brother and co-CEO of Interocean Transportation, Ricardo, was his best friend. "Our experiences growing up were very rich," Felipe said with gratitude. "South Patagonia, where my family's business started, was a very, very faraway place. The only way to get there when I was a child was by ship. It was very perilous navigation."

"Even our family vacations involved taking a ship," Felipe continued. "Whether to Patagonia, Rio, or Europe, a ship was the only way to travel, so we really lived our early childhood on board ships or in contact with ships. It was a very natural way of life for us. It never crossed my mind that I would ever work in any industry besides shipping."

Attending the local university in Buenos Aires, Felipe studied business administration and economics. After he graduated, he enrolled in law school and took classes at night. "When you're young and in the middle of all this learning you don't realize how much of a base that knowledge will give you in business," he said. "The study of economics gives you a rigorous scientific base for understanding problems and for modeling. The theoretical study of law nurtures your discipline. All of this is necessary for a career in shipping."

In 1974, Felipe joined his brother Ricardo working alongside their father at the family companies, then comprising Ultraocean, the bulk carrier operations Casinomar Shipping and Ravenscroft Shipping, and the tanker companies SONAP and Interoceangas. Felipe and Ricardo said the transition of oversight of the family shipping empire was subtle. "We really never noticed that our father was transferring responsibilities to us," Felipe explained. "In the beginning, we were advising him, and he was telling us what to do. Then, the next day, *we* had the responsibility in that area of the company, making the decisions, and *he* was advising us. It was a very intelligent way to prepare us to run the company with his involvement fading out. There was no enormous pressure or sudden change. It was gradual. We would like to pass the torch the same way to our sons."

Felipe's first assignment was a single old tweendecker called the *Caminito*. It was their first Argentinian dry cargo ship. Felipe oversaw the ship and managed everything from the freight contract to crew hires to the consumption of provisions. "Running port operations of a vessel in those days you had to learn a lot about the technicalities of loading and discharging a ship," he said. "The *Caminito* was like a little company. It was during that time that I learned the responsibility of how management could impact a ship."

On a bookcase in his office, a photo of the *Caminito* is displayed alongside an early photo of his grandfather's sailing ship, the *Alejandrina,* in drydock in England.

MV Caminito

Sailing ship Alejandrina

Felipe paused and said, with a lightness in his voice, "I do look at the photo of *Caminito* quite frequently… but not intentionally. It was very good training, and I loved that ship a lot. She was a great ship."

The *Caminito* was originally called the *Tewkesbury* and owned by Houlder Brothers & Co. "She did everything," Felipe recalled. "She loaded bulk cargoes, and as an ordinary tweendecker she carried bales of cotton and paper and all sorts of products. Managing this ship exposed me to the many areas of the shipping business. I think I learned everything I needed to know about shipping by being on that ship."

Felipe's father encouraged his sons to learn by doing. Hands-on knowledge was key to their development as leaders in the family business. Not an engineer by profession, Felipe learned ship engineering by getting his hands dirty on board the *Caminito*, figuring out mechanical problems from the engine in the bowels to the bridge.

Felipe said the experience was invaluable. "The ships were simple back then. There were no electronics, so it was pretty easy to understand physically what was going on," he explained. "I don't think Ricardo's sons, or my sons, will have the same experience because everything today is so electronic. It's very difficult to explore the physics or the mechanics of the workings of an engine these days."

Ricardo started in the shipping business earlier than Felipe, working with his father for a brief period at Compañía Chilena de Navegación Interoceánica and then at the original bulk carrier operation in Buenos Aires. With his talent and entrepreneurial spirit, he helped create a large shipowning and dry cargo operation that owned and operated a large fleet of dry cargo vessels internationally. Ricardo was also a director of the Menéndez family fishing companies, which merged in the mid-1990s with two of its competitors, forming one of the largest fishing company in the world.

From 1970 until 1990, the Menéndez family ran a large international operation of bulk carriers under the names Casinomar and Ravenscroft, in London and New York, headed by Ricardo. Their cargo presence expanded further with the formation of Forward Marine Lines, a liner service from Brazil to the United States, which was later sold. Ultraocean also expanded into reefer vessels in association with the Japanese company Nishiro.

Ultraocean later teamed up in a joint venture with the oil-trading company Interpetrol to form Ultrapetrol. Ultrapetrol started in 1992 with a single oceangoing vessel and grew, as a public company, to close to $1 billion in assets in 22 years.

The brothers organized their leadership roles in the company the same way their father had: They co-direct every effort that they invest in and make all their investment decisions by mutual agreement.

Ultrapetrol was founded as a diversified industrial shipping company. In its origin it owned a single tanker ship. Over the course of its first decade, Felipe and Ricardo grew their ocean business to a fleet of thirteen oceangoing vessels with a total capacity of 1.1 million deadweight tons. The bulk of this fleet was an early version, Japanese 1990 built, Post-Panamax tankers that had been built for captive Japanese crude trading. These ships had extremely shallow drafts and were particularly suitable for the draft restricted ports of South America. As these ships turned of age, Felipe and Ricardo began to sell their entire older single-hull Panamax and Aframax fleets, a process that was completed in early 2004. The company then focused on developing two different ocean fleets: a Capesize/OBO fleet which they had started by buying two 150,000 DWT from Cargill and a product tanker fleet. The OBO vessels traded initially as Suezmax tankers, and when the dry cargo market skyrocketed in 2006, they were cleaned and served as Capesizes until 2010 earning the very high rates available in the dry cargo market at that time. The company secured the earnings of these ships early in 2008 through FFA's and thus enjoyed continuous high rates throughout the 2008/2009 crisis. In 2010, the large order book of Capesizes which anticipated a crisis in the dry cargo market led to the sale of the company's four Capesize vessels.

The ocean business then was focused on its growing fleet of product tankers, and in 2010 the company started its feeder container service in South America, distributing the containerized cargo carried from the Far East by the main world carriers.

Like their father, grandfather, and great-grandfather before them, the brothers were eager to make their own mark in shipping. In 1993, Felipe and Ricardo decided to grow the family's participation in the energy transportation space—but not only on the ocean. Instead, the company expanded into tanker barges on the underdeveloped river operations in South America. Running over 2,200 miles through the hearts of Argentina, Brazil, Paraguay, and Bolivia, the Paraná river system is as large as the Mississippi. Starting with four barges and one pushboat, they multiplied the fleet to just under a thousand barges covering nineteen ports in fifteen years.

"Barging is structured completely differently than other shipping ventures," Felipe explained. "It looks more like a railroad. It was very heavy in administration, but it was incredibly successful. We had our own load ports, our own discharge ports, and we built a fully-automated shipyard to construct the barges."

In October 2000, the brothers formed a joint venture with American Commercial Barge Lines Ltd. (ACL), at that time the largest river-barging company in the world, to expand their river business under the name UABL. From 2000 to 2004, they transformed UABL into the leading river-barge company in the Hidrovia Region of South America.

Over the next two years, the brothers built on that success by securing financing in a series of credit and equity deals. The finances helped fund the company's ocean, river and offshore supply businesses.

Ravenscroft Shipping, headquartered in Miami, was absorbed into Ultrapetrol in 2006, and managed the international fleet in the company's offshore supply and ocean businesses. Through its capacity to manage third-party ships professionally Ravenscroft was entrusted with the administration of two passenger ships by a group of banks. After employing and running these vessels competitively the company acquired these passenger ships from the banks and operated them for its own account for some time.

Calculated Risk

Ultrapetrol thrived under the brothers' leadership, and for the first time in four generations, a Menéndez business would no longer be private and family-controlled. With their sons and daughter at their side, Felipe and Ricardo took Ultrapetrol public in the United States on October 13, 2006. Becoming a publicly traded company was something very different for the brothers, who now had to answer to shareholders and the analyst community regarding their growth plans.

"While we had placed public debt in U.S. and complied with all SEC regulations from as far back as 1998, the experience of having to explain our strategy from a commercial perspective to public investors in 2006 was challenging," Felipe said.

In December of 2008, Felipe and Ricardo decided to discontinue the operations of their passenger business, which had been started as a ship management operation for a group of banks and was later opportunistically acquired by the group.

At the height of commodity prices, in 2014, the brothers agreed it was time to sell and sold their interests in Ultrapetrol to the private equity company Sparrow Capital. "We were very fortunate because we sold it when oil was still at $100 a barrel, commodity prices were booming, and the company was producing very substantial profits. Unfortunately for the buyers, shortly after the acquisition, in an unexpected way, the price of oil and commodities collapsed," Felipe said.

"Those 22 years left us with was an incredible sensation of having participated in something fantastic," he continued. "What started as a local tanker operation became a diversified transportation company that in many ways changed the outlook of a region: On one hand, on the river, we built ports and carried grain cargoes from where nobody had carried them before; at one particular location we built a port that loaded 10,000 tons in its first year of operation and grew to over 1 million tons ten years later. On the other hand, we had the opportunity of launching our offshore division, led by Ricardo, right at the beginning of the development of the offshore exploration in Brazil, where in less than ten years the production grew from virtually zero to close to 2 million barrels per day," he exclaimed. "And the fact that we also grew in oceangoing shipping at the same time was just amazing! The experience of being a U.S. public company was completely different from running a private family-owned business. It gave us the capacity to do things on a different scale and develop transportation projects that changed the landscape of a region."

The timing of Felipe and Ricardo's exit from shipping was as perfect as one could plan. Just one year after the sale, the global dry bulk industry was in complete meltdown. Daily fees, which were once $185,000, plummeted to a scant $4,000 to $6,000. Global commodity orders went bust and so did major players. Companies were forced to file for bankruptcy, divest, or scrap their assets to stay alive. While the sector wallowed in the depressed market conditions, Felipe and Ricardo saw opportunity in the large amount of ships up for sale.

"This industry always overshoots," Felipe said. "The collapse of the freight rates resulted from the over-ordering of ships, and in this case, the overshooting was monumental because China had experienced such enormous growth over a long period that people thought it was going to go on forever, and obviously it didn't."

The number of the Panamax and Post-Panamax vessels up for sale grew. It was time for the brothers to capitalize on the carnage. The brothers formed Interocean Transportation in association with Latin American Partners at the end of 2015, and began cherry-picking vessels they believed had value during the hangover. The company's shopping spree continued through 2017.

"We were trying to buy the ships that would serve tomorrow's needs and do it more efficiently so that when the market recovered to a reasonable level, those ships would really make a difference in terms of earning," Felipe said.

In a nod to their great-grandfather, the brothers named two of their ships that operate a container feeder service to distant Patagonia the *Argentino* and *Asturiano*, after two ships José Menéndez y Compañía had operated a century ago.

Servicing the Needs of Tomorrow

Since walking the decks of their family's ships, Felipe and Ricardo have seen enormous changes in the industry with the opening of new markets. "Over the past 20 or 30 years we saw a boom in the production of commodities in South America," Felipe said. "Now the Asia demand is thriving because of China's appetite for South American imports of bulk commodities. They may not be growing as fast as before, but they are still growing."

Felipe explained that he had received a presentation from a London firm that reinforced his outlook on China. Attached in that presentation was a map of the world with a circle drawn around China, India, and Southeast Asia.

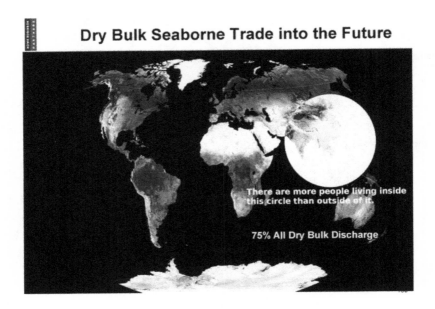

Dry Bulk Seaborne Trade into the Future

There are more people living inside this circle than outside of it.

75% All Dry Bulk Discharge

"That circle is probably no more than 20 percent of the world's surface, if that. But *half* of the world's population live within that circle, and 75 percent of all dry bulk commodities are discharged within it," Felipe said. "Now, if you look at the same circle 20 or 30 years ago, it would have been insignificant. The consumption of bulk commodities was negligible. Today, China alone represents more than 40 percent of all major bulk seaborne imports."

The steady increase of all seaborne imports to China from zero to 40 percent has both Felipe and Ricardo advising their sons to go to China and understand what is happening in the country. "It's just amazing. Everything that they will have to do planning a business over the next 20 or 30 years will have to do with China," Felipe said.

Closer to home, Felipe explained, the South American lack of infrastructure will be a source of opportunity for their sons. The brothers believe that at the rate of growth that the export of agricultural products has experienced in the past two decades we will see South America lead the supply of agricultural products to feed the explosive demand of Asia in the next decade, and they stress the need for the system to be strengthened in anticipation of such significant cargo growth. "The systems are completely antiquated," Felipe said. "Our entire logistical system in South America is a century behind the United State and Europe. There is a great opportunity for them there to develop stronger logistics. Just like the Panama Canal expansion welcomed larger ships, the South American port and river systems need to make way for them as well. Our children will be a part of that expansion. Ships also need to be designed for such expansion. We believe the Post-Panamax will be the workhorse of the future that will increase the efficiency in transportation, which is the key to the long haul carriage of cargo from South America to the Far East."

Since the Panama Canal opened, on August 15, 1914, ships have evolved and been designed around the canal's old width of 32.2 meters. While the $5 billion expansion, completed in 2015, has enabled passage for larger ships, Felipe said the maritime industry is not rising and answering the call for innovation. "The industry still builds ships to 32.2-meter beams!" Felipe said. "It is absurd that we continue to build ships to a specification that is outdated! We are trying to build a fleet of Panamaxes and Kamsarmaxes but also Post-Panamax ships (of 38 meters beam) that make at least partial use of the new width of the canal of up to 45 meters. Half of our present fleet are Post-Panamaxes. It is really the only intelligent thing to do. To service the needs of tomorrow you not only need fuel-efficient vessels but vessels large enough to carry the enormous quantities of cargo demanded. This opportunity wasn't there twenty years ago. It is now."

Looking to the decades ahead, Felipe acknowledged that the shipping world their sons will be operating in will be far more connected and open, and that interest in the capital markets will grow. "Our sons and the next generation in the shipping industry need to realize that in the world they will be operating in they will have competition coming at them from all angles. They need to understand the capital markets and know how to properly use them," Felipe said. "Success in maritime will not be in the common buying and selling of ships. In a few years, that will be gone. Our sons and the leaders of tomorrow need to learn everything about the capital markets and devising solutions to improve logistics. *That* is what will bring them success in the long-term."

This long-term focus is woven tightly within the strands of the Menéndez DNA, Felipe said. "When we were growing up and learning the business," he said, "my father always told us, 'When you go out to hunt a rabbit, the most important thing is to come back with the rabbit,' meaning that one must never lose sight of the objective. This is something I have said to my children. People in business negotiations often get lost in side-track discussions and lose perspective of what they were really trying to achieve. I tell my sons: Never lose sight of what your goal is. Come back with that rabbit."

CHAPTER THIRTEEN

Miles Kulukundis

Shipowner and Industry Executive

In the summer of 1929, the Great Depression hit the United States. Unlike previous depressions, which had been confined to just one country, the Great Depression wreaked havoc on the economies of countries around the world. International trade precipitously dropped 30 percent. Industrial production in the United States declined 47 percent, and the country's gross domestic product fell 30 percent.

During that time, the interconnectedness of the world was felt. The struggling U.S. called in its World War I and post-World War I loans to the Allied Nations, only to be rebuffed because the nations couldn't afford to pay them back. The U.S. downturn quickly became a global contagion. The volume of goods traveling across the seas shrank. Trade was further restricted by new policies like the Smoot-Hawley Tariff Act of 1930.

Source: United Nations Historical Trade Data

177

Consumers were strapped. An estimated 30 million people around the world were unemployed. In the U.K., GDP fell 5 percent. The ripple effect through the rest of the world hit British exports, stripping them in half. Parts of the industrial sector wallowed in poverty. By 1930, unemployment had more than doubled, reaching 20 percent.

Despite the global economic gloom, the entrepreneurial Kulukundis, Mavroleon, and Rethymnis families saw an opportunity. As with many Greek families, they had deep roots in the shipping industry. For well over a century, they had navigated the waters of the Mediterranean and the Black Sea. After the First World War, in 1919, Manuel Kulukundis and his cousin Minas Rethymnis decided to leave Greece and go to London to join the mainstream of the international shipping industry.

"Uncle Manuel, Uncle George, and my father, Nicholas, with their cousins Minas Rethymnis and Basil Mavroleon, opened an office, and they acted as ship managers and brokers," explained Miles Kulukundis, former managing director at London & Overseas Freighters. "During that time, vessels were being sold for very, very, very low figures. My family, together with many other Greek families took advantage of the decimation of the British merchant marine because they were the ones who had actually built the ships."

The ship managing agency was named Rethymnis & Kulukundis Ltd. The company flourished over the years, and its success attracted the talents of additional family members from Greece, including two other Kulukundis brothers, John and Michael.

For over a hundred years, the Kulukundis family had owned tramp steamers, mainly in the Mediterranean and the Black Sea. Now the brothers wanted to replicate that success in the U.K. In 1939 they acquired a number of British vessels and put their mark on U.K. trade. These ships were managed by a new company, Counties Ship Management.

The Kulukundis family were not the only Greeks sailing under the British flag. The Papayannis, the Spartalis, the Schilizzis, and the cargo-trading Rodocanachis were just some of the many major Greek shipping families during that time that did the same.

After the Second World War, the Kulukundis family realized there was an opportunity to set up a company to build and run tramp tankers to participate in the growing oil trade. This opportunity led to the creation of London & Overseas Freighters, which was incorporated on April 8, 1948. The company had nine second-hand dry-cargo ships. On March 20, 1951, the Kulukundises and Mavroleons listed London & Overseas Freighters as a public company on the London Stock Exchange. It would trade on the exchange under the stock ticker LOF.

At that time, there were quite a few shipping companies trading on the London Stock Exchange, mostly British, such as Reardon Smith, Common Brothers, and Ropner, as well as the big ones like P&O and Ocean Steam.

Learning the Ropes

Growing up in the United States, Miles had little exposure to the family's shipping organization, since it was based in London. As a young child, he was able to attend the launching of the company's new vessels, which left a huge impression on him. "This gave me a great thrill," Miles said. "I aspired from a young age to create new vessels. I felt then that it represented the creation of a new entity."

In 1959, Miles joined the family business as a trainee and spent a year in Sunderland at the Austin & Pickersgill shipyard, which was owned by LOF.

Miles learned all the facets of LOF as he moved up the ranks. For three years he served as a chartering clerk on the Baltic Exchange; then, to develop his management skills, he was given the responsibility of running Counties Ship Management. During that time, Miles was responsible for approximately twenty Liberty Vessels. "My father allowed me to learn the business by actively doing it," Miles said. "He didn't advise me on what to do aside from making the final decisions on major questions. My father allowed me to do smaller transactions to learn the business."

Miles served as a non-executive director of LOF until 1976, when his uncle Basil Mavroleon asked him to come to LOF as a joint managing director with specific responsibilities for operations and chartering. "My father and my uncle Basil Mavroleon were both big influences on me. My father had three sayings he often mentioned to me: 'The sea gets sick but it never dies,' 'Everything in moderation,' and 'Vessels are not trains on rails,'" Miles recalled.

"My uncle also inspired me," he continued. "He was a big personality, which made him the center of any gathering. His intense commitment to our companies and industry was something I always admired. I followed their examples during my time at LOF."

Catching a Falling Knife

The line between success and failure in the shipping industry is razor thin. After World War I, the Kulukundis family had seized on the turmoil in the maritime world and established its shipping businesses, which thrived in Britain's shipping ground zero. Through the interwar years, the company rode the highs and lows, consistently finding gainful employment for its vessels.

Following the boom of 1957, LOF found itself, along with the industry as a whole, overextended with newbuilding vessels. For ten years, the company seriously struggled.

In 1962, with the hopes of boosting profits, the company signed three- to four-year charters with the USSR. Unfortunately, according to the United States, the deal conflicted with the U.S. embargo against Cuba because Russia had open business dealings with Cuba.

LOF argued that it was not directly doing business with Cuba—it had an agreement with Russia. The explanation was satisfactory to the U.S. government, but not to the International Longshoremen's Association

(ILA). The ILA had a policy during the Cuban Missile Crisis against working ships trading with Communist Cuba; it refused to handle vessels that had previously traded with Cuba, and boycotted one of LOF's dry cargo vessels in Baltimore. An agreement was finally reached with the ILA when LOF agreed to sail the vessel away without loading, opening the way for the company's other vessels to trade in the United States.

The difficulty with the ILA in Cuba was just one of the challenges facing the company during the early 1960s. In March 1962, for the first time in the company's history, LOF posted a loss and passed on its dividend. The future looked somber. The company had six cargo ships on order, and in June it took delivery of its final tanker. The tanker and ship orders were made before 1960. For five years, the company continued to post losses. The emergence of supertankers also made it hard for LOF to compete.

LOF continued to face hurdles until the Six-Day War and the closure of the Suez Canal in 1967. The closure shut off a vital route, forcing tankers to take longer routes via the Cape of Good Hope. On the longer routes, 200,000-plus-ton tankers were more efficient, which immediately sparked an increase in demand to build such vessels. The canal closed, LOF prospered.

MV London Integrity, 1955

MV London Citizen, 1965

Shipping Depression and Personal Loss

The booms of 1967, 1970, and 1973 were followed by one of the worst depressions for the industry, especially for the tanker industry, as shipowners had ordered an excess of new vessels. Aside from slight improvements, these very difficult trading conditions continued until the late 1980s and led to multiple bankruptcies in the industry.

"LOF had made the same mistakes as others and found itself with a number of unemployed newbuildings," Miles said. "The pessimism was so great that some owners scrapped virtually new vessels. LOF was faced with laying up its new vessels straight from the yard. This was the worst recession I experienced in my career."

In 1977, the company had faced its biggest loss yet when its principal founder and chairman Basil Mavroleon passed away. Then, in 1988, the family lost business founder Manuel Kulukundis. "My uncle Manuel always carried a pocket watercolor paintbox," Miles recalled. "He had a habit of painting pictures on the back of menus at any dinners he attended. He was also a very talented mandolin player. His vast knowledge of the industry was always an asset to me," he added. "He, along with my uncle Basil, taught me the power of having extreme commitment to the industry and to the companies."

While still feeling the loss of Manuel's passing, the family suffered another tragedy. Minas Kulukundis, LOF's CFO and director, was one of the 243 passengers killed in the bombing of Pan Am Flight 103, in 1988. He was flying to America to attend the funeral of his uncle and godfather, Captain Nicholas Kulukundis.

These sad events coincided with a modest improvement in the market, and LOF was able, with the support of the Sumitomo Corporation of Japan, to restructure itself and create a basis for the future.

Tanker Industry's Defining Environmental Moment: The Exxon Valdez Disaster

On Good Friday, March 24, 1989, the shipping industry experienced what was, at the time, the worst oil spill in maritime history. The *Exxon Valdez* struck Prince William Sound's Bligh Reef, spilling 11 million to 38 million U.S. gallons of oil into the water.

This massive man-made environmental disaster was a result of staff breakdown and a failure to use the technology designed to avoid such catastrophes. "I would not have considered the *Exxon* vessel operation substandard or bad," Miles said. "They were unfortunate to have officers who made errors and caused such a major incident that was beyond their control."

The LOF board looked at their best practices and waited to see what government regulations would require in the future. "I knew things were going to change with regulation," Miles said, "but how was not clear. It would be what the government learned from the disaster in terms of how they would create new regulations to make the industry safer."

The historic oil spill was a catalyst for the International Maritime Organization (IMO) to set comprehensive marine pollution prevention rules. IMO member countries voted in favor of amending the International Convention for the Prevention of Pollution from Ships (MARPOL), and under the IMO's new International Safety Management rules, all member shipowners would be required to operate with the mission of having safer ships and cleaner oceans. The U.S. went a step further by passing the Oil Pollution Act of 1990 (OPA-90). One of the changes tanker owners had to conform to under OPA-90 was the use of double hull ships.

"MARPOL has proved a step forward, as oil pollution has been reduced dramatically. It was a step in the right direction," Miles said.

The *Exxon Valdez* disaster left a lasting impression on Miles. One day, he would help shape regulation that would change the way the tanker industry addressed environmental safety.

LOF Restructuring in the Face of Adversity

By 1988, LOF was able to look to the future with confidence. In 1990, the company started a new construction program with the order of a 150,000-deadweight-ton tanker.

In 1992, the board decided to move LOF's corporate operations to Bermuda. Miles, who was managing director at the time, told industry followers the move wasn't a way for the company to pay lower taxes. Rather, it was a way to broaden its capital markets base. "We tried to raise capital as a U.K. company but failed completely," Miles said. "International investors were not interested in U.K.-based operations. We had to relocate if we were to broaden the capital base."

Other tanker companies like Smedvig Tankers, Teekay Corporation, and Frontline Ltd. were based in tax-free environments and were successfully raising capital in the international markets. That had caught the attention of LOF directors. It worked. In the summer of 1993, LOF was able to place 5 million new shares at 15 dollars a share. Of the shares, 60 percent was New York, 40 percent was London.

Lifting the Veil of Transparency

During this transition, in 1990, Miles became chairman of the United Kingdom P&I Club, the largest member of the international group at the time. In 1994 he also became chairman of INTERTANKO. Working through the *Exxon Valdez* disaster, Kulukundis saw firsthand how one company's mistake could label the entire industry. "The industry fought hard together with the P&I Clubs to prevent the passage of the Oil Pollution Act in the United States," Miles said. "It was the biggest problem I dealt with while at INTERTANKO."

Miles explained that the development of oil pollution regulation was motivated by several major oil spills: the *Torrey Canyon*, the *Amoco Cadiz*, and the *Exxon Valdez*.

With that in mind, he set out to establish new regulation and guidelines that would distinguish the difference between a good tanker operator and a bad one, and to try to prevent excessive regulation. Miles wanted to take on the question that the industry did not address: What are the telltale signs of a substandard tanker operator?

In an effort to set standards for safety, transparency was at the forefront of Miles's time as INTERTANKO chairman. For the first time in INTERTANKO history, member shipowners had to disclose safety certifications and adequate insurance. "The industry has a long history of not being proactive," Miles said. "They have never done anything without regulation making them. Honestly, I don't see why it would change even today," he added.

These mandatory measures sparked eleven other marine organizations to adopt similar standards including: Lloyd's Register, Det Norske Veritas (now DNV GL), and the American Bureau of Shipping. The eleven societies were also members of the International Association of Classification Societies (IACS). The IACS had adopted similar resolutions under the IMO. At the INTERTANKO 1994 and 1995 annual meetings, it was mandatory that all tankers owned by new and existing members of INTERTANKO be classed with an IACS member society. "Almost all of our members conformed," Miles said.

In 1995, Adriatic Tankers was forced to resign because it failed to meet the requirements. According to INTERTANKO, the organization had quietly dropped members prior to this point, but this was the first instance of a publicized resignation request made to a member.

Another area Miles wanted to improve was the industry's use of public relations. The industry had long been known for its poor communication with the press. Unfortunately, the *Exxon Valdez* disaster and the American Oil Pollution Act contributed to a further clamp down on media outreach. This was something Miles wanted to reverse.

Financial Challenges

In 1995, the fortunes of LOF turned around yet again. The company saw record profits, bringing in $8.4 million. The drivers behind the profits were the Chevron time charters of *London Spirit, Victory*, and *Pride*. In addition, the *London Enterprise*, which was trading on the voyage market at the time, had increased her daily time charter from $13,500 to $15,000.

The industry was also bullish on the future of oil consumption. OPEC was expected to increase production. The LOF board thought the company was at last in the clear, and that the time was right to continue with its growth plan. Unfortunately, the destination of oil consumption changed. Middle East oil was being transported to the Far East, which reduced voyage time and cut the amount of tankers needed to transport the commodity. The downturn in tanker charters sent around 16 million tons of tankers to be sold for scrap.

In June of 1995, the lucrative Chevron charters came to an end, and with the oil and gas exploration company closing down two of its refiners, there was no need for Chevron to have two tankers chartered. With the tanker cycle in its favor, Chevron was able to negotiate a two-year renewal for *London Spirit*, but at a reduced rate.

During this time, there was a wave of mergers in the container and bulk shipping space. "At the time, LOF was trading on the Nasdaq, and unfortunately, the trading volume was not sufficient enough for active trading to allow for share price movements," Miles said. "In 1997, after a discussion with some of our major institutional shareholders, we placed the company up for sale."

At the time, shipping magnate John Fredriksen declared in the press that it was the right moment for such mergers in the tanker industry.

One London broker said that year that it was "cheaper to buy a company than buy tankers."

In 1997, Fredriksen's company Frontline took a 51 percent controlling interest in LOF. "It ended up as a reverse takeover, as Frontline became part of LOF, but the name was eventually changed to Frontline," Miles explained. "The transaction proved very beneficial to LOF shareholders, who received cash for all their holdings instead of stock. By 1999, Frontline's share price had fallen significantly."

LOF Last Board of Directors, 1996

The Need for Corporate Responsibility During the Cycles

Through the boom-and-bust cycles, Miles said, different actors made the previous mistakes of others hoping for different results. "Every cycle is exactly the same. The market is exactly the same. You have to buy your capital assets at a low price and sell them at a high price. Either sell them to transport cargos on period charters or sell your assets to others," he said. "It doesn't matter if it was the Second World War, the first Suez Crisis, or the oil crisis in the '70s. You need to have gainful employment for your ships to make a profit. You will have overbuying. The outcome is the same. That's why you need to be invested over the long term."

Miles said that the emergence of hedge funds and private equity, with their compressed timeline in the search for return on investment of around five years, has added to the lows of the cycles. "They've made a mess to the industry. They're in a business that they don't understand, and particularly looking for short-term yields. It's ridiculous," he said. "They went into this industry in classically the wrong way—with high-priced assets and newbuildings. You're not going to get a short-term yield on that. I'm not against building new ships, but that's not *always* the way to do it."

Shipbuilders would eagerly take money for newbuildings, Miles said, regardless of creating a glut. "Hedge funds and private equity firms are giving shipowners money and saying, 'Can I get these ships?' Both the shipbuilders and the hedge fund and private equity firms are culprits in this excessive optimism and overbuilding. A lot of damage was done to the industry in 2008 and 2012, in the sense that made private equity think that it would always be a gravy train."

A big believer in corporate responsibility and environmental stewardship, Miles said the maritime industry has done a very good job working with INTERTANKO, and the results have been positive. "While ship operation has been severely regulated, the regulations have been adhered to, and the results have been successful. The environmental impact has been positive."

Miles, who is now detached from the industry, said that while progress has been made on environmental stewardship, it is never over. "As my father once told me, 'This is our heritage, and we must stick with it.' Adhere to new regulations as they develop. The sea gets sick but never dies."

Miles Kulukundis
Source: Original artwork by Johnny Miltiades Kulukundis

CHAPTER FOURTEEN

Richard du Moulin

Hands-on Sailor

In 1918, the great flu pandemic took the lives of 50 million to 100 million people worldwide. During those horrific fifteen months, Richard du Moulin's grandfather Theodore du Moulin, a Wall Street lawyer, and great-grandfather Charles Issar died in the same week, leaving Adele, Richard's grandmother, all alone to raise her three young children, Julia, Edward (Richard's father), and Charles. Adele's distant cousin Sam Lauterbach, a pioneer in sailing and skiing, moved in to help her and became patriarch of the family. It was during that time the du Moulins' passion for maritime was born.

The du Moulin children grew up on sailboats. Their first experience was sailing on Lauterbach's 45-foot yawl *Thora*. In addition to sailing from Block Island to New York during Prohibition with the boat loaded with liquor, the three also enjoyed watching the America's Cup races, little knowing that Edward and his son Richard would be participants half a century later.

After graduating from Far Rockaway High School, being too poor to extend his education by attending college, Edward started work for Bache & Company on Wall Street for five dollars a week, and later joined the Coast Guard Reserve at age 26, in 1941. Edward used his yachting experience to become the bosun's mate skipper of a 47-foot motorsailer named *Bettine*. Their mission was to search for U-boats off the Atlantic coast. During the rough winter of 1941 to 1942 the crew called the yacht "The Rolling Bettine" for the way the vessel behaved with her round bilge at sea. Seasickness became a way of life. After

1942, Edward attended the Coast Guard Academy to train as an officer.

Ensign du Moulin became the commander of a new 83-foot cutter whose sole purpose was to escort tankers along the coast, attacking U-boats and forcing them to submerge so the tanker could escape. Promoted to Lieutenant, Edward was assigned to the 327-foot cutter *Ingham* sailing in the North Atlantic convoys. After the war, he went back to work at Bache on Wall Street.

In 1942 he married Eleanor Lewis, and after the war they had two children, Richard and Cathy. In the footsteps of Lauterbach, Edward shared his love of sailing with his children. At the age of two, Richard started sailing with his father and his World War II North Atlantic convoy buddies. "From my earliest memories, I remembered hearing stories about the convoys, sailing, the Coast Guard and Navy," du Moulin reminisced, "I loved the history. Shipping may not have been in the family, so to speak, but that didn't stop my father from instilling his love of sailing and maritime history into me. Only one of Dad's WWII crew is still alive: Tom O'Sullivan, who at sixteen, in 1941, lied about his age and became a combat artist. I still take Tom to dinner several times a year."

Richard du Moulin enrolled in Dartmouth in 1964 and joined the Navy ROTC. It was a dream come true for his father. "Dartmouth was the college my dad would have gone to if he could have afforded college during the Depression," he said. "I joined ROTC because I wanted to spend time in the service and attend a good liberal arts college. So I kind of had my cake and ate it too."

During his years at Dartmouth, du Moulin was supposed to take summer cruises aboard Navy ships, but he missed them because of America's Cup and Transatlantic Races. "The Navy let me do those instead," he said. "So when I graduated in June of 1969 from the engineering school, I still had to make up a midshipman cruise. My first day in the Navy I arrived in Norfolk, Virginia, and went to the officers' club bar, and the place was going nuts. It was the moment the astronauts were first stepping on the moon!" He chuckled. "That was my first night in the Navy."

Du Moulin served for three years. The ship he was on, the LST *Terrebonne Parish*, got laid up, because at that time, ships were returning from Vietnam. "I spent about six months on the T-bone, as we called her, and then I was transferred to the Naval Academy, where I spent the next two and a half years running a shipyard. The yard maintained all the craft the academy used for professional development (navigation, leadership, seamanship), from sailboats to 110-foot training ships, and even one submarine. The managerial experience was invaluable."

During that time, du Moulin was also given the opportunity to tap into his sailing experience. He coached the Navy ocean racing team and taught navigation and seamanship. After departing the service in 1972, he was appointed to the DeCoursey Fales committee and for 30 years advised the superintendent of the academy on sailing, seamanship, and navigation.

Early Days

After the Navy, du Moulin navigated and skippered the ocean racer *Charisma* in the Bermuda and Transatlantic races. The real world settled in, and in 1972 du Moulin entered Harvard Business School. During the summer between his two years at HBS, he held a job at Moore McCormack Lines working for Jim Barker and Paul Tregurtha. "I was really fortunate with the people I first worked for in shipping. Jim and Paul were two of the most terrific people and businessmen," he said with a smile. "They got me really excited about shipping. They invited me to work for them after I graduated, but I wanted something more international, so I went to work at Ogden Marine (OMI)."

In 1974, du Moulin started to work for Mike Klebanoff, founder and CEO of OMI. It was a turbulent time in the world. It was the year after the Yom Kippur War and the Arab oil embargo. The tanker market was poised for a collapse, and the United States and Russia were in the

Cold War. The Moscow Summit in June and July of that year was overshadowed by the Watergate scandal and the resignation of President Richard Nixon. Being a former serviceman, du Moulin understood the geopolitical tensions.

"When I served in the U.S. Navy, our sole job was to be prepared to destroy the Russian Navy. Russia was our primary opponent. Mike Klebanoff, however, was not particularly concerned about Russia. Mike told me, 'Richard, don't worry about Russia. Russia's so inefficient it's going to collapse. The country to watch as the next world superpower is China.' Mike grew up in China," du Moulin explained. "He said the Chinese are the most efficient, hardworking business people, and when China opens up, they will dominate the world. It was pretty damn smart of him to recognize that back in the early '70s!"

A few years later, the Iranian Revolution shook up the shipping world, and soon thereafter du Moulin's life took another turn. On November 4, 1979, the day the hostages were taken, Richard married Ann Capelli, or as he jokes, "I was taken hostage. Every day for the next 400-plus days, Walter Cronkite told me on the evening news exactly how long I had been married."

Klebanoff, who passed away in 2017, was revered by du Moulin and many others who worked for him, such as current Connecticut shipping executives Charlie Tammara, Kathy Haines, Robert Bugbee, and Craig Stevenson. Klebanoff's parents had run away from Russia during the Russian Civil War in the 1920s. They were Jewish and escaped on the Trans-Siberian Railway. Klebanoff was born at the end of the railroad line in Harbin, Manchuria, and grew up in Shanghai in the Jewish community. His wife, Angelica, had also fled Russia with her family, escaping Communism to settle in China. In 1948, the couple escaped China to settle in Cuba, and when Castro came to power they escaped Cuba to end up in New York.

"Mike had a wonderful background and a whole different worldview from most people because of where he grew up. He was also a kind mentor and teacher," du Moulin said with reverence in his voice.

"Working for him was one of the greatest experiences of my life. He was a short guy without a Napoleon complex. Yes, he had plenty of ego, but it was totally controlled. He gave me so much authority to go out and learn something yet was always there for me to go to and seek his advice. He never put a choker on me. Our charter brokers made huge efforts to teach me the basics. I later found out Mike had told the brokers that he would hold them responsible for my mistakes!"

Even though du Moulin left the company in 1989 to go out on his own, he kept in touch with Klebanoff until the year he died. "The years at Ogden Marine were fantastic, but I really wanted to do my own thing, so I ended up leaving and joining with Mark Filanowski and an investment banker named Paul Gridley, formerly of Lehman Brothers, to form Intrepid Shipping. I called it Intrepid Shipping after the America's Cup boat I sailed on."

Charting a New Course

The goal of Intrepid Shipping was to buy tankers. Du Moulin had friends at Goldman Sachs who wanted to invest in a partner fund with them. They were about to seal the deal when, on June 8, 1990, the *Mega Borg* exploded off the coast of Houston. The bankers at Goldman called du Moulin and with apologies backed out. "We had no plan, so when we heard that Marine Transport Lines, a public shipping company, was in play, we decided to go after it," du Moulin said.

MTL was the oldest shipping company in America, founded in 1816 by the Mallory family in Mystic, Connecticut. Ironically, one of the descendants, Charles Mallory, a partner in the tanker broker MJLF, is a close friend of du Moulin.

To purchase MTL, du Moulin and his team sought funds from a variety of sources. Financing from Norwegian banking friends DNB and Christiania Bank, subordinated debt from the Belzberg family of Canada, and equity from the three partners and friends totaled $144 million, which in 1989 was considered a huge sum. Even so, Intrepid Shipping found itself in a nasty, bruising battle with much stronger buyers. These three other bidders were led by retired Secretary of Treasury Charles Simon, SEACOR's Charles Fabrikant, and a group headed by MTL's then chairman. Intrepid barely survived the fight, but succeeded in closing the acquisition in the waning weeks of 1989, the end of the wild '80s leveraged buyout era.

"We managed to survive the closing," du Moulin said, "but faced a serious challenge with customers upset by the protracted sale of the company, and a staggering amount of debt. We quickly moved to sell an Aframax crude tanker at the market high, half interest in one of the first LR2 product Aframaxes and a 50 percent interest in our British short sea tanker company to P&O. We cut our debt by 60 percent. At that point, the market started to go down. We barely survived."

One of MTL's largest businesses was transporting chemicals, and its most important relationship was with Union Carbide on an American-flagged tanker called *Chemical Pioneer*. "I had to pay a lot of attention to that relationship," du Moulin said. "I traveled to Union Carbide's headquarters in Danbury, Connecticut, to visit Robert Kennedy, the chairman. He was a leader and visionary in chemical industry safety."

Kennedy had taken over Union Carbide from his unfortunate predecessor, who was on watch when the Bhopal gas tragedy occurred in India, killing over a thousand people. "Under Kennedy's leadership, the company turned around, and Kennedy pushed for tighter safety standards," du Moulin said. "His view was that the biggest companies should take the leadership role in safety and share their practices with the smaller companies. It made perfect sense. A disaster by any company hurts all companies."

Du Moulin would remember all the lessons learned from Kennedy about how to create and enforce industry measures for both safety and environmental protection. In 1994 he was elected vice chairman of INTERTANKO, the international organization representing the tanker industry, serving under chairman Miles Kulukundis. Kulukundis and du Moulin, with the new executive director Dagfinn Lunde, made INTERTANKO a far more proactive organization. Du Moulin became chairman in 1996, and for the next three years he was an outspoken advocate for safety and protection of the global environment.

While du Moulin was chairman-elect, he had several lunches with Kennedy, and the two became friends. "Following Kennedy's initiatives in his industry, I would talk about what safety policies I thought the tanker industry should adopt. I wanted to make sure every company was operating safely. I did not want some owner running his tanker on the rocks, and then Congress passing punitive laws that would hurt everyone," du Moulin said. "My goal as chairman of INTERTANKO was to raise the standards of our industry."

But getting all the members on board was not easy. The largest bloc of INTERTANKO members were the Greek owners and operators. They were very unhappy about new regulations and being painted as public enemies, yet were skeptical of industry leadership. So du Moulin flew to Greece to convince them that tougher new standards were in their best interests. "My biggest friend and supporter in Greece was Eric Kertsikoff of Eletson. As he led me into the private dining room, he said, 'Be very careful, Richard. One quarter of the world fleet is owned by these men, and they are prepared to not like what you will say.' As it turned out, our dinner went until early morning, and the outcome was great. We argued about many issues, but the Greek owners realized I was not an empty suit but a maritime man who loved the ships, the ocean, and the mariners. These owners became my biggest supporters and enabled INTERTANKO's global strategy to go forward. Funny that it was Kennedy and the Greeks who opened the door!"

Du Moulin continued: "In the end, INTERTANKO led the way, and it was interesting how well the U.S. Coast Guard, Brussels, and various port states reacted. We learned from the chemical industry how to change the tanker industry, and it had a lasting effect because every statistic you look at now shows that oil pollution is radically, radically down. In January 2018 we did have our first anomaly. That was when the Iranian tanker *Sanchi* blew up and burned in the East China Sea. The Iranians may not have the same safety management systems that the rest of the world has. But other than that, the data has really supported everything we did in the 1990s. We successfully changed the culture of safety and environmental protection in maritime."

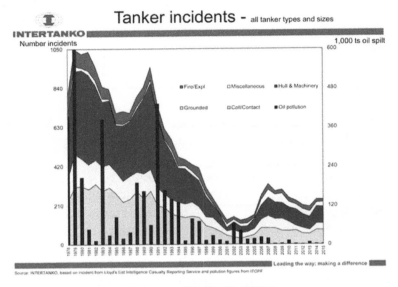

Source: INTERTANKO

But even with industry improvements, accidents could still happen, and du Moulin knew the industry was behind on how to address mishaps in the news. The advice a public relations consultant had given du Moulin years prior was something he would never forget. "He said, 'You know, all news is bad news. If you want good news, read the funny section,' " du Moulin recalled. "He said, 'Nobody's going to want to read about tanker owners being good guys, but the moment there's a disaster it's going to be front page.' "

Based on that advice, as chairman of INTERTANKO, du Moulin made sure the companies started educating themselves on how to deal with crisis response. "You never want a tanker disaster, but once you have one, you are on the television and front pages. A sad form of free advertising, but it is an opportunity to look and be professional, to communicate effectively, giving confidence to the public and the regulators. You must have an effective immediate response to the incident." INTERTANKO required its members to train in crisis response. This is how du Moulin met Jim Lawrence, one of the pioneers in maritime industry crisis response. Jim and his partners in London, together with other PR consultants around the world, were hired to train tanker owners to be prepared to respond to a crisis. This training proved to be a spectacular success for INTERTANKO in the wake of several accidents that occurred in the following years.

Du Moulin's work at INTERTANKO garnered him numerous awards. The U.S. Coast Guard awarded him their highest civilian award, the Distinguished Service Medal. The Connecticut Maritime Association presented him with their Commodore Award, and the unions with the Admiral of the Ocean Sea (AOTAS).

While balancing his duties at INTERTANKO, du Moulin and his team at Marine Transport Lines worked on turning around the company. The immediate deleveraging after the closing in 1989 seemed satisfactory until the chemical and tanker markets crashed in the early 1990s. "We just scraped and scraped for the next five years to stay alive. That's where all the hard knocks from the Navy and everything else began to pay off," du Moulin said. "We managed to keep our team together under terrible stress. Mark, Paul, and the management and staff at MTL were real fighters in terms of never giving up. We made sure to meet and get to know our mariners, which translated into very good customer service by our ships in their dedicated trades. This enabled us to retain virtually every key customer and contract while we struggled to survive. Customers were supportive of our efforts, including our friends at Union Carbide."

When the market turned and started to move back up, du Moulin structured a swap with his old company, OMI, which was then run by Craig Stevenson and Robert Bugbee. In June 1998, MTL and OMI were merged, and then split along U.S. flag and international lines. The strategy of the deal was for Stevenson and Bugbee to take OMI overseas, free of U.S. taxation, and for du Moulin and his team to double the size of MTL. Both companies would then be public, OMI on the New York Stock Exchange and MTL on Nasdaq. This was highly successful for both companies, which then rode improving markets. Three years later, in 2001, du Moulin and the board sold MTL to Tom Crowley.

In 2002, Filanowski and du Moulin departed Crowley and started Intrepid Shipping once again as a private shipping partnership. Du Moulin's college friend Ken Jones, once a major MTL shareholder, brought in new investors, who are to this day still invested in Intrepid vessels.

Leading with Patience and Compassion

Du Moulin's father was known on Wall Street and in the sailing world as a great manager of people in complicated situations. It was his ability to connect with people that opened his son's eyes to the importance of personal support and communication. "Dad was in his best element when he was helping young people find their way in both the sport of sailing and in their lives and careers," du Moulin said.

This leadership trait left a strong impression on du Moulin, and he wanted to lead by his father's example. "I would say one of my stronger suits is dealing with people," he said. "In the Navy I not only had to work with a variety of people, I also had to learn how to deal with a big bureaucracy and the system in which the Navy operates. You learn a lot about dealing with big organizations. Some are good lessons, and some are good lessons because they were bad experiences. In the end, I learned from both."

One of life's teachable moments for du Moulin came while he was serving as a Lieutenant in the Navy. "Because my ship got laid up I did not have battlefield experience, but I had a lot of people working under me who had come back from Vietnam," du Moulin explained. "Senior Chief Petty Officer Gainey, who had the second highest rank you can get in the enlisted ranks, taught me a ton of stuff because he'd been in combat. He got the Silver Star. His lieutenant was killed, and he had to take over the command of three Swift Boats that were under attack on the Mekong River. Gainey was very quiet, but he would take me aside several times to give me little pointers on how to deal with people. He never did it in front of the men."

That relationship deepened his respect for people who were of lower rank but had more years of experience. "I've always found it very easy to talk to the guys working hard on the ship. If you let them know that you want their input, you will get some really good information and feedback," du Moulin said. "But if you talk down at them and show disrespect, they will just shut up. You would never know if there were any problems."

Throughout the years, this leadership strategy helped prevent serious problems for du Moulin and his companies. His knack for developing relationships with employees from every level also provided occasional invaluable insights into steering away from "deals." In 2003 and 2004, du Moulin and Filanowski at Intrepid Shipping were looking to expand their fleet of bulk carriers. Laxman Kumar, the superintendent of their bulk carriers operated by Wallem in Hong Kong, helped them dodge a very expensive bullet. "We were out inspecting ships during the run-up of the dry bulk bull market, and I remember we inspected one Greek-owned ship that was due for drydocking," du Moulin recalled. "The owner shared with us his drydock plan, including his 50 tons of new steel. I called Laxman and told him that we were thinking of buying that ship. He told me he wanted to think about it and would give me his view later in the week. Well, three days later, he called and warned us to stay away from that ship. When I asked why, he said, 'I flew to the shipyard in China where they are planning to drydock, and the owner is lying to you. It's not 50 tons of steel. It's 600 tons of steel they need to put in that ship!' So Laxman took it upon himself to fly to China to check out the shipyard where this ship was heading to find out what was really going on and to safeguard us—his friends and customer. We never would have gotten that if we treated this guy like a servant of our company."

This was something du Moulin had never heard of a ship manager doing before. "You really need to work with people and get to know them and let them know how interested you are in their views. When you've built that trust, people are more forthcoming. Never treat people like your rank and file. That blocks good communication. If you really want complete information, you've got to open up that communication. This is fundamentally important for any manager. Too many executives are afraid of losing their authority and miss important inputs." This style seems more like Silicon Valley than maritime.

Du Moulin's passion for maritime and its people extends beyond business. For twenty years, he has been active on the board of the Seamen's Church Institute (SCI) in New York. As chairman from 2012 through March 2018, he worked with the SCI board and staff to expand the services to mariners, including chaplaincy, seafarer's services, seafarer's rights, and maritime education. One of the saddest and most memorable services rendered by the staff of SCI was the coordination of financial and spiritual help for the families of the U.S. flag *El Faro*. "When she went down in Hurricane Joaquin, in 2015, our board member Jim Lawrence recommended to the shipowner TOTE that they ask us to take care of the families and properly dispense the $800,000 in donations already raised," du Moulin said. "Even though I did not know the young people on board, I felt very close to them because of my own sailing experiences. It was a privilege to get to know some of the families. Our chaplains visited all the families—including the ones in Poland. In February we finally distributed the remaining money to all the families based on the number of children below age 21."

Fundamentals Trump Technology

Over the decades, global trade has gotten deeper, wider, and more intertwined. As a result, vessels have increased in size and speed to benefit from economies of scale. Vessels are also equipped with labor-saving and assistive technologies. Despite these advances, du Moulin stressed that the industry needs to focus on the fundamentals and lead by the common-sense principles of maritime, not by technology. "The fact is the fundamental requirements to go to sea have not changed much over the centuries. I like to use historic comparisons such as the mutiny on the *Bounty* back in Captain Bligh's day, in the 1700s," du Moulin said. "Captain Bligh and seventeen of his crew were put in a longboat—just a long rowboat—and left behind by Fletcher Christian. Captain Bligh led his crew on the longest open-boat journey in history. They sailed over 3,000 miles to Batavia, which is now Jakarta, and only lost one crew member, due to cannibals. That is a great example of tremendous leadership." He paused. "Now, flash forward to 2012 during Hurricane Sandy, with the *Bounty II*, which was a *Bounty* replica. The owner and skipper decided the ship, berthed safely in New London, Connecticut, had to get to Florida for an appointment. They said they could sail around the back of Hurricane Sandy. Well, they couldn't."

The modern *Bounty II* was a classic tall ship with three masts and 10,000 square feet of sail. She was 120 feet long—30 feet longer than the original—with sixteen crew members. The ship departed from New London and sailed into the storm. Captain Robin Walbridge and passenger Claudene Christian, a California beauty queen and professional singer who claimed to be a descendant of Fletcher Christian, both perished.

"The Coast Guard search and rescue teams nearly died while saving the remainder of the crew," du Moulin said. "It's amazing—here you have three centuries separating the two ships. Captain Bligh had terrific seamanship, and the owner and skipper of *Bounty II*, even with all the modern technology and information, made a stupid decision to sail into a storm."

Du Moulin continued: "In the end, it's really about getting back to the core skills of maritime. I am talking situational awareness, seamanship, leadership, and crisis management. It's not about technology," he emphasized. "In fact, technology—if you use it wrong or forget the fundamentals—won't bail you out. We've had two Navy ships get in collisions, and they had plenty of technology! If you have the fundamentals, then you avoid the problems.

"The loss of the *El Faro* in Hurricane Joaquin had all kinds of lessons for anybody who goes to sea. There are certain basic seamanship fundamentals that need to be followed," du Moulin said. "The *El Faro* was very sad—the Coast Guard's pretty much addressed the accident.

One of the contributing causes was bad decision-making by the captain, and lack of communication between the captain and junior officers. The captain was very respected but sadly made some fatal decisions. You might as well be Columbus or Shackleton because you can get into a situation where modern technology doesn't save you. It's seamanship and leadership that has the chance of saving you."

As a member of the U.S. Sailing Association's Safety at Sea Committee and one of nine qualified national moderators of maritime safety seminars, du Moulin is quite familiar with the danger of sailing through heavy weather. He himself has sailed through several hurricanes during his ocean racing career.

Full Circle

Du Moulin is set to compete in his 25th Newport Bermuda Race in June 2018. This ocean racing classic is held every other year. The present record is 30 races, held by one of du Moulin's sailing heroes, the late Jim Mertz of Rye, New York. Du Moulin, the hands-on sailor, said with a smile, "If I keep doing this until I'm 80, I might be able to get to the record!"

Since his first race, in 1966, du Moulin has only missed two—one when his daughter Lora was born, and the other when he raced for the America's Cup with Ted Turner."

"It's a great event," du Moulin said. "My first hurricane was in 1972, when I navigated a boat named *Charisma*. We ended up second out of 180 boats. We were beaten by one British boat by eight minutes! I'm *still* thinking about it," he added with a sigh.

He has sailed his 37-foot *Lora Ann* in the past nine races, usually double-handed, with just two crew including himself. "That's our style nowadays, but this year, with two of my sons available, I will race with a total of seven crew. It's all about preparation," du Moulin explained. "Total focus on safety and seamanship—the same as on ships. What I have learned in my lifetime of sailing all goes back to Dad and Sam."

A regular competitor in international racing events, du Moulin has also competed in four America's Cup campaigns and five Transatlantic Races. Perhaps his greatest sailing adventure was in 2003, with Rich Wilson of Marblehead, Massachusetts. Aboard the 53-foot trimaran *Great American II*, the two Riches raced 17,000 miles double-handed nonstop from Hong Kong to New York, breaking the 154-year-old record of the clipper ship *Sea Witch*. They were at sea for 72 days and broke the record by only 36 hours.

Just as Sam passed his substantial maritime knowledge to Edward, and Edward onto Richard, du Moulin's four children continue in the family tradition. All are sailors. The youngest, Mark, is a third mate in the U.S. merchant marine. "My father had a steady hand and a constant optimism," du Moulin said. "He passed on the importance of responsibility, seamanship, and respect for others. This is something my own children have embraced. It's amazing how a family tragedy in World War I was the start of something so strong and beautiful—the love of sailing!"

CHAPTER FIFTEEN

Mike Hudner

Shipping Finance Pioneer

The shipping industry and the real estate market have a lot in common. Investors of real estate and shipping are long-term. The building of ships and the development of properties take time. When making the multiyear commitment to expanding a fleet, or breaking ground on a property, the health of the economy is closely evaluated. Principals in both industries are naturally bullish in outlook. They must be; their industries rely on that confidence to grow. But as Benjamin Franklin once famously said, "In this world nothing can be said to be certain, except death and taxes." A strong economy is only one crisis away from economic combustion.

In the 1980s, after the devastating economic disaster in the 1970s, the United States went into a severe and deep recession. The real estate and shipping industries were dealing with a laundry list of economic challenges: high interest rates, the 1973 and 1979 oil crises, a steep drop-off in agricultural exports, and the highest unemployment rate since the Great Depression. The U.S. Commerce Department calculated that business bankruptcies had increased by more than 50 percent over the previous year. Both industries were left with half-empty assets. Leaders of industry were looking for ways to revive their zombie holdings with capital that no longer existed.

Shipping Hits the Capital Markets

Date	Company	Deal Type	Size (mUSD)
November 1989	Stolt-Nielsen Limited	Corporate Bond	100
July 1989	MC Shipping	IPO	45
April 1989	International Shipholding Corporation	IPO	15
March 1989	Nortankers	IPO	80
February 1989	B+H Maritime Carriers	IPO	45
December 1988	Global Ocean Carriers	IPO	45
August 1988	B+H Ocean Carriers	IPO	55
June 1988	Stolt-Nielsen Limited	IPO	51
September 1987	B+H Bulk Carriers	IPO	20
June 1987	Anangel-American Shipholdings Ltd.	IPO	45

Source: Marine Money

"The extent and duration of the post-depression low was very important, because each bad day had a cumulative effect," said Mike Hudner, the president and CEO of B+H Ocean Carriers Ltd., who worked in the real estate finance industry in the mid-'70s and has witnessed the similarities between real estate and shipping firsthand. "We had quite a few years of excess capacity. In the mid-'80s there were thousands of ships laid up around the world. Banks closed their doors for financing to shipowners."

The maritime industry during that time was very old school in the way ships were financed and owned. A shipowner would go to the bank and get a mortgage on the ship and put in equity from family and friends. Few outside investors were involved. The shipowner had the full responsibility. But with the banks no longer lending, bulk carrier and tanker owners were under tremendous pressure, and a capital crisis formed. Hudner saw this as a window of opportunity.

While ruin is often the by-product of a crisis, the ingenuity of those who refuse to fail can emerge. Hudner believed he and his Oslo-based Norwegian partner, Arvid Bergvall, could create new ways to finance ships. It would be through the U.S. capital markets, particularly those sectors involved in real estate investment. Their company, B+H, was built on real estate finance concepts and by thoughtfully tracking the capital markets for property. "The Chinese character for *crisis* is made from the characters for *danger* and *opportunity*," Hudner said.

Pioneering Access to U.S. Capital Markets for Foreign-Flag Shipping

In the '70s, while attending law school at night, Hudner worked for Eastdil Realty, the first dedicated Wall Street real estate finance shop. "What I learned during my career at Eastdil is that there's more capital in the world looking for deals than there are good deals to get into," he said. "The same goes for the maritime industry—shipping is a very capital-intensive business. If you're persistent, and if you've got a good project, you will eventually get it funded, in my opinion. It's a lot of work, but you will succeed."

The origins of B+H involved both persistence and chance. In 1975, Hudner and a college classmate, Peter Elrick, who was also an assistant to the chairman of Burmah Oil Tankers, Elias Kulukundis, decided to look for opportunities to put passive investors together with owners of laid-up Very Large Cruise Carries (VLCCs). In November 1975, they had a breakfast meeting with a shipping banker from the Chemical Bank and discussed their concept. In March 1976, they finally got a reply. A Norwegian shipping man, Arvid Bergvall, was coming to New York from Oslo to look into the U.S. capital markets to see if there was money available for distressed Norwegian shipping projects. Bergvall, Hudner, and Elrick met on St. Patrick's Day. They had a very general discussion and agreed to be in touch. Late that fall, Bergvall was back in touch, and for the next year he and Hudner had sporadic conversations on alternative ways to generate capital for maritime projects.

Their first small pilot project was in the fall of 1977. The success of that deal gave Hudner the push he needed to leave his comfort zone and the certainty and security of his real estate investment banking job on July 1, 1978, to start B+H with Bergvall.

The new chapter he was writing in his business book of life was exhilarating and scary. "I left the W-2 income world for something strange and unknown," he said. "I was working with a partner I hardly knew and who was based in Oslo, in an industry about which I knew nothing. But I believed we could make distressed shipping projects similar to the real estate deals I used to make with investors looking for ways to enhance their capital investments."

For the first four years, B+H was based out of a small room with just a telephone and an electro-mechanical telex machine off the kitchen in an apartment Hudner shared with his wife, Hope Freeman Hudner. Hudner said the very uncertain beginnings of B+H were more than a defining time in his life. "Jumping into the unknown with nothing but your wits and persistence to sustain you was one of the most gratifying, humbling, and satisfying experiences I have ever had," he said. "Combining my passion for ships with innovative finance was like finding my personal star in the heavens and following it."

Hudner took the capital challenge head-on and created various ways to raise equity for shipping workout deals and asset plays. "I gave a talk in Oslo at one point and explained that we had developed about fourteen different ways to get money into ships that were all sort of equity equivalents," Hudner said. "I was intrigued when I went through that catalog of how you can make things happen if you are flexible and think creatively about ships and money."

From 1978 to 1985, the main focus of B+H was to pioneer U.S. limited partnerships for foreign-flagged vessels. In 1987, the company pioneered the move into the public securities markets with a blind pool IPO for bulkers. Investors would own listed shares that could be freely traded in New York. Three of these companies went public in 1987, 1988, and 1989, respectively. This was followed by the first ever single B-rated shipping bond, in 1997. All of these innovative financings caught the attention of Wall Street and the shipping industry. Once the trail had been blazed, there were many followers.

These low-leverage ship-owning IPO entities were not allowed to invest in additional ships after the initial purchases. The original amount raised in the public market offering was paid out, plus a preferred return from all cash flows, and then management received a success fee or carried interest. A great many other companies followed B+H into the public arena. The goal of public investors was not to become shipowners over the long-term, but to participate in a cyclical opportunity. The company's sole purpose was to acquire and operate ships and exit as the market improved. These public companies that opened the doors on Wall Street in the late 1980s became known as "self-liquidating companies." They paved the way for Anangel-American Shipholding, Ltd., Pacific Basin Shipping Limited, Nordic American Tanker Limited, Nortankers, Inc., and others to invest in ships as a combination of current yield vehicles and asset plays in the public equities arena.

Hudner knew it would be a challenge to educate the capital markets on this new investment vehicle. How can you convince someone to invest in a ship when they can't see or touch it, let alone have an understanding about the business in which they would be investing? Hudner hoped his passion for maritime and his hands-on experience in the industry could transcend that barrier and help motivate investors.

Breaking Out the Blueprint

Growing up on Mount Hope Bay, on the northeastern region of Narragansett Bay in Rhode Island, Hudner started sailing at a young age. The family had a small, sixteen-and-a-half-foot sailboat. "I was sort of a wharf rat. I just fell in love with the marine world," he said. "As a kid, I was always looking at the horizon, wondering what it would be like to go beyond it on a boat."

Hudner worked on boats for a couple of summers in college and started ocean racing. "I loved the marine world, but I also got intrigued by the financial aspects of real property—particularly distressed property, where you could pick up real estate and get a lot of sellers' credit, or take distressed assets off the hands of the banks and buy them at a fraction of the original cost."

Hudner understood why investors and portfolio managers were attracted to real estate. It was an investment physically accessible at any time. In addition, the cachet of owning real estate sent investors into what they perceived as a more exotic alternative, asset investment, which was uncommon at the time. The tax incentives that come along

210

with real estate investing didn't hurt either. But investing in an asset literally floating somewhere around the world was a hard concept to convey, much less to sell.

"The first guys I did a deal with had to send somebody over to Norway to make sure the ship was there," Hudner said. "People normally verified the existence of the ship by getting its registration and documentation. These guys wanted to go and sort of touch it. It was smart because this was their first maritime investment. To investor types, the industry seems virtual. To owners, it's intensely tangible."

The first deals B+H made were limited partnerships. "We actually pioneered the first American limited partnerships for foreign-flagged ships," Hudner said, adding that B+H used Delaware limited partnerships with Panamanian corporations as general partners.

The limited partnerships were at first very successful, but because of new tax laws B+H was not able to organize them after 1985, and each year the structures got more convoluted. They were not widely repeated, but they did circulate in the New York investor market. Hudner and Bergvall evolved their plan into the investment concept of shipping IPOs. "In 1987 we did our first IPO for B+H Bulk Carriers," Hudner recalled. "We had a single underwriter, Mabon, Nugent & Co., which was actually a bond house trying to break into equity underwriting, and we bought a bunch of older Handysize bulk carriers. The concept was largely derived from seeing how Public Storage, a mini-warehouse developer, was funding its projects."

Once the first IPO was brought to market, the learning curve for investors was leveled out. In the late '90s, in rapid succession, B+H rolled out two more IPOs: B+H Ocean Carriers Ltd. (a deal to acquire the nineteen-vessel Canadian Pacific fleet of bulkers and medium-range product tankers) in 1988, and B+H Maritime Carriers Ltd. in 1989. In 1989, Hudner personally bought the Marathon Oil Company's fleet of Aframax and Suezmax tankers, several of them in joint ventures with Phibro Energy (then part of Salomon Brothers), with the intention of carrying the project to a fourth IPO as B+H Crude Carriers.

The spigot of public equity was open, and capital was flowing, but fitfully. It was October of 1989. B+H was in the process of arranging an IPO for B+H Crude Carriers. "I'll never forget it," Hudner said. "I went out to lunch from my lawyer's office on Friday, October 13. The book for this deal was about half put together, and when I came back from lunch the whole thing had blown up. United Airlines had announced the cancellation of the employee buyout due to lack of financing. That was the bell ringing telling you that the 1980s junk-bond-fueled leveraged buyout game was finito. It wasn't that much later when Drexel Burnham Lambert, one of the ringmasters of all this, went broke. The equity window slammed hard, right on our fingers."

After that, B+H's deals were done privately for almost a decade.

The '90s: Junk Bonds Become High-Yield

The early to mid-1990s saw the dissolution of the original, 1978 Bergvall-Hudner partnership. It took more than three years for Hudner to get the charter of B+H Ocean Carriers Ltd. amended to make it a mainstream owning and operating business, with the ability to reinvest and retain its cash flow from operations and capital events. Hudner and his team, including director and capital markets guru John M. LeFrere, saw the growing high-yield bond market as possibly ripe for development by a single B-rated shipping offering. High-yield bonds were the successor to the 1980s junk-bond market dominated by Drexel Burnham Lambert. High-yield bond funds were now a major part of the investment landscape. Hudner and LeFrere teed up an offering with Jefferies & Co. and Credit Suisse First Boston as co-managers and went out to raise $100 million. The June 1997 roadshow was highly successful, and $125 million was issued, with Equimar Shipholdings Ltd. (a B+H subsidiary) becoming the first single B-rated shipping bond. It was like opening a floodgate: The whole industry flowed into the newly developed market for shipping capital, courtesy of another innovative B+H ship finance deal.

New Decade, New Crisis: The Commodity & Shipping Supercycle and the Credit Bubble Bust

In 2004, the shipping industry was booming, with world trade growing at an exponential rate. The world's fleet carried around 90 percent of the total global exports, with a value of $8.9 trillion.

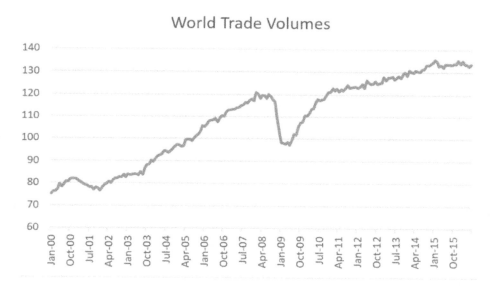

World Trade Volumes

Profits of shipping firms were brimming with a total of $80 billion.[20] Fueling that growth were the emerging markets. China's dynamic economic expansion triggered a rabid demand for raw materials, which created more manufactured products exported out of China. The growth rate climbed to a dizzying 9 percent in 2004, compared to 5 percent in 2003 and 3.5 percent in 2002. China was hailed as the new world economic driver. The markets were looking for ways to capitalize on the growth of world trade.

---

[20] Clarksons, 2004

China's Exports of Manufactured Goods
Log scale, 2001 = 100

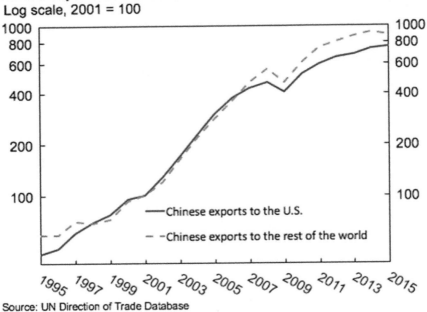

Source: UN Direction of Trade Database

On August 9, 2005, the public markets welcomed the largest shipping IPO that year. Seaspan Corporation, the containership firm spun out by Canada's Washington Marine, was listed on the New York Stock Exchange for $600 million. "Things were really quite good," Hudner said. "In 2007, my family owned between 70 and 80 percent of B+H. The company was still listed, but it was almost a de facto private business by that time because there was no meaningful float. We were maintaining the public listing basically for access to public funding with the possibility of making a deal."

Hudner and his team looked for pockets of prudent opportunity to buy in the sky-high environment of early 2008. "Dry cargo values and earnings were pretty well matched up, but so high you couldn't believe that it was sustainable," he said. "So we said, 'No more dry cargo,' and we started selling and lightening up our dry fleet." Tanker market fundamentals didn't pique Hudner's acquisitive appetite either, with their values well ahead of their earnings. "While it was not a good time to invest further in wet, we thought that the earnings were going to be increasing, so we didn't want to sell."

Once that was decided, Hudner looked around for the next big thing in shipping, and started to focus on offshore. "It was just getting going for its first big rally in about 30-some years, so we developed an offshore project," he said. "We were building a 400-person dynamically positioned accommodation barge that was perfectly suited for Mexico or West Africa."

There were other projects that looked like good opportunities as well. In 2005 and 2006, in China, B+H converted four single-hull product tankers they owned into double-hull IMO 2 and 3 product/chemical vessels so they could stay in a commercially dynamic trade that Hudner and his team at Protrans built up—an around-the-world service with two vegetable-transporting legs and one clean petroleum products (CPP) leg. It was a sweet business for B+H.

The company took three other single-hull product tankers and converted them into geared bulk carriers. "In real estate," Hudner said, "the formula for development of big construction projects is cost plus cost equals cost-plus—you're creating value simply by putting it all together and getting something built. That was what we were doing with these conversions—creating actual current value through one-off vessel conversions. This was highly unusual in shipping. We showed the industry and the banks that conversions can add value. The value creation was not when the ship was originally built in the yard; rather, the *true* added value was after the ship was modified." These were exceptionally intense projects.

B+H's first conversion was a 60,000-ton single-hull product tanker that became, in effect, a Supramax bulker. B+H picked up cranes in India from a Constructive Total Loss (CTL) and had them barged over to China, where the ship was being converted. The hull that was put into the vessel was valued at about $10 million. "This was a $20 million conversion, so you've got a $30 million cost. But the ship on paper was now worth $44 million," Hudner explained. "We got into three sets of negotiations about selling this ship in the low $40 millions in the spring and summer of 2008, but the banks were starting to tighten up that summer, and things were starting to get sticky in a hot market. Our buyers could not get financing."

Despite the equity-evaporating conditions, the company was able to ink a three-year charter on the ship. It averaged $44,000 a day for three years, with the first year at $54,000 a day. "We thought we had created a value of up to 50 percent of our cost basis, which we were happy to cash in on," Hudner said. "We also bought some puts on a dry cargo index that was sort of an insurance policy that, in effect, guaranteed the level of the freight market." Hudner said there was some cause for concern, as one-year time-charter rates soared in excess of $60,000. "It was unbelievable. You couldn't imagine these were Panamax rates, let alone guess how long these high rates would last," he said.

The floor finally did fall out, with the global financial crisis triggered by the sudden Lehman Brothers collapse. The Panamax bulk carrier day rate crashed from $54,000 a day to $4,500 a day. B+H charterer Industrial Carriers Inc. went bankrupt in the fall of 2008. "It was a huge, spectacular, global bankruptcy," Hudner said, adding, "It was like we were walking a dark hallway toward a down staircase, and were aggressively lightening up, when a trapdoor opened underneath us." At that time, B+H had a $30 million loan from the bank. "They said, 'How about you pay that down to $12.5 million in the next couple of weeks?'" To meet the bank's demands, Hudner sold off their dry cargo index put portfolio. But in the end, it wasn't enough. The financial markets were so roiled that there was serious concern that the counterparties for the dry cargo puts, Goldman Sachs and HSH Nordbank, might also default. "Shipping is still affected by those problems," Hudner said.

B+H had four counterparty defaults in a period of about three weeks. Two of those defaults cost B+H more than $80 million. "Unfortunately, we lost so much money in those three weeks that it made the whole business vulnerable to any further downturns," Hudner said. Things stabilized at a low but manageable level for about 30 months, into late 2011.

Then, the dry cargo market took another big downturn. In addition, many traditional shipping banks were broke. Hudner said it became an intractable situation. "I felt my job was to protect everybody as much as possible. My equity was gone. I also didn't see the equity coming back in those ships, given the historic magnitude of the problems. I felt that if we didn't get this quickly under control, we would be seeking a protection of the court," he said. "A lot of people helped us build up this business, and the relationships we had with most of the banks and vendors were very long and deep. I wanted to give back to those who supported me. It was the right thing to do. You have to stand for something in life."

Every evening, Hudner and his wife would sit down and look for solutions. To visually lay out all options, Hope created a whiteboard on the floor. "She put out these big white sheets of paper, and we listed the pros and cons of different things that we might be able do," Hudner recalled. "This concept was her idea, God bless her. She was desperately trying to help me to see a way to avoid having to put B+H Ocean Carriers Ltd. into Chapter 11."

Hudner's daughter, Bay, was working overseas at the time. "That was the wonderful part of my parents' partnership and marriage," she recalled. "They both believed you should always do right by people. You may be forced to interact with plenty of people or situations you don't like, but that doesn't exempt you from acting with decency. Nothing that is going on in your life should give you the license to denigrate someone else or take advantage of them."

After many late nights and much soul searching, Hudner filed privately owned B+H Ocean Carriers Ltd. for Chapter 11. "It became the best thing we could do," he said with a sigh. "It was the only responsible way to deal with the matter. It was agonizing, and Hope understood how brutal this was for me personally. For 35 years I had built up B+H. People backed me, and while now I had to draw a line under the business, it was best thing I could do for them to be able to settle things up."

B+H Ocean Carriers Ltd. went into bankruptcy in May of 2012 and came out twelve months later. The main bank loan was paid in full.

"It took me 35 years to get to a point where I had really the basic ownership of a meaningful balance sheet with a diversified fleet," Hudner said. "It was like being a third-generation Greek, Norwegian, or Hong Kong shipowning family. And then, in three years, it was all gone."

Hudner did not move fast into pursuing new shipping opportunities. It was a difficult personal time. After B+H's last six ships were sold off at the end of June 2013, the company closed its technical and commercial operations. "It was just a lot to take on board. And on top of that, I was trying to figure out the best way to move forward," Hudner said. "I knew what was commercially interesting to me, but it was difficult to find that psychic energy you need so you can have real conviction moving forward. It was just very challenging; we needed some time to regroup. We have owned and operated over 140 vessels, wet and dry, since 1978. We know how to do this and will do it again."

In the middle of 2014, things started to turn around. Hudner and a longtime colleague and close personal friend, commercial manager Gerard H. Potier, were trying to raise money. Hudner was interested in the product tanker market and was spending a lot of time in New York. Then, in December of 2014, his world was turned upside down again. Hope suffered three seizures on a Sunday afternoon. She was diagnosed with grade-four glioblastoma, one of the most aggressive forms of brain cancer. By this point, Hudner's daughter, Bay, had left her job at Barry Rogliano Salles (BRS) in Paris and was living in New York pursuing her own venture. The family had already lost their son and brother, Rip, in September 2004. It was immediately clear that they should all be together to help Hope battle the terrible illness she faced. For thirteen months, Hudner and Bay took care of her. "During that time, I was able to spend a tremendous amount of time with Hope," Hudner said. "Raising money for a new venture was not my top priority. I went through the motions." Hope passed away on January 14, 2016.

New Beginnings

While home acting as her mother's primary caregiver, Bay asked her father what she could do to be helpful on the shipping front. "Work with me," Hudner said with a smile.

Bay said that for years she had tried to avoid the family business because she wanted to make her own way. "I had grown up with shipping, through dinner table conversations, visits to ships and yards, even stints at the office in Rhode Island and Singapore. While I thought it was all fascinating, I was wary of joining B+H because I didn't want to be known as the boss's daughter. I wanted to make sure I would be my father's *partner*, and that we would build something *together*. I wanted to make sure I would really add value." Having spent several years cutting her teeth elsewhere—followed by the emotionally intense time at home with family—Bay accepted her dad's offer to be his partner, and the two have not looked back.

"She's working with me full time now. And we're out shaking the money trees together," Hudner said with a smile. "I must say, Bay's a much better networker than I am. She's a much more fun person to be with." He laughed. "I'm sort of quiet and thoughtful. She is very thoughtful, too, but she has a way of making everybody feel better when they spend time her. My wife was like that, too. We'll be coming around again soon. Ships on the water. People like to work with us."

The road back to rebuilding has been challenging, but the father-daughter pair is determined to come out on top in the product tanker market. "We've had a number of near misses with very serious investors," Hudner said. "We've got several ongoing discussions, and I think that, as for the product tanker market, which has had its ups and downs in the last couple of years, things have really been fairly flat, which means we haven't missed anything. The big order book that everybody was worried about in 2014 is just about fully delivered now, so I think the product tanker market is really ripe for the harvesting."

"One thing I've noticed working closely with my dad," Bay said, "is how many times I've been pulled aside at industry conferences or after meetings for someone to tell me what an upstanding guy my dad is. The way he handled the bankruptcy—that he elected not to walk away just to save his own hide—has been widely respected in the shipping community. There's a long list of shipping types who have done just that: bow out just in time to save themselves and no one else. The fact that he can walk into a room five years after B+H filed for Chapter 11 and people gladly talk to him, welcoming him back to the table with a hug—that's incredible to me."

After working in the public markets, staying private this time around sounds like the best option to Hudner. "While the public markets offer you money where you might not get it otherwise, there is a big trade off," he warned. "These hedge funds and private equity firms are not really interested in investing for long-term returns. They want a big investment rate of return (IRR) in a much shorter time. Shipping doesn't generally offer the high teens and twenties of IRR they've gotten addicted to," he said. "Shipping is more of a very high-single-digit, low-double-digit rate of return business. Long term, I don't think the current finance shop solutions are a viable approach to raising the large amounts of money needed in shipping. I think the industry has a problem. Other sectors of the capital markets, beyond the shorter-term *hot money* investors, need to be developed. A lot of education will be required. It happened in real estate."

The pressures of making earnings estimates and listening to investors talk about how to take over your business or leverage it up to get higher rates of return didn't sound charming to Hudner either. "I would not go public unless there was some really compelling reason. The people I know in the shipping industry who have the most satisfaction in their lives have been owners of successful privately owned businesses. Their culture and values dominate the company. They work with who they want to work with. They are not forced to do things. That's what I want."

Hudner's personal and professional crises would have left many men waving the white flag and quitting. But Bay said that was not in her dad's DNA. She credits his persistence in life as a cornerstone in his foundation. "My father, like many shipping people, is an optimistic and resilient creature. You have to be in order to survive this business."

Hudner added that, in the end, you need to put things into perspective. "If I had gotten back the money I lost and multiplied it by ten, it's not going to bring back my son from his car accident or cure his schizophrenia," he said. "All that money wouldn't have cured my wife's glioblastoma. It couldn't bring her back. So, while, yes, the money is nice to have because it adds more colors to your palette, it's not everything. It's more artful to have laughter and joy on your palette of life. We all need to know what we stand for."

EPILOGUE

Thoughts on Half a Century of Shipping Cycles

Dr. Martin Stopford was kind enough to share some of his thoughts on the markets after 50 years scrutinizing the world economy and the maritime industry. These market cycles and events form the backdrop to the challenges faced and successes enjoyed by every person interviewed in this book, and so they are included here to provide additional context as well as an excellent shipping history.

"Sea trade has played an amazing part in the world economy," Martin Stopford said. "It lies right at the heart of economic development. For starters, the growth has been massive. In 1950, the maritime industry moved about 0.5 billion tons of cargo a year, but now it moves over 11 billion tons. Sea trade grew 60 percent faster than world GDP and includes energy, minerals, food, chemicals, and manufactures—everything needed by global economies to share in the good life. Even at a personal level, the volumes are enormous. In 2016, the industry moved 1.5 tons for every man, woman, and child on the planet and four to six tons per capita for the rich OECD countries. There are 60,000 ships at sea, with a capacity of 1.8 billion deadweight tons, carrying this cargo. They represent an investment of $930 billion. Yet the cost of moving a barrel of oil by sea from the Middle East to the U.S. has hardly changed since 1950—it is still about $1 per barrel. Shipping performs an epic task and is a major contributor to the world economy. Everyone involved should be proud of the job they do."

Why Trade Grew So Fast

The explosive trade growth was part of the 1950s free trade revolution. The world moved from the prewar era of European empires to global free trade supported by the General Agreement on Tariffs and Trade (GATT), International Monetary Fund (IMF), and the World Bank.

"As trade restrictions were lifted, multinational companies could access global markets and sources of raw materials," Stopford said. "This supercharged trade growth, but to achieve this the shipping industry had to become more efficient. The liners and tramps of the previous era were swept away and replaced by much bigger bulk carriers, tankers, container ships, and fleets of specialized vessels to carry vehicles, chemicals, gas, forest products, and heavy lift cargoes."

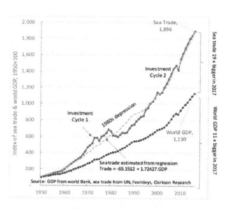

Figure 1: Sea Trade Expanded 60 Percent Faster than World GDP

Over the next 50 years, "waves of growth" in the world industrial economy drove economic expansion. The first wave, in the 1960s, was generated by Europe and Japan as they rebuilt their economies after WWII. Raw materials like iron ore, oil, coal, and forest products were now sourced overseas, and this boosted their imports. There was explosive growth from 1960 to 1973, followed by a sudden stagnation as the 1973 oil crisis pushed both regions into deep recession (see Figure 1). In the 1970s, the Southeast Asian countries set off along the same path, producing more trade growth. Then, in the 1990s, domestic policy changes in China triggered an even bigger wave of development. These successive waves of growth drove demand for bulk commodities such as oil, coal, and iron ore and encouraged exports of manufactures.

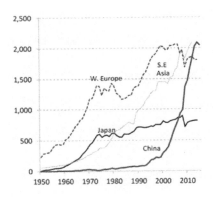

Figure 2: Regional Waves of Sea Imports Drove Sea Trade

But as industrial economies mature, economic activity generally becomes less resource-intensive, and demand switches from construction and consumer durables to services such as medical care and recreation, which have a lower requirement for imported raw material. By 2016 the import share of the OECD countries, which accounted for 80 percent of sea imports in the 1960s, had fallen below 40 percent, and the trade growth was coming mainly from the non-OECD countries.

Perspective on Shipping Cycles

Throughout this period, the investment needed to expand the world fleet was coordinated by the shipping market cycle. "These cycles breathe life into the industry," Stopford said. "They come in all shapes and sizes, so there is never a dull moment. But this makes life difficult for shipping investors and professionals, who really need to get to grips with this aspect of the industry. It's a full-time job; with shipping cycles, investors can't just string along for the ride—they need to get their hands dirty."

The 70 years between 1947 and 2017 saw a continuous sequence of cycles. Like waves hitting a beach, each had a different length and intensity. There were nine dry cargo cycles, with an average length of 7.4 years. But these dry statistics disguise the pain and euphoria experienced by investors. Most peaks lasted two years, but there was a long, drawn-out peak from 1988 to 1997 and very strong peaks in 2004 and 2007. On the negative side, there were two very severe recessions. The seven-year recession from 1958 to 1964 was severe, and the notorious six-year recession from 1981 to 1987 ranked just behind the 1930s depression as the worst of the century.

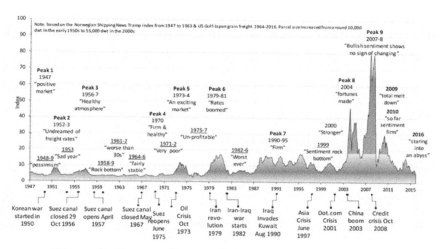

Figure 3: Seventy Years of Shipping Market Cycles:
Driving Investment and Keeping Investors on their Toes

Naturally, the relentless succession of cycles shown in Figure 3 preoccupied analysts and investors alike, creating a constant state of tension in which every conversation seemed to end with the question "When will the market recover?" in bad times, or "How long will the boom last?" during booms. But Stopford believes that predicting these cycles, except in the most general way, is a futile strategy. The business cycles and crises in the world economy that drive them are unpredictable, and even more unpredictable is sentiment-driven investment, which can quickly change the outlook. A short burst of high freight rates can trigger new orders, changing the future market. This often happens during recessions, when shipyards with spare capacity offer bargain prices. "This is tricky for analysts," Stopford said. "Shipowners with their finger on the pulse of the market are often quicker to pick up these market inflections."

The Long Investment Cycles of 1947 to 2017

But Stopford believes there is another dimension to shipping cycles. "During the 65 years since Bretton Woods and World War II, there were two very long investment cycles, measured by orders placed for new ships as a percentage of the current fleet. These cycles give a completely different perspective on what was really going on," Stopford said. "Let me explain. Over those 60 years, trade grew at about 5 percent per annum, so investors ordered more than 5 percent of the fleet in a year when things were heading for trouble." Stopford's analysis, shown in Figure 4, reveals that, during both investment cycles, ordering massively overshot the 5 percent safety margin. The first started at 5 percent in the 1950s and built up to a peak of 30 percent in 1973, after which it collapsed. "If you include the collapse, the whole cycle lasted over 30 years," Stopford said. Then, over the next 30 years, the whole thing was repeated. Investment surged from below 5 percent of the fleet in the mid-1980s to a peak of 28 percent in 2007, followed by a collapse triggered by the Lehman Brothers crisis in 2008. "We are still on the way down from this peak," Stopford said.

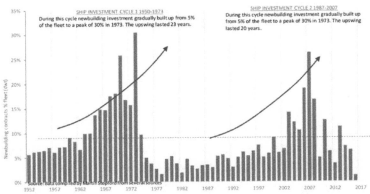

Figure 4: Long Lasting Ship Investment Cycles-a Hidden Force in Driving Shipping Cycles

Stopford is not surprised that analysts pay little attention to these very long cycles. "Investors are more concerned with the next six months, and telling them that market recovery might take seventeen years is a tough message to deliver! When you get to my age, you can say these things, but it's hard for a young analyst," he said with a chuckle. "Anyway, these long cumulative changes are deep and not visible in the freight cycles. But it is where the real market story is played out."

Nevertheless, Stopford believes the real value to studying long cycles is the insight they provide into changing ship investment strategies.

The First Ship Investment Cycle: From Industrial Shipping to Speculation

The first investment cycle, from 1950 to 1973, was a classic innovation cycle, triggered by the new global trading system. It was a period of unbounded innovation. Shipping's enormous vigor was underpinned by multinational companies needing bigger and more efficient ships. They were prepared to use their balance sheets to get them. The emerging Eurodollar market was tailor-made for the job, providing independent owners with fast access to capital for the construction of supership newbuildings, backed by time charters. The old imperial liner companies were driven out by containerization, and virtually every specialized shipping system in use today was developed during this period—supertankers, bulk carriers, gas tankers, chemical parcel tankers, vehicle carriers, wood chip carriers, and most important, container ships all appeared in the 1950s and 1960s. The multinationals were also deeply involved in the logistics, which were more efficient than many we have today.

But in the late 1960s the investment cycle got out of control. The shipyards expanded capacity to meet the seemingly endless demand for ships, and banks, with easy access to the Eurodollar market, started lending against a first mortgage on the hull. Meanwhile the surge of innovation was slowing, and investment became increasingly speculative. For example, tanker owners who had previously ordered ships against time charters started ordering for their own account. Banks were happy to lend—even without a time charter, the ship provided apparently bulletproof security because ship prices had increased steadily. By the early 1970s ship finance was dubbed "floating real estate."

This investment cycle collapsed after the 1973 oil crisis. Shipyard overcapacity and slower trade growth created a deeply toxic market, and by 1983 most tanker and bulk carrier companies were in trouble. Some tankers went straight from the shipyard into layup, and in September 1983, one major oil company sold a four-year-old VLCC, which had cost about $60 million, for demolition at $3 million. The only buyers were demolition brokers; independents with cash, like John Fredriksen; and a few outsiders, like James S. Tisch, of the Loews Corporation (Figure 5), who started buying "fabricated steel for the price of scrap" and naming his 400,000-deadweight-ton ships, bought for $3 million to $4 million each, after film studios.

Figure 5: Jim Tisch bought tankers at the bottom

The Second Ship Investment Cycle: Trading Ships, Not Cargo

The second investment cycle started in the late 1980s, and from the outset was driven by speculative investment. Initially investment was weak—about 5 percent of the fleet per annum. But by the late 1990s, after the Asia crisis, investors got their confidence back and momentum picked up, reaching a peak in 2007. In that year orders were placed for $240 billion worth of new ships, representing 28 percent of the fleet. "The 2007 to 2008 peak was driven by a torrent of cash," Stopford observed. "In June 2008 a Capesize bulk carrier worth around $150 million was chartered for $300,000 per day. To put that in context, for most of the previous 25 years a Capesize had earned less than $25,000 per day, so this was new territory. No wonder investment got out of control. But that was the peak, and in fall 2008 the whole speculative edifice came crashing down. In November 2008 a similar Capesize was chartered for $3,000 per day and its value had fallen to $45 million, in the unlikely event that anyone would buy it. Now that's a cycle!" History repeated itself, and this time the collapse was triggered by the credit crisis. As letters of credit became difficult to obtain, trade was shaken to its foundations. In 2009, sea trade fell for the first time since the early 1980s, and the shipping industry was pushed into a long, deep recession.

Unlike the first investment cycle, the second was not driven by innovation. The size of ships continued to creep upward, and the container industry built up a fleet of 5,000 ships. But the basic technology did not change significantly, and there were no major ship-type innovations, so investors in new ships did not have much commercial advantage. Many trades were now handled by traders and freight forwarders who were more interested in arbitrage than efficiency. With few time charters available, investors turned to speculation, and as the industry emerged from the 1980s depression, a new investment strategy emerged: trade ships, not cargo.

During the second investment cycle, the industry supplied plenty of ships and speculative investment kept freight rates low. There was little innovation, as compared with the previous cycle, which seems to have been fine with the cargo owners and traders chartering the ships. But today attitudes have changed and the industry is under new pressure to improve quality standards, reduce harmful emissions, and contribute to reducing climate change. All of which led to the question "How will the next maritime investment cycle develop?"

The Next Investment Cycle

"In 1956, Malcom McLean started to dabble in containerization. He put the first ships into the deep-sea trade across the Atlantic in 1966, but it was probably not until the mid-1980s that you could say

229

containerization was well established. It was such a disruptive change that few of the existing liner companies could cope with a complete change of fleet and business model."

Embracing digital technology may be less disruptive, Stopford said, but some tricky organization and personnel issues must be resolved. One is the time-honored practice that each ship and its crew operates as a standalone business unit, reporting vertically to the ship's captain. "Effective digitalization needs teamwork across the company, and organizations will need to be 'flatter' than is the current practice in the industry so that the fleet can operate as an integrated transport factory [Figure 6]. It all comes back to the business culture and the people in it. You can't buy digital systems off the shelf, companies have to build them, which needs time and persistence."

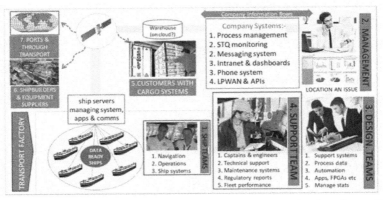

Figure 6: Using Information & Communications Technology (ICT) to Manage a Fleet of Ships as a Transport Factory

There will be other changes in the global trade, Stopford added thoughtfully. Geopolitical turmoil and the security issues can never be ruled out. "If we get some sort of maritime flare-up in the Asia area, that would be a big problem. It could cause economies to become introverted," he said. "But I believe there is still great maritime growth potential in Asia.

"China is an enormous economy with ongoing development potential, but there is much more to Asia than that," Stopford said. "You have the South China Sea coast and President Xi's One Belt, One Road investment program. That could lay the foundation for future trade. South Korea and Japan are very sophisticated technology manufacturers. That's also good for trade. India is a massive market and Southeast Asia has enormous potential, if supported by a cheap, fast, and efficient maritime logistics system."

Don't Be a Sucker

The shipping industry has always been big on optimism, with overbuilding resulting from that irrational exuberance. But, Stopford said, shipping investors need to adjust their timeline. "It is not about predicting what will happen 30 or 50 years from now. It is about identifying the things we can do *today* to make a better *tomorrow* possible." Using digital technology to build organizations capable of using resources more efficiently and developing tightly integrated logistics systems should be high priority.

But the shipping cycle will still be with us. For almost five decades, Stopford has lectured on this subject to thousands of conference attendees around the world. "There are seasonal cycles, short cycles, and long cycles, lasting up to 35 years," he said. "So, while building their new smart shipping businesses, investors must also be smart about how they play the market and the cycles."

In a recent Marine Money presentation, Stopford ended with a poignant quote from world champion poker player, Amarillo Slim:

"Play the players, not the cards. Watch them from the minute you sit down. Play fast in a slow game, slow in a fast one. Never get out when you're winning. Look for the sucker, and if you can't see one, get up and leave, because the sucker is you." Stopford added: "Shipping, in the end, is about people doing their jobs. Each generation must try to do it better than the last. That's our duty. And hopefully, along the way we all make a few bucks."

ACKNOWLEDGEMENTS

My life as a journalist has given me the opportunity to meet some of the world's most inspiring and successful individuals in society, business, and politics. I have learned that it's not the number of zeros in your bank account that defines success; it's the way you live your life and how you give back that exemplify your prosperity.

Of all the industries I have written about, I have found the maritime industry to be a great example of leaders who have contributed to society with genuine thankfulness—not a puffing of the chest, bragging about "philanthropic giving." From the humble beginnings of James Chao, who lived during war and didn't let hate extinguish his spirit, to Richard du Moulin, whose family suffered a debilitating loss in the flu pandemic, these leaders were not traditionally born into the maritime industry; instead, they carved their own path and not only made their own name in one of the hardest cyclical industries, but changed the lives of others in the world with their work *outside* of the boardroom.

I would like to thank these men and women for taking the time to tell me their stories. I hope their chapters inspire and educate readers about what leadership skills are needed to be a success in business. The how and why and the strategies they employed leapt out of the conversations I had with them. After every interview, I was excited to get to my computer and write. Without their contributions, this book would not be possible.

Jim Lawrence, thank you for giving me the opportunity to write the sequel to *Dynasties of the Sea*. It was an experience I will never forget.

Thank you to CNBC for giving me the proverbial green light for writing this book.

I would like to thank my three children, Nicholas, Declan, and Abby—thank you for understanding and supporting me when I was writing these chapters. While I tried to write in the early hours, my work did bleed into "mommy time." I love you all very much, and I hope the three of you chase your dreams, live a happy life, and make your mark on this world. And to my husband, Michael, thank you for your understanding, love, and support. Every writing project I do, I do for my family.

I hope you enjoy reading this book as much as I had the distinct privilege and pleasure in writing it.

APPENDIX

Major Lessons Learned from the Shipping Leaders

Chapter One: Cesare d'Amico

"Unfortunately, I had to be eighteen years old to legally put my signature as a personal guarantee on bank loans. Paolo's dad, my uncle Ciro, told me, 'Remember, any dollar that we are taking from the bank is a dollar we have to give back, because as long as you are able to give back the money, you can remain in this business. The moment that you do not give back the money, you are out of this business. It's your choice.' I have never forgotten that."

"At the time it was more half-village, half-town. My uncle Ciro wanted me to go with our technical inspector and stay there because he believed Singapore could grow a lot in the next ten, fifteen, twenty years and would become very important for oil trading. He said the atmosphere of Singapore was the driver. Also, my uncle Antonio had a vision about Genoa and the success of the liner service in the '70s. I am proud and impressed to tell these stories, because my uncles had a vision of this city's growth, and shipping is always about vision. The successful shipowners are the ones who have a vision in their life. No illusions but real, concrete visions. And when shipowners have a concrete vision, and they act on that vision, they are always successful."

"In the old days, you would see the captain on deck supervising the loading or the unloading of the vessel. Nowadays, the captain, he's confined in his office, always filling out papers. He's becoming a bureaucratic guy. His experience is to fill out papers to do with audit and costs, and to make sure that everything is in order instead of overseeing what is going on inside the port."

"The family gives a long-term interest in the company, what they do, in what they pursue, and so on. That long-term interest can be seen in a company's culture."

"They board our vessels and become third officers for our vessels, but also for other companies. This is a big commitment. The investment in this academy is very important. Investors in a public company would not value that kind of spending. But this is an investment in the long-term success of your crews. More generally, d'Amico Group is very committed to the development and growth of its people, because this makes the success of the company."

Chapter One: Paolo d'Amico

"My father told us never to believe in our own hype. You may be smart, but there will always be others who are smarter. We needed to work hard and show our board we had earned the right to lead the company."

"My father taught us one of our greatest lessons, and that was to be humble. Don't pretend to know everything, because you don't, and even if you think you know it, question yourself five times. He also said to try to take things the way they are. Never hide things. If there are problems, don't run away, because even if you run away the problem will run after you, so it's not a solution. And of course, be extremely transparent with your people and in the job you are doing."

"When you are at the bottom, things can only go in one direction. You know that the opportunities are out there, but you have to be extremely careful about at what point of the cycle you move in. Even if the assets are devalued, it doesn't matter. This is not an easy game. It's very much up to how much debt you take on your assets, when you buy your assets, and if you can liquidate them easily. You don't want to get stuck with assets you cannot sell, because at the end of the day, capital is most important."

Chapter Two: Sabrina Chao

"One of the biggest pieces of advice [my father] gave me was to never be personal about your assets—when it's time to sell, sell. Don't get emotionally attached to what you own. It is a very cyclical business."

"Shipbuilding for countries like Korea and China is a strategic industry because it generates employment, and the building is supported by government money. So even with no orders they are still building ships."

"[Private equity] has changed the whole game plan for shipping altogether. Before private equity, it was big news for the markets to hear a shipowner ordering six ships. With of all these PE funds entering the market, you were seeing orders of 20, 30 ships! The sad reality is that the fund may have come and gone, but the ships they have ordered to be built remain. These are the ships we will have to deal with over the next twenty years. Between the government money and private equity money, there are no real commercial principles at play here. Low interest rates have also prolonged the problem."

"There's so much inefficiency within shipping right now, but Big Data, if used correctly, could change all that. We have layers of charterers and layers of agents that we are dealing with day to day. We need to be able to comb through the data better and use that information to improve communication. Unfortunately, though, I think it will probably take an outsider to come in and make that paradigm shift. If we can do that, efficiency would be enhanced."

"My father was a man of few words, but he always had wonderful pieces of wisdom for me. One of the most important was, 'You always need to build a long-term relationship through fair deals.' It was needed for the *long-term* success of the company. We don't want to earn every penny from a partner or from a business venture, because we want people to come back. These long-term relationships help Wah Kwong thrive in good or bad markets because we stick by each other."

Chapter Three: Peter Keller

"It's all about the time, distance, and money. When you look at what it costs a particular company, whether it's Procter & Gamble, or Walmart, or Home Depot, or anybody else, for them to first develop a product, manufacture the product, move the product, store and distribute the product, and then finally try to sell the product, that's a huge, huge amount of time and investment. And on top of that, they have to consider the cost of transportation as well as all the other supply-chain costs. That is something customers and service providers are always looking at, trying to find the best time value for their product. One way to try to enhance the process and make it more efficient has been the recent introduction of ever larger vessels. The other is expediting the individual supply-chain links, but that must be undertaken with a view to the entire supply process, not just pieces. The answer is cooperation and transparency across the intermodal range so everyone benefits."

"I still believe very strongly that the large container ships are possibly going to go the way of the Airbus 380. If you look at the latest production of the 380, I think Airbus is now down to about one a month, and the order book is not terribly healthy. None were ordered in 2016. They're likely going to lose a lot of money on that program. I think there's a strong possibility that this could also be happening with these extra-large containerships. The environmental and logistical issues associated with these vessels are huge. Just as the 380 can only operate in certain airports, only the largest deep-sea ports can accommodate the mega-ships. The amount of money that a port needs to spend on infrastructure to accommodate these ships is hellacious."

"When I started, the transportation manager was usually somebody on the dock who was actually moving the freight. Today it's somebody with an M.B.A. and advanced degrees in data processing, process optimization, and transportation management. That represents a huge, huge change that we often do not think about. That level of sophistication is the reason we have all this emphasis on productivity and optimization of process in the appropriate time-money equation.

Then how do I optimize again, and again. A key to logistics is really this continual optimization."

"We've been able to bring in many organizations from across the value chain of LNG—from the molecules all the way to the Port Authorities that facilitate bunker operations, as well as original equipment manufacturers (OEMs), shipyards, and shipping and cruise lines. We want to address and break down the market barriers to the adoption of LNG, a more environmentally friendly marine fuel. Together we can turn this into a global reality."

"The environmental rules facing the shipping industry are coming like a freight train going downhill. Shipowners need to be able to move more quickly to get ready for these rules. They are not ready. It all goes back to a preoccupation with the here and now as opposed to the longer term. They won't be able to react quickly to the new emissions rules if they don't start strategizing about it now."

Chapter Four: Herbjørn Hansson

"When I started my own business, in 1989, after I stepped out of that big Norwegian company where I was CFO, I saw that if you should come anywhere in the world in terms of shipping you had to work internationally. Norway is a nice country, but the stock exchange in America is 85 times larger than Norway's. In order to grow my business from a global competitive standpoint, I had to go to America."

"Many didn't understand what we were doing. A rule for me has always been to do the opposite of what others are doing. Yes, it's a way of contrarian thinking. Few would have touched the BP deal in the first place, but that was one of the reasons why we went for it."

"Bottom line, we are three things: We are ships, we are capital, and we are people. Together they make a round circle. We are complete."

"I have met people who believe they can see into the future. I have not met anybody who can actually see into the future. All cycles are the same."

"I have been told ever since I started out in shipping as a young man that I was in the wrong industry, but based upon the business principles we follow, Nordic American Tankers has been able to prosper and build a decent company that is about the largest tanker company in the world. And I have no intention of changing a thing."

Chapter Five: Dr. Martin Stopford

"While the past 30 years have been great fun, and the mantra 'We trade ships, not cargo' worked well for some individuals, this philosophy was the product of the 1980s.... Trading ships is *not* the answer. Adding value and dealing with problems like efficient through transport and climate change is where the industry should be focusing."

"Digitalization adds value because it allows companies to use their resources more efficiently. Just adding ships to the fleet does not."

"It's not just a single technology that is needed to take a step forward. It's a bundle of technologies, which I call the smart shipping toolbox."

Chapter Six: Claus-Peter Offen

"I never forgot that feeling I had. I said to myself, Wow, now I am a shipowner! I spoke with a private banker who was helping me finance the ship in the beginning a little bit, and he congratulated me and gave me one piece of advice I will never forget: 'You are a lucky man today. If I were you, I would go out on the street and the first poor devil you see, give him a hundred dollars, just to say thank you to your God for helping today.' And I thought this was good advice. When I walked home through the streets there was some poor guy sitting there.

I pulled a hundred dollars out of my wallet and gave it to him. He looked at me puzzled."

"A crisis always has its victims, but a crisis also provides a good chance to start something new or to expand. I decided that this was the moment to expand the company."

"Nobody ever tells you this is a good moment to buy, and nobody will tell you this is a good moment to sell, and that makes the life of a shipowner quite fascinating. You need a lot of knowledge and experience about the world markets, yes, but you need a lot of stomach to say this is the right moment or the right ship to buy or sell."

"Standing still is *always* a step back."

"An entrepreneur is the main engine that drives the company. It's always easier to work with your own money than to work with other people's money, because you don't want to lose it for them. But I think opportunities are all about taking risks."

"Just like shipping, [sailing is] all about building the right team. I put the yacht crew together. It's all about the people coming together for the common goal of coming out on top."

"You need top people, and they have to be able to make decisions on their own, whether it is for the company or on board the race boat."

Chapter Seven: Dr. James S.C. Chao

Through it all, Dr. Chao learned from his father, a school principal, Yi-Ren Chao, and his mother, Yu-Chin Hsu Chao, that a good education was necessary for what he called "the toolbox of life."

"We also invest in our crews. We have very good, strong crew development programs. We raise them from cadet to officer and finally to captain. They are very, very loyal. We have crew members who will stay with us for more than 25 years. No other company has this history. Nobody can compete against this."

"Nobody can control the market. We never speculate on the market."

"Be courteous to others. Live with honor and respect and you will get it back in return. That's how I raised my daughters and built my company."

Chapter Seven: Angela Chao

"It's something we really need more of right now. We are suffering from a fundamental lack of trust in the world. I believe this is great advice for everyone to live by."

"This is not the time to be cutting corners and saving money on crewing or saving money on maintenance. These are the times, actually, when we double down. We invest in crewing because we're now able to retain crew at a higher rate. We can do longer drydocks because the opportunity cost is lower, so we can sandblast all the cargo holds. Yes, it takes more money, but it's during these tough times that we are investing for the future. That's why we also have a healthy newbuilding order book that will be coming out over the next two to three years."

Chapter Eight: Clay Maitland

"Our opposition to efforts to get rid of open registries had the support of the U.N. General Assembly, so part of the battle was actually fought in New York. The U.S. and Britain vetoed the Security Council's attempts to eliminate the open registries. This was a political exercise fought not only in the halls of the U.N. but in the media as well. We took to the media and did lots of interviews. You are not going to convert people to your point of view by sweet reason. You convert them by making it clear that their economic interests are being threatened. Our big enemies were European countries and European academics hoping to get jobs running a sort of U.N. superagency governing shipping. They would say flags of convenience were the tool of Western imperialism. A tool of Western domination. If they had succeeded, and had flags of convenience eliminated, they would have failed miserably because it would have cost too much to operate. They didn't understand the business benefits of an open registry."

"We would like to see a revival of the U.S.-flag merchant marine, ships painted gray, with enough sealift capacity. Why would we like to see that? Because we believe there is going to be another war in the Pacific, probably involving North Korea. When I say this to people they look at me as though I'm absolutely nuts, but you know the average American attitude is that, Well, everything is hunky dory today so it will be hunky dory tomorrow. But that's the wrong type of thinking. I think this crazy little fat guy [North Korea dictator Kim Jong-un] who's firing off missiles regularly is eventually going to try to hit San Diego. I think Jong-un can do it. And I think that there are a lot of people in Washington who agree. When Ronald Reagan started to talk about Star Wars everybody laughed at him. They're not laughing now. So we need military sealift capacity. We need more seafarers—American ones. We need American flag ships that can carry cargoes of various kinds to the Far East and probably elsewhere in the world. But all of this is neglected and allowed to go to seed."

"We always believe we're going to make a profit and that business is going to be better tomorrow than it is today, and in relying on that optimism, we go out and build too many ships, we sometimes hire too many people."

"Unlike Silicon Valley, which bases its business on research and planning, shipping goes simply by its belief. We don't plan. We just believe that we don't have to do anything to plant fertile seedlings for the future. Very little thought is given to the next month, next year, or even the years after that."

"If I would offer some advice, as a sort of an imaginary commencement speaker, it would be: Don't try to plan ahead too much, because it's likely that what you're going to end up doing in terms of your career is going to be determined by chance, coincidence, and luck—especially luck."

"You never know what the next turn in the road is going to be. Even now, at my age, there are things happening that I never thought would happen, and there are advantages that come my way that I didn't anticipate. Most of the people who do well in life do well because they keep it up. They do not quit or become discouraged."

Chapter Nine: Kishore Rajvanshy

"If you reward people well and develop a sense of family at work, they like to work harder. They feel a part of the organization. That's the secret to creating a culture that promotes hard work and all-around growth. The results? Success."

"Chairman Deng Xiaoping, the Communist Party leader, was trying very hard for reforms. And he opened China up so much that Hong Kong shipping companies greatly benefited because more ships were needed to transport commodities and goods to China. It was a high growth time in those days, as people who were investing in ships needed ship management companies to oversee their vessels."

Chapter Ten: Rod Jones

"I remember I was so frustrated by the captain of my ship because he was always so unsure of himself. He was afraid something bad would happen if someone else was driving the ship. Therefore, he never delegated the conn when the ship was in a maneuvering situation. This was something all junior officers wanted to do. But because of his lack of self-confidence, he would not allow it. We were on our way to the western Pacific from San Diego when he had a stroke on the bridge and was helicoptered off. A chief of staff of the squadron was helicoptered in. He was an old, experienced hand who really knew what he was doing, and the first thing he said was, 'Okay, who's driving the ship into Hawaii?' It opened my eyes. I really saw the difference between someone who was incredibly self-confident, had done it all, and didn't need to prove anything, versus someone who was afraid to empower others because of his or her own lack of confidence. The chief of staff was going to let us develop ourselves. That was the kind of leader I wanted to be."

"While shipping has changed a lot over my career, some of the problems it faces are still the same. The biggest problem is the boom-and-bust cycle. I am not naive enough to think this will change any time soon. However, the future leaders of this industry have to try to find ways to make the industry and the companies they operate more sustainable."

Chapter Eleven: Jim Dolphin

"Shipping has always been an industry of creative destruction."

"We have a long history of living with risk and investing our own money in deals, so we view everything we do through that lens. If our advice leads us to not getting paid for something because we thought our client shouldn't do a deal, or if they needed to take an alternative route because we couldn't help them, that's fine with us. We're very consistent with that. We review up and down the balance sheet so we understand the alternatives, and we always tell people what we think their best option is."

"All restructurings are essentially about information, about the assets, about the documents, about the jurisdictions, etcetera—and leverage. With information and relationships, you can create options. You can then use whatever leverage you have to push the option that works best."

"The object for financial guys is to make money. If it's not in shipping, it's something else. Families who have been in shipping for generations are beholden to the industry. Some families will take a lower return on equity because they think they can manage the risk better. They are thinking about the long term."

"We are, by and large, cycle analysts of the industry, which sometimes has hurt us on our investing decisions. We tend to look at the industry as a reversion to the mean in terms of rates and values."

"Shipowners make money primarily by buying and selling ships, *not* by operating ships. But it's hard to sell ships in any real quantity these days. There just aren't buyers or access to capital. With any investment you do these days you need to be convinced you are buying at a good price but at the same time also figure out how you are going to exit."

Chapter Eleven: Peter Shaerf

"Chaos tends to be good for shipping. Think of the closing of the Suez Canal, or the Gulf Wars. The short-term disruption of trade lanes and stockpiling of oil drove up short-term rates."

"There have been times when we've told prospective clients that we wouldn't consider recommending a particular investment and maybe it ended up being successful. It's okay we walked away from it. We've tried to talk people *out* of doing certain things more than *into* them on many an occasion."

"Whether it's the objectives of your clients or the objectives of the people who sit across the table from you, when you are negotiating you need to understand both of their endgames. Listening is an important part of making deals."

Chapter Eleven: Paul Leand

"You need to recognize *where* you are in the market. Keeping clear focus on your objectives and executing before the market moves on you, even if you have to give up the last dollar, is just incredibly important."

Chapter Twelve: Felipe Menéndez Ross

"Our experiences growing up were very rich. South Patagonia, where my family's business started, was a very, very faraway place. The only way to get there when I was a child was by ship. It was very perilous navigation."

"Even our family vacations involved taking a ship. Whether to Patagonia, Rio, or Europe, a ship was the only way to travel, so we really lived our early childhood on board ships or in contact with ships. It was a very natural way of life for us. It never crossed my mind that I would ever work in any industry besides shipping."

"We really never noticed that our father was transferring responsibilities to us. In the beginning, we were advising him, and he was telling us what to do. Then, the next day, *we* had the responsibility in that area of the company, making the decisions, and *he* was advising us. It was a very intelligent way to prepare us to run the company with his involvement fading out. There was no enormous pressure or sudden change. It was gradual. We would like to pass the torch the same way to our sons."

Chapter Thirteen: Miles Kulukundis

"My father had three sayings he often mentioned to me: 'The sea gets sick but it never dies,' 'Everything in moderation,' and 'Vessels are not trains on rails.'"

"My uncle Manuel always carried a pocket watercolor paintbox. He had a habit of painting pictures on the back of menus at any dinners he attended. He was also a very talented mandolin player. His vast knowledge of the industry was always an asset to me. He, along with my uncle Basil, taught me the power of having extreme commitment to the industry and to the companies."

"We tried to raise capital as a U.K. company but failed completely. International investors were not interested in U.K.-based operations. We had to relocate if we were to broaden the capital base."

Chapter Fourteen: Richard du Moulin

"I've always found it very easy to talk to the guys working hard on the ship. If you let them know that you want their input, you will get some really good information and feedback, but if you talk down at them and show disrespect, they will just shut up. You would never know if there were any problems."

"You really need to work with people and get to know them and let them know how interested you are in their views. When you've built that trust, people are more forthcoming. Never treat people like your rank and file. That blocks good communication. If you really want complete information, you've got to open up that communication. This is fundamentally important for any manager. Too many executives are afraid of losing their authority and miss important inputs."

"In the end, it's really about getting back to the core skills of maritime. I am talking situational awareness, seamanship, leadership, and crisis management. It's not about technology. In fact, technology—if you use it wrong or forget the fundamentals—won't bail you out. We've had two Navy ships get in collisions, and they had plenty of technology! If you have the fundamentals, then you avoid the problems."

"My father had a steady hand and a constant optimism. He passed on the importance of responsibility, seamanship, and respect for others. This is something my own children have embraced. It's amazing how a family tragedy in World War I was the start of something so strong and beautiful—the love of sailing!"

Chapter Fifteen: Mike Hudner

"Jumping into the unknown with nothing but your wits and persistence to sustain you was one of the most gratifying, humbling, and satisfying experiences I have ever had. Combining my passion for ships with innovative finance was like finding my personal star in the heavens and following it."

"The first guys I did a deal with had to send somebody over to Norway to make sure the ship was there. People normally verified the existence of the ship by getting its registration and documentation. These guys wanted to go and sort of touch it. It was smart because this was their first maritime investment. To investor types, the industry seems virtual. To owners, it's intensely tangible."

"Shipping is more of a very high-single-digit, low-double-digit rate of return business. Long-term, I don't think the current finance shop solutions are a viable approach to raising the large amounts of money needed in shipping. I think the industry has a problem. Other sectors of the capital markets, beyond the shorter-term *hot money* investors, need to be developed. A lot of education will be required. It happened in real estate."

"I would not go public unless there was some really compelling reason. The people I know in the shipping industry who have the most satisfaction in their lives have been owners of successful privately owned businesses. Their culture and values dominate the company. They work with who they want to work with. They are not forced to do things. That's what I want."

PROFILES

Chapter One: Cesare d'Amico and Paolo d'Amico

Cesare d'Amico

Cesare d'Amico joined the family-owned company d'Amico Società di Navigazione S.p.A. in the technical department in 1976. He soon moved to the liner department, where he became general manager in 1978, and in 1982 he was appointed chief executive officer, a role he continues to hold to this day. Since 1997, he has played a leading role in the development of the activities of d'Amico Dry d.a.c., and in 2007 he took part in the listing of d'Amico International Shipping S.A. on the STAR segment of the Italian Stock Exchange. He was appointed president of the advanced technical education school Fondazione ITS Caboto (Gaeta, Italy).

Paolo d'Amico

Paolo d'Amico joined the family-owned company d'Amico Società di Navigazione S.p.A. in 1971 and was appointed as a director in 1981 with a focus on the product tanker aspects of the business. He was appointed as chairman of the board of directors in 2002, a role he continues to hold to this day. In 2007 he took part in the listing of d'Amico International Shipping S.A. on the STAR segment of the Italian Stock Exchange. He is a board member of the Confitarma, the Italian Shipowners Association, and in 2013 was awarded the title of Labour Knight by the Italian government.

Chapter Two: Sabrina Chao

Sabrina Sih Ming Chao began her career in finance working for Jardine Fleming and PricewaterhouseCoopers. In 2001 she joined the shipping industry by enrolling in the Galbraith's Shipping Course in

London. She subsequently gained experience in various shipping sectors, working with Tanker International, Britannia P&I Club, and Bureau Veritas, before joining the family business, Wah Kwong Maritime Transport Holdings Limited, in 2002. She was appointed chairman in 2013, and assumed the role of chairman of the Hong Kong Shipowners Association in 2015.

She is the daughter of Mr. George Chao and the granddaughter of Mr. T. Y. Chao, and is the third-generation owner and chairman of Wah Kwong Maritime Transport Holdings Ltd.

Chapter Three: Peter Keller

From 2000 to 2010, Peter Keller was executive vice president and chief operating officer of NYK Group Americas Inc., where he oversaw policy matter for all the NYK Group operating companies in North America. He was then the principal of Peter I. Keller and Associates, LLC, a consulting and advisory practices serving the international maritime industry. He joined TOTE in 2012 as president of TOTE Maritime Puerto Rico, and has been leading the conversion of the company's fleet to LNG. As EVP of TOTE, he now assists in the oversight of both TOTE Shipholdings and the TOTE Maritime Division. He is also currently chairman of the board for SEA\LNG, a multisector industry coalition focused on the use of LNG as a maritime fuel. He was one of the founders of the Coalition for Responsible Transportation, now an industry-wide organization committed to environmentally responsible practices across the supply chain, and was inducted into the International Maritime Hall of Fame in 2006 at the United Nations in New York.

Chapter Four: Herbjørn Hansson

Herbjørn Hansson began working for the Norwegian Shipowners' Association in 1974. From 1975 to 1980 he was chief economist and research manager of INTERTANKO, the tanker industry association whose members control about 70 percent of the world's independently owned tanker fleet, excluding states and oil companies. During the 1980s, he was chief financial officer of Kosmos/Anders Jahre, a large shipping and offshore group based in Norway. In 1989 he founded Ugland Nordic Shipping AS, which became one of the world's largest owners of specialized shuttle tankers. He served as chief executive officer of that company from 1993 until its sale to Teekay Shipping Corporation in 2001. He continued working with Teekay until leaving in 2014 to work full-time at Nordic American Tankers Limited, where he continues to serve as chairman of the board, president, and chief executive officer.

Chapter Five: Dr. Martin Stopford

Dr. Martin Stopford began his shipping career in 1971 at Maritime Transport Research in London. His first year as an analyst convinced him of the need to learn more about economics, and in 1979 he earned his Ph.D. in international economics. In the meantime, he had started work in 1977 as group economist at the newly formed British Shipbuilders. In 1981 he became director of business development. In 1988, Dr. Stopford joined Chase Manhattan Bank as global shipping economist, and in 1990 he took the opportunity to head up Clarkson Research Services Ltd. This would prove to be a long-lived position, and in 2004 he joined the board of Clarksons plc. He retired from Clarksons in May 2012 and is now nonexecutive president of Clarkson Research Services Limited (CRSL) and director of MarEcon Ltd.

Dr. Stopford is a visiting professor at Cass Business School in London, Dalian Maritime University in China, and Newcastle University. He has an honorary doctorate from Solent University, and received a lifetime achievement award at the 2010 Lloyds List Global Shipping Awards. In 2013 he was Shipping Personality of the Year at the Seatrade Global Awards Dinner in London, and in 2015 was awarded the Onassis Prize for Shipping. His publications include *Maritime Economics,* third edition, the widely used shipping textbook published in January 2009, and many papers on shipping economics and ship finance.

Chapter Six: Claus-Peter Offen

Claus-Peter Offen acquired his first vessel in Hamburg in 1971, marking the founding of Reederei Claus-Peter Offen (RCPO), of which he is the founder, sole shareholder, and chief executive officer to this day. From that one ship he has built the current RCPO, which, after its most recent takeover of the Conti Group, has a fleet of 95 containerships totaling 631,000 TEU, 37 bulkers totaling 3 million DWT, and 37 product tankers totaling 1.8 million DWT. Under his leadership, the company has grown and prospered through changes including the widespread adoption of containerization and several major shipping cycles.

Chapter Seven: Dr. James S.C. Chao and Angela Chao

Dr. James S.C. Chao

Dr. James S. C. Chao began his study of navigation in China and completed his college coursework in 1949, before the Civil War in China resulted in his relocation to Taiwan. By the age of 29 he was an oceangoing sea captain, and in 1958 he received a record score in the Master Mariner Examination, which resulted in a government sponsorship for further study in the United States. He founded Foremost Group in New York in 1964 and remains honorary chairman to this day. He has been an advocate of environmentally friendly designs and technology in modern ships. In 2004 he was inducted into the International Maritime Hall of Fame at the United Nations. He has also served as an advisor, adjunct professor, and member of the St. John's University Board of Trustees for decades, and as chairman of the Chiao-Tung University Alumni Association in America and the Chiao-Tung University Alumni Foundation of America.

He has received awards and recognitions for both his professional achievements and contributions to civil society too numerous to list in entirety. These include the Horatio Alger Award, the St John's Medal of Honor, an honorary Doctorate of Law from Niagara University, an honorary Doctorate of Letters from Nyack College, and lifetime achievement awards from communities across the United States and China recognizing his contributions together with those of his wife and family. Dr. Chao also serves as chairman of the Chao Family Foundations, and he and his wife, the late Ruth Mu-Lan Chu Chao, have presented their own awards to others in the form of thousands of scholarships to students in the United States and China.

Angela Chao

Angela Chao is the Chairman and C.E.O. of Foremost Group, an international transportation and shipping company. Additionally, Angela is an active philanthropist and President of the Foremost Foundation, one of the Chao family's philanthropic organizations. Angela is a board member of many international organizations. She received her undergraduate degree in economics from Harvard College, graduating manga cum laude in only three years. Upon graduation, Angela entered the investment banking industry, where she was engaged in mergers & acquisitions at Smith Barney, now a part of Morgan Stanley Smith Barney. Angela is a published author on the topics of economics, international trade and finance, and education.

Foremost Group is an industry leader in incorporating fuel-efficient designs and technologies in its fleet of modern and eco-friendly bulk carriers and has a worldwide reputation for its commitment to reliability, exceptional performance and high ethical standards. Foremost's core values are: Honor. Integrity. Performance.

Chapter Eight: Clay Maitland

Clay Maitland began his work in the maritime industry upon graduation from law school in 1968. He was admitted to the New York Bar in 1969 and became associated with the admiralty law firm Burlingham, Underwood & Lord, where he worked until 1974. After a brief stint as admiralty counsel at Union Carbide Corporation, he joined what is now International Registries, Inc. (IRI) in 1976. At the time, IRI managed the Liberian ship register, which was then the largest in the world by tonnage in number of ships. Around 2000, IRI parted ways with Liberia and began administering the Marshall Islands Ship Registry, which is now the third largest registry in the world. He is presently a managing partner and owner of IRI. He is on the boards of the Maritime Industry Museum at Fort Schuyler (SUNY Maritime College), the King's Point Maritime Museum at the U.S. Merchant Marine Academy, and the Sea Research Foundation, which operates, among other things, the research vessel Nautilus. He has been a delegate to a number of international maritime conferences, including the United Nations Conference on the Law of the Sea and the International Maritime Organization. He received the honorary degree of Doctor of Letters from the State University of New York Maritime College in 2006, and was decorated with the U.S. Coast Guard's Distinguished Public Service Award in 2010. He has also endowed two scholarships for students entering the maritime industry.

Chapter Nine: Kishore Rajvanshy

Kishore Rajvanshy began his maritime career at the Shipping Corporation of India in Mumbai. From 1971 to 1978 he spent most of his time at sea, working his way to the rank of chief engineer. He came ashore in 1978, as he progressed toward the post of superintendent, and in 1979 he embarked upon a fifteen-year career with Univan Ship Management in Hong Kong. He worked from superintendent to technical manager, technical director, and finally director and general manager. In 1994 he joined Noble Group to establish Fleet Management Ltd. He continues as managing director of Fleet Management, which is now a Caravel Group Company. He sits on the Technical and Regional Committees of all major classification societies, and is a director on the board of the West of England P&I Club.

Chapter Ten: Rod Jones

Rod Jones was immersed in shipping from an early age growing up in Nassau, Bahamas. While in college, he sailed as a deckhand for three summers on the Great Lakes on self-unloaders for Cleveland-Cliffs and Oglebay Norton. After college he entered the U.S. Navy's Officer Candidate School. After four years in the Navy he began looking at commercial opportunities in shipping and joined Navios Corporation, where he worked for two years as a vessel operator in New York. He then went to business school, where he gained an appreciation for niche business models. In 1985 he began work at Canada Steamship Lines (CSL). He would spend the next three decades working to transform what was a Great Lakes-focused shipping business into the largest owner and operator of self-unloading ships in the world, expanding its operations from Canada and the Americas to Australia, Asia, and Europe. He became president and chief executive officer of the CSL Group in 2008, a role he held until his retirement in 2017. Shortly before then, he was selected as the co-personality of the year by Women's International Shipping and Trading Organization for his solid ethics and values around diversity, safety, and the environment, and for his inclusive leadership style.

Chapter Eleven: AMA—Paul Leand, Peter Shaerf, and Jim Dolphin

Paul Leand

Paul Leand worked at First National Bank of Maryland before joining AMA in 1998. He was appointed chief executive officer of AMA in 2004, a role he continues to hold to this day. At AMA he led the development of the firm's restructuring practice and was involved in the restructurings of numerous high-yield issues including Golden Ocean, ACL, Global Ocean, Pegasus and Enterprises, and Horizon Lines. On the offshore side, he led AMA's efforts in the restructurings of PetroMENA ASA, Sevan Marine ASA, Remedial Offshore, and Equinox Offshore. He has been involved with numerous M&A roles, including Golden Ocean, SFL, and TECO Transport, and spearheaded the firm's private equity investments in Chembulk, PLM, and Lloyd Fonds. He currently serves as a Director of Eagle Bulk Shipping Inc., Golar LNG Partners LP, Lloyd Fonds AG, North Atlantic Drilling, Seadrill Limited., and Ship Finance International Ltd.

Peter Shaerf

Peter Shaerf has worked in the shipping industry for over 40 years, including as a shipbroker for container and dry cargo vessels with the Commonwealth Group, a company he founded. He also operated a small Caribbean liner service while working for a firm of British shipowners, and has extensive experience in vessel valuations. Immediately prior to joining AMA in 2002, he was a co-founder of specialist maritime boutique Poseidon Capital. At AMA he has worked primarily advising hedge funds and investors on a variety of maritime investments in equity and distressed debt, and is actively involved in transaction origination. He is currently deputy chairman of Seaspan Corporation, a director of privately held Interlink Maritime, and chairman emeritus of the New York Maritime Association.

Jim Dolphin

Jim Dolphin led the global maritime management consulting practice at Booz Allen Hamilton before joining AMA Capital Partners in 2001. At AMA he has been actively engaged in the firm's principal investing activities as well as mergers and acquisitions and restructuring efforts. He recently led AMA's efforts in the restructurings of CMA CGM, Eitzen Chemical, Nexus Floating Production, ZIM, TMT, Master Marine, and Marine Subsea. He was also heavily involved in the creation of the new cruise line Oceania. Within AMA's fund activities, he led the investment in four 2,500-TEU containerships and was active in the oversight of the financing of the portfolio company Chembulk. He currently serves as a director of Genco Shipping & Trading Limited.

Chapter Twelve: Felipe Menéndez Ross and Ricardo Menéndez Ross

Felipe and Ricardo Menéndez Ross grew up immersed in the shipping industry in south Patagonia, which at the time was accessible only by ship. Ricardo's career began alongside his father, Julio, at Compañía Chilena de Navegación Interoceánica and then at the origin of the bulk carrier operation in Buenos Aires. In 1974, Felipe joined his brother and his father at Ultraocean-Casinomar-Ravenscroft and in tanker companies Sonap and LPG Interoceangas. His first assignment was to oversee a single old tweendecker. The brothers gradually learned the business and took over oversight of the family companies.

In 1993, the brothers decided to grow the family's participation in the energy transportation space and expanded into tanker barges on the underdeveloped river operations in South America. They grew this business to just under a thousand barges covering nineteen ports. In 2000 they formed a joint venture with American Commercial Barge Lines Ltd. to further expand the river business. Their company Ultraocean expanded into reefer vessels and later teamed up in a joint venture with the oil company Interpetrol to form Ultrapetrol. Meanwhile, as regulations tightened, the two brothers began to sell off their single-hull bulk carriers, completing the process in 2004. Over time they shifted focus to product tankers and feeder container vessels.

In 2006, Ravenscroft was absorbed by Ultrapetrol, which then managed the company's international fleet in their offshore supply, ocean, and passenger business. The brothers took the company public in the United States. After eight years this business was sold to the private equity firm Sparrow Capital in 2014. By the end of 2015, the collapse of dry bulk freight rates had created new opportunities, and the brothers formed Interocean Transportation Inc. in association with Latin American Partners. The brothers continued to grow this company through 2017, and currently serve as co-chief executive officers.

Chapter Thirteen: Miles Kulukundis

Miles Kulukundis began his career in shipping in 1959, when he joined the family business as a trainee in Sunderland at the Austin & Pickersgill shipyard owned by London and Overseas Freighters (LOF). He worked three years as a chartering clerk on the Baltic Exchange and was then given the responsibility of running the family company Counties Ship Management, where he was responsible for approximately twenty Liberty Vessels. He served as a nonexecutive director at LOF until 1976, when he joined as a managing director with specific responsibilities for operations and chartering. In 1990 he became chairman of the United Kingdom P&I Club, and in 1994 he became chairman of INTERTANKO. The *Exxon Valdez* disaster and subsequent Oil Pollution Act inspired him to use this position to set standards for safety and transparency that sparked eleven more maritime organizations to step up. In the meantime, he saw the LOF through market peaks and troughs and family crises until 1997, when a 51 percent interest was sold to Frontline and Frontline was reverse-merged into LOF.

Chapter Fourteen: Richard du Moulin

Richard du Moulin joined the Navy ROTC while in college and served for three years upon graduation. After completing his time in the Navy, he attended business school and held his first commercial job over the summer at Moore McCormack Lines. From 1974 to 1989 he worked for Ogden Marine, which would later be known as OMI Corporation. In 1989 he set up Intrepid Shipping with the goal of buying tankers. Intrepid's first deal was a leveraged buyout of Marine Transport Lines (MTL). In 1994 he was elected vice chairman of INTERTANKO, where he served under chairman Miles Kulukundis. He became chairman in 1996, and was an outspoken advocate for safety and protection of the global environment with the goal of raising industry standards. Intrepid managed MTL through 1998, when it was merged with OMI and the companies were split along U.S. flag and international lines. Intrepid retained the U.S. flag business as MTL and was listed on the Nasdaq until it was sold in 2001 to Crowley Maritime. Du Moulin and his partner Mark Filanowski re-launched Intrepid Shipping as a private shipping partnership, which they continue to manage to this day.

Du Moulin currently sits on the board of trustees of the Seamen's Church Institute, where he has served as chairman for the past six years. He is also a member of the U.S. Sailing Association's Safety at Sea Committee. He has been awarded the U.S. Coast Guard's Distinguished Service Medal, the Connecticut Maritime Association's

Commodore Award, and the unions' Admiral of the Ocean Seas. He is an avid sailor and has competed in 24 Newport Bermuda Races, four America's Cup campaigns, and five Transatlantic Races.

Chapter Fifteen: Mike Hudner

Mike Hudner's career began at real estate finance shop Eastdil Realty. He had a longstanding interest in ship investment, however, and in 1977 he executed his first small pilot project with partner Arvid Bergvall. In 1978 they established B+H. From 1978 to 1985, the main focus of B+H was to pioneer U.S. limited partnerships for foreign-flagged vessels. In 1987, B+H pioneered the move into the public securities markets with a blind pool IPO for bulkers. In 1988, B+H Ocean Carriers went public, followed in 1989 by B+H Maritime Carriers. In 1992, the original partnership was dissolved, and Hudner amended the B+H Ocean Carriers charter to turn it into a mainstream owning and operating business. In 1997, B+H interests issued the first ever single B-rated shipping bond. He continues to serves as chairman and chief executive officer of the B+H Shipping Group to this day, having been primarily responsible for the acquisition and financing of over 140 product tankers, combination carriers, bulk carriers, crude oil tankers, and offshore support vessels. He also heads Navinvest, the investment arm of the company. He is a member of the New York Bar and the Council of the American Bureau of Shipping. He is also active in many philanthropic and community organizations including Mystic Seaport Museum and Coastal Resources Management Council.

ABOUT THE AUTHOR

Lori Ann LaRocco is senior editor of guests for CNBC business news. She coordinates high profile interviews in business and politics as well as special multimillion-dollar on-location productions for all shows on the network. She specializes in politics, working with titans of industry. LaRocco is the author of *Opportunity Knocking* (Agate Publishing, 2014), *Dynasties of the Sea: The Shipowners and Financiers Who Expanded the Era of Free Trade* (Marine Money, 2012), and *Thriving in the New Economy: Lessons from Today's Top Business Minds* (Wiley, 2010).

GLOSSARY

Aframax – The largest tanker size reported in the original Average Freight Rate Assessment (AFRA). These tankers carry between 80,000 and 119,999 DWT.

American Depositary Receipt (ADR) – A financial vehicle in which a domestic bank issues a receipt for shares of a foreign company, which are traded in a domestic market and are priced and pay dividends in the local currency.

Articulated Tug Barge (ATB) – A type of tug boat and barge combination, where the tug pushes the barge by fixing itself into a notch at the stern of the barge.

Association of Southeast Asian Nations (ASEAN) – A group of ten Southeast Asian nations (Brunei Darussalam, Cambodia, Indonesia, Laos, Malaysia, Myanmar, Philippines, Singapore, Thailand, Vietnam) to promote economic and cultural development.

Backhaul – The return voyage to the port of loading. Securing a cargo on this return voyage, even if for a charter rate that only covers bunkers, will significantly reduce costs and improve profitability.

Ballast – Heavy material placed low on a vessel to improve stability. Modern cargo ships use water for this purpose. When empty, a ship must take on ballast to improve stability and performance. A ballast leg is a voyage without cargo, often for the reason of reaching a load port.

Basel Accords – Three accords written by the Basel Committee on Banking Supervision, and implemented by federal banks, holds banking institutions to capital, leverage, and liquidity requirements. The purpose is to ensure that financial institutions

261

remain financially sound in the event of an economic downturn. The accords have the side effect of reducing the amount of money banks can lend.

Berkshire Hathaway – An American company controlled by Warren Buffett, who is known as the Oracle of Omaha, and has consistently been one of the world's largest, as well as top returning, investment firms.

Bond – A certificate of debt that is auctioned off to raise capital. Bonds issuers pay interest (fixed or variable) to bond holders at regular intervals and pay the face value ($1,000 for corporate bonds) upon maturity. Many other features exist which can be applied to make the terms of the bond more favorable to the issuer or to purchasers, depending on the strength of the market. Purchasers of bonds can either hold them, collecting interest payments and principle upon maturity or trade them as their market based price fluctuates.

Box – A colloquialism for container.

Brent Crude – A crude oil benchmark comprised of oil from North Sea oil fields.

BRICs – Brazil, Russia, India, China. This informal grouping comprises the world's largest fast growing economies.

British Thermal Unit (BTU) – A unit of energy equivalent to quantity of heat required to heat one pound of water from 39 to 40°F.

Bulk carrier – A ship designed to carry unpackaged dry (ore, grain, etc.) cargos.

Bunkers – Any fuel used by a ship, this is most commonly a heavy fuel oil, but can also be diesel, LNG, or otherwise.

Capesize – Used in reference to dry bulk carriers, these ships are too large to transit the Panama Canal or Suez Canal, and therefore must travel around the Capes of Good Hope or Horn. They carry greater than 100,000 DWT and the largest today over 400,000 DWT.

Capital – Financial and physical assets of a company.

Catamaran – A multihulled vessel with two hulls. Ships of this design have greater stability, reach higher speeds, and consume less fuel than a comparable monohulled vessel.

Chemical tanker – A ship built to carry multiple bulk liquid cargos in individual tanks. The pipes and tanks of these ships are usually constructed of stainless steel or lined with high tech coatings to resist corrosion from, or contamination of, the cargos they carry. A state-of-the-art parcel tanker can carry as many as twenty different liquid cargos, fully segregated and individually heated or cooled as needed. These ships are generally smaller in size than other tankers.

Connecticut Maritime Association (CMA) – The CMA is a non-profit organization based in Stamford, Connecticut with over 1,300 members from 35 countries and over 450 companies and organizations, making it the largest international commercial shipping association in the U.S. The CMA is perhaps best known for its annual CMA Shipping conference.

Container – A standardized box, typically 40' in length though other sizes available include 20' 45', 48', and 53', which can be transported by ship, truck, or rail. These are most commonly used to transport finished products such as electronics and home goods, rather than bulk cargo. Small amounts of liquid cargos can be carried in tanks fitted in frames which match the dimensions of a container. They are carried by container ships, tractor trailers, and trains.

Container ship –Ships designed to carry containers stacked in holds and on deck. Container ships are measured in TEU capacity and come as small as 100 TEU and as large as 18,000 TEU. These ships and intermodal containers were developed by an American trucker, Malcolm McLean, in the 1950s.

Credit – An agreement to receive something now and pay for it later.

Deadweight ton (DWT) – The carrying capacity of a ship, including bunkers, water, stores and cargo, in metric tons.

Deep Sea Shipping – Also known as blue water shipping or ocean shipping, this industry carries cargo in large volumes across oceans.

Drill ship – A vessel equipped with a drilling rig and support equipment used to drill offshore oil and gas wells or for research purposes.

Dry bulk – Unpackaged solid cargos such as iron ore, grain, or scrap metal. Contrast to containerized, bagged, or palletized cargo.

Earnings Before Interest, Taxes, Depreciation, Amortization (EBITDA) – Revenue minus expenses without interest, depreciation, or amortization payments. This is a non-GAAP (Generally Accepted Accounting Principles) measure of a company's ability to service debt.

Equity – The owners' share of capital in a company; total asset value minus debt.

European Union (EU) – A confederation of 27 European countries: Austria, Belgium, Bulgaria, Cyprus, Czech Republic, Denmark, Estonia, Finland, France, Germany, Greece, Hungary, Ireland, Italy, Latvia, Lithuania, Luxembourg, Malta, the Netherlands, Poland, Portugal, Romania, Slovakia, Slovenia, Spain, Sweden, United Kingdom. The EU has its own supranational government and is a single market. 17 EU members, Austria, Belgium, Cyprus, Estonia, Finland, France, Germany, Greece, Ireland, Italy, Luxembourg, Malta, the Netherlands, Portugal, Slovakia, Slovenia, and Spain, use a common currency, the Euro.

Flag – The country in which a ship is registered. Countries have unique requirements placed upon ships they register including crews, inspections, and taxes. Ships may be regulated on where they can trade based on their flag.

Floating Liquefied Natural Gas (FLNG) – A vessel which is moored over an offshore natural gas field and equipped to produce, liquefy, store, and then offload natural gas into tankers. The first of these ships is currently under development.

Floating Production Storage and Offloading (FPSO) – A vessel, often a converted VLCC, that is used for processing and storing crude oil from nearby offshore oil wells and then offloading into tankers.

Floating Storage and Offloading (FSO) – Similar to an FPSO, but without any equipment for processing of the crude oil.

Freight Forward Agreement (FFA) – A contract for future carriage of goods which can be bought and sold to hedge the future price of freight.

Gross Domestic Product (GDP) – The value of goods and services produced within a country.

Gross Registered Tonnage (GRT) – A measure of the internal volume of a ship's enclosed spaces. One GRT equals 100 cubic feet.

Handymax – A subset of the Handysize class that carry between 40,000 and 59,999 DWT

Handysize (dry bulk) – The smallest size dry bulk ships, these carry between 10,000 and 39,999 DWT. These ships are considered the dump trucks of the sea.

Handysize (tanker) – The largest size vessels capable of berthing at a Type II pier, these ships are up to 180 meters and carry 30,000 DWT.

Initial Public Offering (IPO) – The sale of equity in a company to the public on an exchange for the first time.

Inland shipping – The industry of carrying cargo on rivers and lakes, often utilizing a tug and barge combination.

International Maritime Organization (IMO) – The United Nations body dedicated to regulating the international maritime industry.

INTERTANKO – This is the working name of the International Association of Independent Tanker Owners. The organization has a mission to provide leadership to the tanker industry in serving the world with the safe, environmentally sound and efficient seaborne transportation of oil, gas and chemical products. It was founded in 1970.

Jones Act – A U.S. law passed in 1920 that requires ships operating between U.S. ports to be built, flagged, crewed, and owned by U.S. citizens.

Key Performance Indicators (KPI) – Measurements to determine the performance of an activity. Shipping KPI's include health and safety, environmental performance, navigational safety, technical performance, etc.

Level 5 Leadership – Coined by Jim Collins and the subject of his book "Good to Great," level 5 leaders are great leaders. They possess the skills and knowledge to organize and lead groups, as with competent leaders, but great leaders are most importantly humble and attribute a company's success to its people or luck.

Leveraged Buyout (LBO) – The acquisition of a company using debt to fund the majority of the purchase price.

Liberty Ship – Cargo ships built by the Allies during World War II to transport war supplies from the United States to Europe. These ships were hastily built as they were only expected to make the journey once as survival rates were low due to German submarine warfare. Many surviving Liberty ships were made available to Greek shipowners who had lost their ships during the war. These ships successfully traded around the globe for many years and established the Greeks' dominance in shipping.

Liner shipping – The industry of carrying cargo between designated ports on a fixed schedule. This typically includes ferries, cruise ships, and some container ships.

Liquefied Natural Gas (LNG) – Natural gas liquefied by chilling it to between -120 and -170°C. Natural gas is 600 times denser as a liquid than a gas, allowing LNG to be economically transported or used as transportation fuel.

Liquefied Petroleum Gas (LPG) – LPG is a mixture of hydrocarbon gasses, primarily either propane, butane, or a mixture of both, that liquefies under moderate pressure. Petroleum gas is separated from natural gas or a byproduct of crude oil refining.

Liquidity – Cash or assets that can be quickly sold for cash.

LR1 – Tankers that carry between 45,000 and 79,999 DWT.

LR2 – Tankers that carry between 80,000 and 159,999 DWT.

Management Buyout (MBO) – The purchase of a company by its management.

MR – Tankers that carry between 25,000 and 44,999 DWT.

Natural Gas – A hydrocarbon mixture primarily composed of methane that is gaseous at normal temperature and pressure.

New Panamax – The largest size ship that will fit through the new Panama Canal locks (to be opened in 2014). These ships are up to 366 meters by 49 meters with a laden draft of 15 meters and air draft of 57 meters and carry approximately 120,000 DWT or 12,000 TEU.

Newbuilding – Ships under construction or newly launched.

North American Free Trade Agreement (NAFTA) – A 1993 agreement between the United States, Canada, and Mexico with to eliminate tariffs between the signatories.

Offshore – Refers to the industry and equipment engaged in subsea oil and gas (can also include any maritime based energy production, such as offshore wind, wave, and tidal) exploration, construction, production, and support.

Order book – The number of commercial vessels currently on order at shipyards.

Organisation for Economic Co-operation and Development (OECD) – A group of 34 nations, including many of the world's most advanced nations, which collaborate to promote market economies. Member nations are Australia, Austria, Belgium, Canada, Chile, Czech Republic, Denmark, Estonia, Finland, France, Germany, Greece, Hungary, Iceland, Ireland, Israel, Italy, Japan, Korea, Luxembourg, Mexico, the Netherlands, New Zealand, Norway, Poland, Portugal, Slovak Republic, Slovenia, Spain, Sweden, Switzerland, Turkey, United Kingdom, and the United States.

Organization of Petroleum Exporting Countries (OPEC) – Comprised of the oil and gas producing nations of Algeria, Angola, Ecuador, Iran, Iraq, Kuwait, Libya, Nigeria, Qatar, Saudi Arabia, United Arab Emirates, and Venezuela with the intention of setting production targets for its members to manage oil prices. The group produces 19 percent of the world's natural gas and 43 percent of crude oil.

Panamax – The largest size ship that can fit through the old Panama Canal locks, typically 290 meters by 32 meters with a laden draft of 12 meters and air draft of 57 meters. These ships can carry between 60,000 and 100,000 DWT or 5,000 TEU.

Parcel tanker – A ship built to carry multiple bulk liquid cargos in individual tanks. The pipes and tanks of these ships are usually constructed of stainless steel or lined with high tech coatings to resist corrosion from, or contamination of, the cargos they carry. A state-of-the-art parcel tanker can carry as many as twenty different liquid cargos, fully segregated and individually heated or cooled as needed. These ships are generally smaller in size than other tankers.

Post-Panamax – Ships larger than Panamax size.

Private Equity (PE) – Equity that is not publicly traded. Associated with private equity firms which make investments on behalf of individual or institutional investors.

Product tanker – Tankers which carry refined petroleum products as opposed to crude oil, typically of a smaller size than crude carriers.

Scrapping – The demolition and recycling of ships.

Shale Gas – Natural gas that is trapped in porous shale rock. Recent technological advancements have allowed for economical extraction of the gas through hydrofracking, a process of breaking open underground rock formations using high pressure fluids. As a result, there are ongoing booms in shale gas production around the world, most notably in the United States.

Short Sea Shipping – An alternative to road or rail transport, this industry carries cargo along coasts (and therefore is also known as coastwise or marine highway) and does not cross oceans.

Sovereign debt – Debt owed by national governments, agencies, or government backed industries.

Spot charter – Chartering a ship for a single voyage. In this type of charter, the owner pays all operating and voyage expenses.

Strategic Petroleum Reserve (SPR) – The largest oil stockpile in the world. SPR is owned by the United States government for use in emergencies. The oil is kept in salt caverns in Texas and Louisiana with a total capacity of 727 million barrels.

Suezmax – The largest size ship that can fit through the Suez Canal, typically used in reference to tanker. The canal allows ships of unlimited length (typically around 275m), a maximum beam of 77 meters, a maximum draft dependent on the beam (for a ship with a typical beam of 50m is limited to an 18m draft), and a maximum air draft of 68 meters.

Tanker – A ship designed to carry liquids in bulk. Cargo types include crude oil, gasoline and other refined oil products, chemicals, vegetable oil, fruit juice, fresh water, etc. Tanker ships may be designed to carry a single type of cargo or a variety.

Time charter – Chartering a ship for a specific period of time. The charterer is responsible to all voyage costs during the charter including bunkers, port fees, canal expenses, and any additional insurance required. The owner is paid on a per day basis, regardless of how the ship is utilized during the charter.

Ton-mile – The number of tons of cargo carried multiplied by the distance is transported. This is a useful macroeconomic indicator to understand demand in the shipping market.

Tramp shipping – The industry of carrying cargo without a fixed route or a fixed schedule.

Triangulate – When backhaul cargos are not available, a ship can triangulate to reach the original port of loading by combining three or more voyages.

Twenty-foot Equivalent Unit (TEU) – A unit used to measure the cargo capacity of a container ship based on the number of twenty-foot long containers which could fit in holds and on deck. Container ships can carry the equivalent of this measure in various container sizes. In other words, a 10,000 TEU container ship could carry 10,000 twenty-foot containers, 5,000 forty-foot containers, or 4,000 forty-foot containers and 2,000 twenty-foot containers.

Ultra Large Crude Carrier (ULCC) – Tankers which carry between 320,000 and 549,999 DWT. Many were built in the 1970s and they are among the largest ships in the world. Few remain in service today.

Very Large Crude Carrier (VLCC) – Tankers which carry between 160,000 and 319,999 DWT (roughly 2 million barrels or 10 percent of the United States' daily oil consumption).

Very Large Gas Carrier (VLGC) – Liquefied petroleum gas carriers which carry greater than 60,000 cubic meters.

Very Large Natural Gas Carrier (VLNGC) – Liquefied natural gas carriers which greater than 200,000 cubic meters.

Very Large Ore Carrier (VLOC) – Dry bulk ships specifically designed to carry heavy ore. These carry greater than 150,000 DWT and are a new development, primarily trading long haul distances.

West Texas Intermediate (WTI) – An oil benchmark of light sweet crude, first priced at Cushing, Oklahoma. WTI is the most common benchmark used in the U.S. and the basis for most other oil prices in the country.

World Trade Organization (WTO) – An international organization with 167 member countries, committed to reducing barriers to trade.

Worldscale – Published rates for voyages between any world ports used by the tanker industry. These rates take into account port fees, canal expenses, bunker costs, and a daily hire (all of which are updated regularly). Charter rates are then negotiated as a percentage of the worldscale rate for that voyage.

MARINE MONEY, INC.

INDEX

Page numbers in *italics* indicate photographs; page numbers followed by *f* indicate figures

CPSIA information can be obtained
at www.ICGtesting.com
Printed in the USA
FFHW022143111118
49358460-53651FF